Detroitland

DETROITLAND

A Collection of Movers, Shakers, Lost Souls,
and History Makers from Detroit's Past

RICHARD BAK

A PAINTED TURTLE BOOK | Detroit, Michigan

15 14 13 12 11 5 4 3 2 1

Library of Congress
Cataloging-in-Publication Data

Bak, Richard, 1954–
Detroitland : a collection of movers, shakers,
lost souls, and history makers from Detroit's
past / Richard Bak.
p. cm.
"A Painted Turtle book."
Includes index.
ISBN 978-0-8143-3499-7 (pbk. : alk. paper)
1. Detroit (Mich.)—History. 2. Detroit
(Mich.)—Biography. I. Title.

F574.D457B349 2011
977.4'34—dc22 2011005436

∞

Designed and typeset by Ashley Muehlbauer
Composed in Scala and Museo

To Rosie and Minnie

CONTENTS

FOREWORD

Before Detroit became the lab school for everything that can go wrong with a city, we were a pretty good case study for everything that can go right.

A living wage? Check. An international exposition? Check, in 1889, even if almost no one but Richard Bak still knows it ever happened. A major industry that put the city on the map? Another check mark: it was stoves, paving the way for cars.

It's easy to forget all that when Detroit loses 25 percent of its population in the ten short years between census tallies, when the only thing worse than the unemployment rate is the dropout rate, when occupied houses on some blocks stand out like the squared-off teeth on the gumline of a jack-o-lantern, and when an arrogant and larcenous former mayor is in prison.

Richard Bak remembers. Or at least, if he wasn't around to be a witness, he's aware. A politician headed for the slammer? Old news. Bak can tell you about Daniel West, the fascinatingly fraudulent state representative who was facing a maximum sentence of 755 years in federal prison before he vanished one day in 1965. As Bak puts it, West has been "unavailable for comment" ever since.

Bak has been writing about this stuff for a quarter-century, often for publications that have become history themselves. Fortunately, he kept copies, which is how we have been blessed with *Detroitland: A Collection of Movers, Shakers, Lost Souls, and History Makers from Detroit's Past.*

For this thoroughly engaging assemblage, we can also thank Miss Troshynski—not a major historical figure, but one lovingly remembered by the fifth-graders at Epiphany Grade School on the west side. Her class of fifty or so students in 1964 had a Secret Santa program, which for most of the kids meant buying and ultimately receiving some Taiwanese trinket from Dave's Dime Store on West Chicago. Bak's name, however, was drawn by the teacher, and his gift that December was something extraordinary: a Landmark Books biography of Alexander the Great.

Young Mr. Bak had already developed a taste for reading history, courtesy of the bookmobile that rumbled to a stop at the corner of Orangelawn and Meyers every Tuesday. Paul Revere, Kit Carson, Davy Crockett—these were great tales, and they were even *true*. (Or at least inspired by truth, and it made for better reading if the author imagined Crockett swinging the butt of his musket at the advancing hordes at the Alamo.) But the book about Alexander the Great was fresh and new, and more important, it was his.

Miss Troshynski spent probably $3.95 on it, a staggering sum. The binding cracked and the fresh ink smelled better than Aqua Velva. Bak read it, by conservative estimate, 136 times, and his parents took note. Eddie Bak, who worked the line at Dodge Truck, had a fifth-grade education. Lillian, who stayed home with five kids in a tidy 900-square-foot bungalow on Pinehurst, had lasted only a few school years longer. Seeing their son's interest in the printed word, they fed it, and books became the standard Christmas and birthday presents.

Ultimately, Bak—after a few career detours as an autoworker, cab driver, and Marine rifleman—graduated from Eastern Michigan University with a degree in secondary education and began selling articles to magazines. An event or a person or a juicy crime from the past would intrigue him, he'd do some research and find a few people to interview, and he'd drop a manuscript in the mail. He'd sold five or six pieces that way before an editor finally said, "Um . . . you know you're supposed to ask us first, right?"

So he learned the art of the query letter and kept going. He had minored in creative writing, but with history, the plots came ready made. The trick was to make the past palatable in the short-attention-span present—and heck, it wasn't that hard. He's not a professional historian, he'll tell you; he's just some galumphing guy who likes to write about what he likes to read about. After half a lifetime of ferreting out obscure names, facts, and incidents, the first twenty minutes at the microfilm reader still makes him queasy. But the payoff is learning that the Marvelettes' "Please Mr. Postman" was in fact written by a letter carrier.

If the devil is in the details, so is the delight. By 1928, eight years into Prohibition, the smuggling, distribution, and manufacture of illicit booze was the second-largest industry in Detroit, with annual revenues of $400 million. Amazing. And that old slogan about how when better cars are built, Buick will build them? GM founder Billy Durant actually said it, to racecar driver "Wild Bob" Burman, on a tour of the Buick plant in Flint.

A British bomber crashed in the middle of an east side neighborhood in 1958. How can we not all know that? Bak not only located witnesses, he found someone with snapshots. Topics come in ways large and small; a name or a scrap of information in one archeological dig through a library or a used-book store will turn into a story of its own a year or a decade later.

The Black Legion marches through *Detroitland,* and so does the first white lead singer at Motown, Stuart Avig of the Valadiers. There's the Purple Gang, homegrown thugs so vicious they kept Al Capone out of Detroit, and Johnny Miler, a scrappy Olympic hopeful who once pummeled the Brown Bomber. Joe Louis was not deterred after his first amateur bout, fortunately, and became so renowned and revered that he was featured after his death on a postage stamp. "It was issued before self-adhesive stamps became the norm," Bak writes, "giving millions of ordinary Americans the opportunity to do what Johnny Miler did in such convincing fashion one long-ago winter day: lick Joe Louis."

Perfect. And there's this, about Tom Tyler, who went from Hamtramck to Hollywood to become a star and have a fling with Marlene Dietrich, only to die in pain and anonymity back home: "Just one more obscure laborer in the dream factory of American cinema."

Detroitland is, like the city, a place of mayhem, magic, and mystery. Bak refers to it whimsically as "my greatest hits." Give it a spin, and I suspect you'll wind up wearing out the grooves. And then you can do what the kids did in those long-ago days before iTunes: hold your breath and wait for Volume II.

—NEAL RUBIN
The Detroit News

PREFACE

Detroitland is a collection of writings about Detroit's past, culled from the many feature-length historical articles I have contributed to various publications over the years. These chapters originally appeared in such periodicals as *Detroit Monthly, Hour Detroit, Michigan History,* and the Sunday magazine section of the *Detroit News.* For this collection, most of the articles have been updated, corrected, expanded, and otherwise changed as I saw fit. There is no thematic or chronological pattern to their arrangement; rather, each chapter is a separate story about a personality, event, or era to be enjoyed (hopefully) on its own. During my journalism career I have been grateful to the many editors who have shared my enthusiasm for local history, and I am obliged to Wayne State University Press, one of the country's leading publishers of regional history, for bringing out this compilation. As someone who was born and raised in Detroit, I have come to appreciate that my hometown, now in its fourth century of existence, offers writers and readers an inexhaustible supply of stories, a few of which are related on these pages.

—*R. B.*

The poetry of history lies in the quasi-miraculous fact that once on this earth, once on this familiar spot of ground, walked other men and women, as actual as we are today, thinking their own thoughts, swayed by their own passions, but now all gone, one generation vanishing into another, gone as utterly as we ourselves shall shortly be gone, like ghosts at cockcrow.

—*GEORGE MACAULEY TREVELYAN*

A trade card from the 1890 Detroit International Exposition & Fair. Visitors calling on the cigar manufacturer's booth could purchase a barrel of souvenir cigars for one dollar. (Author's Collection)

ONE

A Fair to Remember

The ambitious Detroit International Exposition & Fair of 1889 put the growing, pre-automobile city in the spotlight, drawing attention to its prosperity and potential.

Fiji Jim was there. So were Professor Woodward and his trained seals. Professor Bartholomew, acclaimed "Balloon Ascension Specialist," arrived in time to make his daring leap through the clouds. Miss Ida Williams, "The Female Colossus of Fat Women," also came to town, as did tens of thousands of salesmen, hustlers, stock handlers, city slickers, and country cousins. It was Detroit's great fair, and everybody was welcome.

Nobody alive has a personal memory of the Detroit International Exposition & Fair of 1889. No physical traces of the great exhibit hall—at the time, the largest such building in the world—remain. The attractively arranged grounds in Delray that fair patrons once strolled across in their starched blouses, sailor hats, pressed pants, and tight shoes are today part of the most polluted neighborhood in the city. But for a spell, the now forsaken area was host to a growing community's grandest dreams and the site of its coming-out party to the world.

Detroit's "big show" of 1889 belonged to an era of ambitious fairs. The Eiffel Tower was unveiled that year at the Exposition Universelle, which commemorated the centennial of the French Revolution, but Detroit's fair was unusual in that it did not celebrate a significant anniversary; rather, it was principally an exercise in good old-fashioned civic boosterism, headed by a group of leading citizens whose names today grace various streets, parks, and buildings. "It is not to be an agricultural fair alone," promoters explained in a circular, "it is not to be merely an industrial fair; nor is it simply an exposition; but it is a grand combination of all these features, which makes it the greatest institution of its kind in the world." The popular New York–based magazine *Harper's Weekly* thought enough of the undertaking to devote much of a single issue to Detroit and its fair. "It is a beautiful city," the journal's correspondent noted approvingly, "strong in resources, full of life, and rich with opportunity."

Detroit in 1889 was still seven years shy of the first automobile appearance on its streets and a full decade away from the opening of its first auto factory. Industry in the future Motor City was more diversified during this big-shouldered period than at any other stage in its long history. Hundreds of companies, large and small, produced an array of products: shoes, stoves, varnishes, paints, drugs, cigars, patent medicines, boats, railroad cars, steel rails, brass fittings, soap, and seeds for local consumption and export.

In the process of flexing its muscles, Detroit "had lost most of its small-town characteristics and had become a real city, big and bustling," wrote historian Arthur M. Woodford. Within a decade, the population had nearly doubled to 206,000 people, making Detroit the fifteenth largest city in the country. Development had pushed north, east, and west from lower Woodward Avenue, with the new residential sections, as Woodford wrote, "planted in what only a short time before had been corn fields and wood lots. Huge elm, maple, and chestnut trees shaded the streets, and gracious homes, most of them frame and painted either white or dark green, gave the new residential areas an air of comfort and well-being." The streets were paved with cobblestones and cedar blocks, and the sidewalks were made of wood. The widespread use of electricity was literally just around the corner—garish 125-foot towers illuminated intersections throughout the city—but in 1889 homes and businesses still used gaslight, and trolleys still were drawn by horses. Major symbols of progress—a new art museum, the city's first skyscraper, a second train depot—had either just opened or were underway.

For years Detroiters of means and influence had been talking of holding a permanent annual event on a much grander scale than that of the Michigan State Fair, which rotated among various cities. Their imaginations had been stoked by the Centennial Exposition in Philadelphia in 1876, the country's first official world's fair. The idea of wedding an agricultural fair to an industrial exposition seemed to make sense. By the middle 1880s, thanks principally to the unflagging efforts of local booster Eber Cottrell, enough of Detroit's movers and shakers had signed on to the dream to make it an actuality. By early 1889, the exposition company had a capital stock of $500,000 to draw on. The goal was not only to showcase the products of the city and the state, but to draw attention to Detroit and boost its stature among other great cities. And, of course, this being an era of unbridled capitalism, the men planning Detroit's exposition fully intended to make money while doing so.

The president of the exposition company was U.S. Senator James McMillan, who had made his fortune manufacturing railroad cars. Other notables among the hundred or so stockholders were ex-governor Russell Alger, a Civil War general who'd also grown rich off rolling stock; Thomas W. Palmer, a former U.S. senator who had been appointed minister to Spain in early 1889; and Dexter M. Ferry, who operated the largest catalog seed company in the country. Rather than paying the sky-high real estate prices that were the going rate in the growing city, officers of the enterprise purchased seventy-two acres of unincorporated land at the juncture of the Detroit and Rouge rivers, just south of Fort Wayne and about a thousand yards beyond Detroit's western boundary. The bucolic area, valued at $150,000, had long been enjoyed by canoers, fishermen, and hunters. Based on his experience with several New York fairs, C. W. Robinson, known as "a cultivated, well-informed gentleman of liberal tastes," was hired as general manager. By the time the exposition ended, he would be described as being in a state of near collapse.

In the spring of 1889, a small army of laborers moved in to drain the marshes and clear the farmland. Contractors followed, and soon the grounds began to acquire a profile. Railroad tracks were laid on the grounds to accommodate exhibitors and visitors alike. Two separate docks were built to handle excursion boats. Meanwhile, Robinson signed up

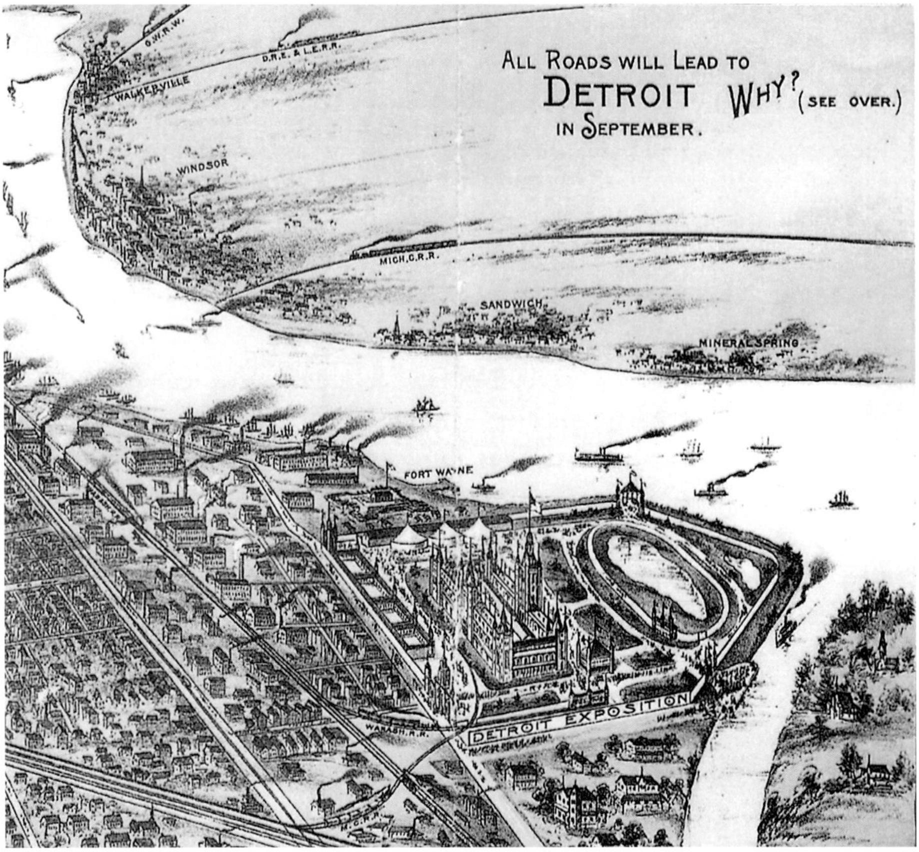

A sketch of the fairgrounds depicts the exposition's location at the juncture of the Detroit and Rouge rivers, just south of Fort Wayne. (Author's Collection)

hundreds of firms, most of them from Michigan and Canada, eager to display their wares. The announcement that $100,000 in cash prizes would be awarded in various competitions created great interest. With nearly a month to go before opening, would-be exhibitors were turned away due to lack of space in the main hall. Dozens chose to build small cottage-size structures at private expense all around the grounds, which were surrounded by a high fence. The livestock buildings also rapidly filled up. As opening day approached, a "babel of bleating, cackling, mooing, and grunting" arose from the stalls, which housed "the finest breeds of cattle, sheep, swine, and poultry," reported a daily newspaper. The final catalog of entries in the horses, cattle, and sheep categories alone filled seventy pages of fine print.

The main exhibit building, constructed of wood, sprang from the drawings of local architect Louis Kamper. Prior to the fair, the young German immigrant had designed a forty-nine-room turreted mansion on Woodward Avenue for Frank J. Hecker, president of the Peninsular Car Company, and Kamper went on to design such landmarks as the Book-Cadillac Hotel. Kamper's great hall resembled a grand European palace. It had a frontage of nearly five hundred feet, a twenty-story main tower, four corner towers, almost five acres of glass, and it boasted 200,000 square feet of exhibition space—enough room to hold two or three ordinary state fairs.

In this pre-aviation age, where ordinary folks could gain a bird's-eye view of their surroundings only by climbing to the top of a hill or a tall building, the main tower proved to be a resounding hit. William Willard Howard, in town to report for *Harper's Weekly,* was allowed an early peek. "From the tower of the Main Building may be seen a panorama worth an hour's study," he wrote a month before the exposition opened. "To the left, reaching out to the horizon, lies the city, tinged over with the smoke of industry. To the right the green fields of Canada stretch up from the eastern shore of the Detroit River, and go out to meet the lower rim of the distant sky. Close at hand the stately river flows past, with its fleet of barges, its casual schooners, and its steam craft, while all alongshore the giant elevators and the prosaic warehouses give a strong contrast to the dim beauty of Belle Isle and the farther stretches of river and woodland, and the drifting sails of commerce."

America was in the midst of changing from an agrarian to an industrial nation, with mechanized advances improving productivity on the farm and at the factory; however, the majority of its citizens still lived in rural areas. In 1889, Michigan had 160,000 farms (more than three times 2010's figure), including the largest number of small farms—those between twenty-five and fifty acres—of any state in the union. The activities of communities such as Royal Oak, Rochester, Milford, and Ortonville continued to revolve mainly around agriculture. Entertain-

Visitors to Detroit's great exposition disembark from one of two boat landings. (Burton Historical Collection)

ment options were minimal and rudimentary by urban standards. The provincial country "rube" was a stock character on stage and in print. For many, a visit to the "big city" was a rare treat; for some, it was literally a once-in-a-lifetime experience.

Detroit was an accommodating host. Red, white, and blue bunting, streamers, flags, and pennants decorated the doors, windows, and cornices of businesses along the major thoroughfares. On the eve of the fair's opening, the crush of tourists caused several leading hotels, including the elegant Russell House (at the corner of Woodward and Michigan avenues) and the new Wayne Hotel (at Third and Woodbridge, opposite the original Michigan Central Railroad depot), to place guests three and four to a room while the overflow slept on cots in the hallways and parlors.

The Detroit International Exposition & Fair opened its forty gates at 8 a.m. on September 17, 1889, a blustery Tuesday following two days of cold rain. It was Children's Day. Schools were closed, and an estimated six thousand youngsters were let in free. Thousands of adults joined them, arriving by trolley, steamer, train, buggy, bicycle, on horseback, and on foot. "Let Detroit put on her best holiday attire and sweetest smile and make everybody happy," a reporter for the *Detroit Tribune* declared. "They used to call Detroit 'old fogy.' Let those who think that term is applicable now come here and repent and be saved before it is everlastingly too late."

The fair's debut was anything but smooth. With many exhibits still unfinished, visitors spent the first day maneuvering around workers lugging in furnishings, hanging drapes, and sawing wood. Opening ceremonies were delayed for more than an hour until several lost members of Cappa's 7th Regiment Band, which had been hired to provide music throughout the two-week event, finally arrived. With a stiff wind blowing his words right back in his face and hammers echoing in the background, Senator McMillan addressed the throngs from the veranda of the main hall. In his judgment, "Detroit had entered upon a new era in her history. Her businessmen have shown that when it becomes necessary to undertake a great public enterprise, they can act in harmony. . . . It has also been demonstrated that among our citizens we have architects who can design and mechanics and workmen who can execute with as much energy and skill as can be done in any city."

Following a bit more speechifying by other dignitaries, McMillan pushed an electric button, signaling the engine room of the massive $30,000 power plant. An engineer's young daughter pulled a lever, and the entire machinery of the exposition was put into motion.

Visitors discovered a city within a city. Employees of Harper Hospital staffed an aid station, and there also were a jail, post office, and train depot on the grounds. For those who might be tempted to stray from the straight and narrow path, there was a "tabernacle gospel tent," as well as a booth manned by members of the Women's Christian Temperance Union. Landscapers had created a miniature lake, and a racetrack had been installed around it. The band gazebo and a merry-go-round both saw heavy duty. The various buildings dripped with gingerbread bargeboard and colorful bunting, all of which were illuminated by soaring towers topped with electric lamps. The transformation of the area in just five months was remarkable. It prompted one fairgoer, a Frenchman from Ecorse, to exclaim: "My God, look a dat! I shoot duck in 'e mash here last spring!"

All of Detroit's iconic names of the period were out in full force. Mabley & Co., long the city's largest retailer, spent $20,000 on a trio of glass-enclosed booths. One featured a facsimile of the Statue of Liberty, which, in 1889, had been on its pedestal in New York harbor for three years. The Detroit Soap Company could boast of the most fragrant cottage on the grounds, the entire structure being carved from giant cakes of its popular Queen Anne soap. Workers at the Pingree & Smith exhibit made hundreds of pairs of shoes each day for the benefit of onlookers. "Each exhibitor has striven to out-do his neighbor," a wide-eyed attendee who walked the corridors and galleries marveled, "and the class of goods and the varieties are almost bewildering."

Adjacent to the main hall was an art gallery. The T-shaped building housed some three hundred paintings, including Konstantin Makovsky's *The Russian Wedding Feast.* Fair managers had been so anxious to display Makovsky's famous painting that they agreed to pay its owner, a New York diamond merchant, three thousand dollars plus all of his expenses during his stay in town—a shakedown that helped persuade management to reluctantly charge an admission fee of twenty-five cents per person to view the gallery.

There was so much to take in: fifteen acres of steam engines, threshing machines, presses, and other machinery, and a seemingly endless succession of mechanical and industrial halls. Features included a palm garden, a floral palace, and miles of stalls displaying horses, sheep, cattle, pigs, poultry, and pets. There were band concerts and piano recitals and competitions of all sorts: yachting, riding, shooting, track and field, horse racing, baseball, and lacrosse. Attendees could gaze at giant prize squashes and pumpkins while being entertained by a clarion player performing an aria from *Rigoletto* or sit on the veranda of the main hall and try to bounce peanut shells off a passerby's derby.

The grounds were open daily, except Sundays, from 8 a.m. to 10 p.m. Admission was fifty cents for adults, a quarter for children. Steamboats

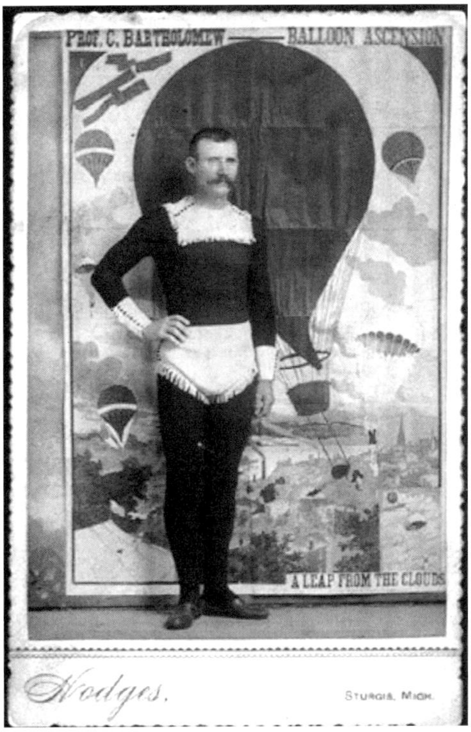

Professor Bartholomew, acclaimed "Balloon Ascension Specialist," made his daring leap through the clouds at the 1889 fair. (Author's Collection)

and trolleys disgorged visitors to the exposition in five-minute intervals. Businesses, both legal and otherwise, looked to take advantage. Keepers of boardinghouses cashed in by lodging strangers everywhere from the cellar to the garret. Few concerned themselves with fire-escape regulations. On the fairgrounds, beer was sold only in the main hall's restaurant, so enterprising citizens stepped in to fill the void. "The thoroughfares leading to the main entrance to the exposition where cheap beer joints are springing up by the dozen are known as No Man's land because nobody seems inclined to make the keepers of the joints obey," complained one newspaper reporter. "The police can't interfere because the joints are outside the city limits, the sheriff's powers doesn't extend far enough for him to enforce the payment of a license, and the township board is too slow to prevent any infraction of the law."

More than one worldly "drummer" (salesman) or unsuspecting yokel found his way into the sporting houses of the riverfront vice district known as the Potomac. "It extended eastward from Woodward about a mile to the vicinity of the railroad crossing on Dequindre Street," recalled city councilman John C. Lodge. "It was filled with saloons and dives of every degree of villainy, whose operators preyed upon the sailors and others in search of entertainment who were unwary enough to enter the district." Visitors were on their own in the neighborhood, which was so notorious, the police department assigned only one officer to patrol it.

As expected, there was an influx of out-of-town prostitutes and other criminal types. One high-ranking police official warned that he had issued orders for his men to "run in every pickpocket, gambler, confidence man, sneak thief, porch climber, and burglar they see, whether they are working or not. I shall keep them locked up until after the exposition closes and photograph them for the rogues' gallery. It is cheaper for the city to board them than to arrest them after they have committed a crime. Their friends can habeas corpus them as much as they please, but if we are compelled to release them they will be rearrested at once and the same proceedings can be taken over again."

Law enforcement on the fairgrounds was a bit wobbly at first, with a night watchman (who happened to be an ex-policeman) fired after being caught pilfering merchandise from the Newcomb-Endicott exhibit on the eve of the fair's opening. That same night, unknown persons snuck onto a flatcar containing an out-of-state exhibitor's collection of West Indies cocoanut and banana trees and picked them clean of fruit. But after a few days, the sheriff in charge of the seventy uniformed officers assigned to the exposition grounds was able to report a quiet time of it. "Everybody seems to be on his good behavior. If there is a pickpocket or crook of any kind on the grounds, the detectives have been unable to find him."

Looking to capitalize on interest created in their goods at the exposition, business owners extended promotional offers and their operating hours. Mabley's was representative of such expanded offerings, hosting free balcony concerts and stereoptican exhibitions at its stores every evening. Tobacco merchants displayed the greatest flair for publicity. The cigar store of J. S. Thompson & Bros. on Woodward, near City Hall, attracted large crowds by displaying what appeared to be a wooden Indian in its front window; closer examination revealed that the counterfeit seated in full paint and feathers was a living, breathing being. Moebs & Co. took a considerably more animated approach, hiring a circus performer in a tin Roman helmet to drive around a white chariot drawn by four black horses to promote its Ben-Hur brand of cigars.

Professor J. C. Chambers invited fairgoers to drop in at the Electric Sanitarium and Institute on Washington Boulevard for a free treatment. The professor, whose advertisements cited no credentials beyond noting that he had "spent one-quarter of a century relieving suffering humanity," employed a patented apparatus "whereby the Galvanic, Magnetic, and Electric induced currents are quickly infused all through the system." This, he claimed, enabled him to cure such varied and chronic cases as "brain exhaustion," kidney troubles, memory loss, headaches, impotence, and back pain, as well as "threatening insanity, blood poisoning, and skin diseases of any kind."

At Detroit's leading theatre, the Wonderland, showman Enoch "Pop" Wiggins promised fair patrons "Everything New and Startling for Exposition Week!" The imported freak show featured Miss Ida Williams, who was billed as "Mammoth, Mountainous, Half a Ton of Womanly Loveliness," and a boxing match between a 490-pound man ("A Human Jumbo!") and a bladelike 49-pounder ("A Giant of Lankiness!").

Without having to worry about such twenty-first-century notions as political correctness, any arguments concerning similar circus-style sideshows on the exposition grounds centered on money, not sensitivity. Fairgoers grumped about spending an extra quarter after already paying to enter the grounds. An elderly hermit farmer with a straw hat and a long flowing beard, identified only as "Uncle Josh" in the newspapers, made the trip from Washtenaw County to Detroit for the first time in twenty years. "Ain't yer ashamed of yerself," he yelled while wagging an old umbrella at a sideshow attendant, "ter charge people wots paid money ter get in here?"

Exposition managers, looking to avoid too much criticism, limited the number of sideshows and offered their own free museum. Featured were a working miniature harbor and train yard, stuffed and live birds, a magician, and a card-playing pig. The most popular act was Professor Woodward and his trained seals and sea lions, one of which had suffered severe injuries six weeks earlier when it jumped out of a moving train in Indiana. Like a true trouper, though, the scarred, battered sea lion joined its companions in putting on first-rate shows daily. Their tank required a barrel of salt and a ton of ice each day to keep the water in an acceptable living condition.

Another popular attraction was Fiji Jim, who was either a cannibal or a warrior or possibly both, depending on the individual fairgoer sizing him up. A genuine Fiji Islander whose real name was Ruto Sernm, he had been lured to the United States by a circus promoter who soon abandoned him. Fiji Jim worked sideshows in a futile attempt to make enough money to return home. He was destined to die seven years later inside a freezing Brooklyn flat, having caught pleurisy after saving a swimmer from drowning. At the Detroit fair, though, the exotic-looking specimen from the South Pacific spoke "gibberish" to gawkers.

At one point a troublemaker leaned over and whispered a few words to Annie, the woman advertised as Fiji Jim's wife. Whatever was said was enough to stir the bushy-haired, gaudily painted woman out of character. "If yese waz in Boofalow," she exclaimed in an Irish brogue, "yese wouldn't dare to tawk loike that to me at all." As the crowd laughed and Fiji Jim frowned disapprovingly, Annie stopped shaking her fist and resumed her role as a submissive native of the Fiji Islands.

George Bailey of Buffalo, New York, was press superintendent of that city's annual exposition. Reporters and officials sought his expert opinion. He had just returned from the Paris world's fair, which was winding down its six-month run, and he was determined to say nothing but good things about Detroit's fair in comparison. "In your show of horses, cattle, swine, and agricultural implements," he said, "the Detroit is superior to the Paris exposition."

Bailey was fascinated with the Eiffel Tower, which had been built as the gateway to the Paris fair and was the tallest structure on earth. "I really think that the erection of a similar tower at the Detroit exposition would be a practical undertaking and a very lucrative one," he said. He figured one could be built for $500,000 and was convinced that this "marvelous attraction" would be "one of the permanent sights of Detroit." If an Eiffel Tower could not be built in Detroit, Bailey offered a downsized alternative. "I think a captive balloon capable of holding eighteen or twenty people would prove a great attraction."

On the same day Bailey spoke of these possibilities, several thousand people arched their necks to watch Professor C. Bartholomew—the seemingly suicidal balloonist and parachutist—perform trapeze tricks while ascending into the overcast sky in his hot-air balloon. He was still recovering from a recent bad fall in which he had bounced off a building in Australia. However, the daredevil aeronaut insisted that the show must go on. When he reached an altitude of 9,000 feet, he climbed out of the basket and jumped into the clouds. The professor missed the exposition grounds completely but landed without mishap on the outskirts of Windsor. "I have looked down upon a great many cities," he said upon his return, "but I have never seen a prettier city than Detroit. To fully appreciate its beauty one must look at it from an elevation that will enable him to see it all at one time."

The exposition's final day was September 27, 1889, a wet Friday. For two weeks, the city's four daily newspapers had been filled with items like this: "Charles Grant of Thornburg, Ont., made Michigan farmers' eyes bulge out with his elegant display of grains and seeds." Now it was time to close the gates and the books. Despite the almost consistently inclement weather, during those two weeks in September between 20,000 and 37,000 people had visited the fair each day. Total attendance topped 300,000.

Detroit's big show ended with a big bang when a battery of cannon punctuated a martial tune that final afternoon. The ground-shaking explosions caused people in the main building to come tumbling out the doors. Most thought the roof or a tower had given way. "A force of waiters employed in the exposition restaurant, wearing white aprons and tall, round hats, rushed out of the restaurant and across the open space toward the river as if pursued by fiends," a bemused witness reported. "At their head was a jolly little red-faced man with short, stubby legs. His hat was set back on his head and as he ran his white apron fluttered in the breeze like a signal of distress."

The fair, which returned a $5,000 profit to its investors, was viewed by some of its most upbeat supporters as proof that Detroit could handle

A marksmanship demonstration during the Detroit International Exhibition & Fair. The Louis Kamper-designed exhibition hall, at the time the largest such building in the world, stands in the background. (Burton Historical Collection)

Visitors to the inaugural Detroit fair, held September 17–27, 1889. The Detroit Soap Company's entire structure was carved from giant cakes of its popular Queen Anne soap. (Author's Collection)

the Columbian Exposition, the world's fair being planned to celebrate the 400th anniversary of Columbus's arrival in the New World. However, the city was never a serious contender. Congress accepted Chicago's bid over those of New York and St. Louis. Detroit assumed its more familiar role as foundry to pre-automobile America, with the star attraction of the 1893 Columbian Exposition—George Ferris's massive passenger wheel—being built largely in its shops.

The Detroit International Exposition & Fair continued as an annual affair for three more years, always turning a small profit, before the land was sold to the Solvay Process Company. At that point, the heavy industrialization of the area began. Delray was formally incorporated into Detroit in 1906. A century later, it is a toxic landscape of smokestacks and blown-out houses with the bleakest future of any neighborhood in the city. Such decline would have been unthinkable to the exhibitors and fairgoers of 1889, when all the talk was of the community's rapid progress, its beauty, and its boundless potential. The "promoters of this enterprise have scored a proud triumph," the *Tribune* trumpeted on the day Detroit first threw open its gates to tomorrow, "and secured permanently to Detroit an institution that will add to her fair fame and prosperity through all time to come."

Brace Beemer, the longtime voice of the Lone Ranger, delivers his lines inside the WXYZ studio. John Todd, the voice of Tonto throughout the radio show's entire run, stands at left of center. Others in this circa-1948 photograph are (*from left*): actors Harry Goldstein, Bill Saunders, Bob Dale, Jay Michaels, Ernie Winstanley, Jimmy Fletcher, and announcer Fred Foy. The man working the engineering booth is unknown. (Paul Carnegie Collection)

TWO

The Lone Ranger Rides Again!

Radio's greatest fictional lawman had his origins not in the wide-open West but inside a cramped Detroit studio. Return with us now to those thrilling days of yesteryear. . . .

The panel of *I've Got a Secret* was stumped this particular Monday evening in 1964. So was the national television audience. Who was this tall, heavyset man with the craggy good looks? It didn't help matters that host Garry Moore would not let the mystery guest answer any questions himself. Finally, Moore allowed him to utter a single word—"No"—and millions of ears around the country instantly perked up at the sound of an old friend's voice.

"Brace Beemer!" panelists shouted. "The Lone Ranger!"

Such was the influence of radio during its golden age, and such was the remarkable staying power of the medium's greatest fictional lawman.

"Brace Beemer had a voice that was unforgettable," recalled Mert Oakes, who grew up in Iowa during the 1930s. "We had a three-foot-high cabinet radio in the living room, and I'd sit there on the floor and listen to every episode. It wasn't like television. You had to use your imagination as to what was going on."

From 1933 to 1957, a period that spanned the Great Depression, World War II, and the early Cold War years, *The Lone Ranger* threw an enormous electronic lasso over a country hungry for heroes, roping in as many as fifteen million listeners every Monday, Wednesday, and Friday night.

America's sweetheart, child star Shirley Temple, gushed that it was her favorite program. FBI director J. Edgar Hoover loved the simple cowboy morality sandwiched between pitches for Silvercup bread, one of the show's sponsors. Even atomic spy Julius Rosenberg was tuned to the Ranger on the evening that real-life lawmen burst through the door of his dingy flat to arrest him for selling secrets to the Russians.

Over time the Lone Ranger franchise grew to include movies, books, comics, and the first made-for-TV Western series. A saddlebag full of merchandise found its way under Christmas trees, including cap guns, clothing, lunchboxes, radios, watches, board games, puzzles, flashlights, and toothbrushes. "I had to have everything—the Lone Ranger outfit, the guns, the mask, everything," said Oakes, now living in Vancouver, Washington. "I was crazy about the show. I memorized the preamble and I never forgot it."

That preamble remains the most famous in radio history. Each episode began with the horn blast from the rousing "cavalry charge" finale of Rossini's *William Tell Overture* and continued with the announcer's breathless introduction:

"A fiery horse with the speed of light, a cloud of dust and a hearty Hi-Yo, Silver! The Lone Ranger. With his faithful Indian companion, Tonto, the daring and resourceful masked rider of the plains led the fight for law and order in the early western United States. Nowhere in the pages of history can one find a greater champion of justice. Return with us now to those thrilling days of yesteryear. From out of the past come the thundering hoof beats of the great horse Silver! The Lone Ranger rides again!"

The Lone Ranger debuted on the evening of January 30, 1933, live from WXYZ studios in the Maccabees Building on Woodward Avenue in Detroit. The show's exact origins have been the source of eternal debate; however, it's safe to say that the principal creators were station owner George W. Trendle, who had made his money managing local vaudeville houses and movie theatres; Buffalo-based writer Fran Striker, who fleshed out the characters and story lines for a few dollars per script; and WXYZ's drama director, James Jewell, who, like several others involved in the show's beginnings, went to his grave feeling that he had been robbed of proper credit.

"The Masked Man of the Plains" was a ubiquitous pop culture figure appearing in, among other things, this 1940s comic book. (Author's Collection)

To accommodate different time zones, each half-hour episode of *The Lone Ranger* was performed live three times. Although Beemer's voice is the one most closely associated with the show, he actually was just one of several radio Rangers. A dapper little actor named Jack Deeds played the title role in unconvincing fashion for the first six episodes. When Deeds arrived at the station drunk one evening, he was fired on the spot by Jewell, who took over for that night's broadcast.

By the following episode a new masked man was in place—George Stenius, a soft-spoken twenty-one-year-old stage actor more comfortable with writing than performing. Stenius soon left Detroit for Hollywood, where, as George Seaton, he achieved success (including a pair of Oscars) as the writer and director of such movies as *Miracle on 34th Street* and *Airport*.

Earl Graser next settled into the saddle. Graser was a young law student who enjoyed badminton and singing in his church choir. According to the late Dick Osgood, a longtime WXYZ staffer who wrote a history of the station, Graser had "blue eyes, fair skin and was inclined to be chubby. Born in Canada, he had never been west of Michigan, couldn't ride a horse, and shot a gun only once in his life."

Nonetheless, starting on April 16, 1933, and continuing for the next eight years, the mild-mannered Graser was the voice of the hard-riding Ranger. Meanwhile, Beemer—a strapping six-foot-three Illinois native who could handle horses, guns, and bullwhips with ease—portrayed the character outside the studio. When seventy thousand kids showed up on Belle Isle one July day in 1933 for the Lone Ranger's first public appearance, Trendle realized he had an emerging hit on his hands. The program quickly moved from Trendle's fledgling statewide network of stations to a coast-to-coast feed. He offered Striker, who had been mailing in his scripts, a full-time job at one hundred dollars a week. As a condition of employment, the writer reluctantly surrendered all rights to the character. Striker moved his family to Detroit just in time to see the windows of Hudson's fill up with Lone Ranger merchandise for the 1933 Christmas season.

Trendle's coffers filled up as well. He quickly copyrighted *The Lone Ranger* and raked in millions of dollars over the life of the show. To discourage employees looking for a raise, he kept a doctored ledger showing the profitable program losing money. The show's dizzying success eventually begat *The Green Hornet* and *Sergeant Preston of the Yukon*, WXYZ dramas that borrowed many of their themes, story lines, and voice actors from *The Lone Ranger*.

Trendle issued strict directives regarding the Ranger's comportment. He was to speak in perfect English, could never cuss, drink alcohol, or tell a lie, and he had to be respectful of all nationalities and religions. In this theatre of the mind listeners were to see a level-headed pursuer of justice, not some vigilante wildly blasting his trademark silver bullets off saloon ceilings and canyon walls. "I'll shoot if I have to," the Lone Ranger would say. "But I'll shoot to wound, not to kill. If a man must die it's up to the law to decide that, not the person behind a six-shooter."

To which Tonto would reply, "That right, kemo-sabe!" The much-parodied word, which in the show was interpreted as "faithful friend," was borrowed from the name of a Camp Ke-Mo-Sa-Be Jewell's father-in-law owned in northern Michigan. It's worth noting that, pidgin English aside, Tonto's character was a departure from the stereotypical treatment of Indians in that and later eras. His role was written in a respectful fashion that made him the Lone Ranger's equal, not a subservient sidekick. For the first year or so the two even rode Silver together until Tonto got his own horse, Scout.

To Patsy Horan of Lansing, the noble and loyal Tonto was simply "good ol' Uncle Fred"—a pudgy, balding, veteran Shakespearean actor who happened to be her godfather, Fred McCarthy. He was born in Pennsylvania in 1877 and went by the stage name of John Todd and had, during his vaudeville days, met Buffalo Bill.

"He'd come over to our house in Detroit for Sunday dinner," said Horan. "I remember sitting on his lap. A real kind man. He'd give us kids elocution lessons. I thought it was kind of funny that Tonto always had shiny, manicured fingernails and smelled like cologne. But then I figured, well, he was an actor."

Todd played Tonto throughout the radio show's entire run. He often said he was grateful for such steady work, especially during the Depression. "We were the stars of the neighborhood," Horan said. "The family next door had a priest. But we had Tonto."

The classically trained actor John Todd made an unconvincing Tonto in person. Even his young niece noticed that the Lone Ranger's "faithful Indian companion" had manicured fingernails and smelled of cologne. (Peggy Horan Collection)

Few people even in Graser's Farmington neighborhood knew of his secret alter ego. But the Ranger's identity was tragically exposed in the early morning hours of April 8, 1941. While driving home on Grand River, the thirty-two-year-old actor—who had urged millions of kids to join the Lone Ranger Safety Club—fell asleep at the wheel and plowed his car into a parked trailer. Graser's untimely death rattled a country grown comfortable with his deep, rich voice and shocked children who had been convinced of the Lone Ranger's invincibility. Warmhearted obituaries were published coast-to-coast, and ten thousand people attended the funeral.

With a schedule of live broadcasts looming, the tragedy had station officials scrambling to rewrite scripts while searching for a permanent replacement. Several candidates were considered, including a staff announcer recently graduated from the University of Michigan—Myron "Mike" Wallace of future *60 Minutes* fame.

In the end Beemer—who by now was the station manager and longtime public face of the Ranger at parades, rodeos, and school functions—was the logical choice. Looking to soften the transition to a different voice, Striker's revised story line had the Ranger seriously wounded and unable to speak in anything other than an occasional moan or whisper. Tonto carried much of the action for several episodes until finally, a couple of weeks after Graser's death, a healed Lone Ranger was able to speak with bold, renewed vigor.

With Beemer at the reins, *The Lone Ranger* continued to ride righteously through the ether, picking up sponsors, listeners, and merchandisers along the way. By 1947 the program was heard on nearly two hundred and fifty radio stations. One giveaway that year resulted in a record three million letters and postcards, many bearing postmarks from places as far-flung as Mexico, New Zealand, and Singapore.

"My memory goes back to Brace as 'my' Lone Ranger on Monday, Wednesday, and Friday nights," recalled Chuck Ingraham, then an impressionable youngster growing up in New York. "I would wait for that wonderful voice in our lower east side tenement, get a kitchen chair, turn it around and sneak a pillow out of the bedroom (that was 'Silver'). I would set myself up in front of the old Majestic radio with the eagle on the dial and then I was in another world—away from the cold water flat, the hard times of winter in gloomy New York City during the early war years, with tipped-over trash cans in the alleys, and streets covered with blackened snow. The Lone Ranger changed my world for that half hour and I will always remember him and the mental images of prairies and mountains, western saloons and dusty trails." Ingraham ultimately made it out West, settling in California. "Brace started the dream," he said.

Beginning in the late 1940s, Detroit native Dick Beals played the role of the Ranger's nephew; he later lent his distinctive high-pitched voice to the famous "Speedy" Alka-Seltzer commercials as well as to numerous cartoon characters. "Brace drove a Cadillac convertible from his ranch, northwest of Pontiac, into work each day," recalled Beals, who today lives near Los Angeles. "A rather large, shiny, loaded six-shooter was just beside him, between the seats. He'd walk into the studio thirty seconds before airtime, always ready. Brace never missed a cue, blew a line, lost his place in the script, or criticized an actor."

The virile, strong-willed Beemer, who liked to wind down after shows with a few martinis and beer chasers at the Van Dyke Club, could be a handful when mask-less. But he was the perfect role model while in character, making unpublicized visits to hospitals and nursing homes and always putting on spirited public performances. He had been wounded while serving as an under-age soldier in World War I and absolutely believed in every syrupy syllable of the Lone Ranger's code, especially those homilies concerning duty, honor, and patriotism. He was the ideal pitchman for the show's major sponsor, General Mills, which offered such premiums as the Lone Ranger Atomic Bomb Ring. Kids ate it all up—the cereal along with the myth.

Announcer Bob Hite recalled one appearance at Madison Square Garden in 1951. Beemer, who by then was approaching fifty, "rode around the whole runway, and then he dismounted and walked to the microphone, and he was all alone in this huge arena, with a white light down on him, with his white hat on, the white horse, the silver guns—very impressive. The kids just went wild."

Over the years the show featured its share of "before they were famous" names. In addition to Beals, other actors included future screen star John Hodiak of Hamtramck ("one of the best villains on the station," recalled Osgood) and a Lebanese-American entertainer born Muzyad Yakhoob, who was destined to find fame as actor-philanthropist Danny Thomas. Another now-familiar voice belonged to a local college student named Kemal "Casey" Kasem, who years later made his pop-culture mark as host of the long-running *American Top 40* countdown show.

Paul Carnegie, known as "Paul Cannon" during his years as a disc jockey and program director at WKNR ("Keener 13") radio in the 1960s, is another alum. "I remember sitting on the floor, playing with my toy cars and listening to the show," said Carnegie, born in Detroit six months before *The Lone Ranger* first aired. In early 1951—by which time the show's production had shifted to studios inside the converted Mendelssohn mansion in Indian Village—the Southeastern High grad was hired to work in the sound effects department, considered one of the best in the business. That was "pretty heady stuff" for the teenager, who got paid a dollar an hour.

Brace Beemer (*left*) and Detroit movie-show host Bill Kennedy on March 1, 1965. A few hours later, Beemer was dead. For years afterward, Kennedy aired the radio Ranger's last interview on the anniversary of his death. (Ed Golick Collection)

The sound effects department at WXYZ in 1951 included Paul Carnegie (*far right*), who produced the sound of galloping hoofbeats by pounding plungers into a box of gravel. (Paul Carnegie Collection)

"Whenever some character was socked on the jaw, I'd smack the palm of my hand with this little pad of rubber," he said. "It hurt like hell." Galloping hoofbeats were created by pounding bathroom plungers into a box of gravel.

Carnegie's most important duty was making sure Tonto was awake to say his lines. "John Todd was in his seventies by then, and he'd sit in this chair in the corner. So on my script I'd always write 'John' in big letters a couple pages before one of his scenes. That reminded me it was time to go over and nudge John. He'd say, 'Sheriff ride to town, kemo-sabe,' or something like that, and then doze off again."

Beals recounted one memorable incident that highlighted the occasional danger of Todd's advancing age and also showcased Beemer's unflappability. During one particular live episode, the Lone Ranger had been wounded and was desperately crawling across the desert, moaning, "Tonto . . . Tonto . . . Tonto . . ." At that precise moment, the dozing Todd leaned the back of his chair into an electrical sound-effects button, causing the wall-rattling horn of the 20th Century Limited to blast across the airwaves. The explosion blew the dazed actor out of his chair and sent him stumbling through the studio door and into the hanging mike. "Brace didn't blink an eye," Beals said. "He kept reading, ad-libbed John's lines into his script and the show continued."

Trendle also was getting on in years and growing concerned with certain estate implications of owning the Lone Ranger franchise. On August 3, 1954, all rights to the property were sold to Wrather Corporation, the Texas-based production company that had already brought the radio show to television. Out of that $3-million windfall Trendle wrote Striker—the man who at one time mass-produced 60,000 words of copy a week for the various Lone Ranger commercial properties—a "bonus" check for $4,000.

The final live broadcast of *The Lone Ranger* took place on September 3, 1954, ending a twenty-one-year run that featured some three thousand original episodes. Afterward Todd simply said, "It's just as well. We were getting into a rut." WXYZ continued to broadcast repeats of old shows until 1957, the year Todd died, but the era of the live radio Ranger was over.

One by one, the rest of the show's principals joined Todd in that Great Bunkhouse in the Sky. Striker died in a car accident in upstate New York in 1962. Three years later, Beemer succumbed to a stroke while playing bridge with friends at home. Trendle passed away in 1972; to the very end he threatened to sue anyone who challenged his claim as the sole creator of *The Lone Ranger.*

Meanwhile, TV's version of *The Lone Ranger* (with the lead role played by Clayton Moore and featuring Jay Silverheels as Tonto) took hold in the public consciousness. The show ran on ABC from 1949 to 1957; the same actors also appeared in a pair of Lone Ranger movies. "You watch those shows today and they're just terrible," said Carnegie. "You get sick of seeing the same phony rocks and phony trees. That was the advantage of radio. You saw things in your mind, not with your eyes."

An aging George W. Trendle holds the Lone Ranger's calling card: a silver bullet. Until his death in 1972, the tight-fisted radio pioneer threatened to sue anyone who challenged his claim as the sole creator of *The Lone Ranger*. (Author's Collection)

Nonetheless, thanks to countless syndicated reruns and thousands of personal appearances by Silverheels and Moore until their deaths in 1980 and 1999, respectively, the characters from the TV show are the ones best remembered by baby boomers today.

All modern remakes of the Lone Ranger story—including a made-for-TV movie that featured kung fu and rap sequences—have flopped. Although technology has the ability to enrich creativity in ways that would astonish the original cast, fans of old-time radio say it's impossible to improve on a classic Western drama whose clomping hooves and signature line—"Who was that masked man?"—came out of a cramped studio in Detroit.

"The show had all the right elements," Carnegie said. "There were great sound effects and a wide variety of voices, so you could identify characters. There was fine acting, good writing, and a little bit of mystery.

"And good triumphed over evil. Always."

Frank Murphy in 1930, the year he was elected mayor of Detroit. (Author's Collection)

THREE
The Saint

During a long and notable career in public service, Frank Murphy wore many hats. Some thought he should have been fitted for a halo.

Frank Murphy had been one of the most famous men in America, and now he was dead.

On a warm summer day in 1949, some twenty thousand Detroiters quietly shuffled through the marble expanses of old City Hall to say goodbye to the beetle-browed crusader. Another twenty thousand were turned away. "They came in shirt sleeves and they came with dinner pails," observed a reporter. "There was sadness in their faces and many wept publicly, unashamedly."

The rank and file had a special affection for Murphy, whose mediation of the landmark 1937 Flint sit-down strike had given the fledgling United Automobile Workers a breakthrough victory. At Dodge Truck, where workers had observed one minute of silence when company president Walter Chrysler died, factory hands paused at their workstations for a full five minutes to honor Murphy. When management declared it would dock workers fifteen cents each for what amounted to excessive mourning, they responded in a way that would have drawn a sympathetic nod from the recently departed. They went on strike.

Murphy was a friend to the disadvantaged, a guardian of the downtrodden, and a hero to the working class. As Recorder's Court judge, mayor of Detroit, governor-general of the Philippines, governor of Michigan,

U.S. attorney general, and associate justice of the U.S. Supreme Court, his life intersected with some of the great issues and events of his time. The *New York Times* described him as "one of the most earnest, interesting and able men in public life," an idealist who was "a searcher after the Grail if ever there was one." Twenty years after his death, the new Recorder's Court was named after him. It has since been expanded into a judicial center known as the Frank Murphy Hall of Justice. Outside is one of the last works by noted Cranbrook sculptor Carl Milles, *The Hand of God,* which the UAW commissioned to honor Murphy.

Among the pallbearers who accompanied Murphy to his final resting place in his hometown of Harbor Beach was Jim Lincoln, who was on Murphy's staff in Lansing and Washington before going on to a long career in Detroit as a city councilman and judge. "One of his finest qualities was his easygoing way with people," recalled Lincoln. "Anyone could speak his mind to him and feel at ease. In his eyes, every person, no matter what their skin color or station in life, had dignity and was worthy of respect."

Murphy had led a full life even before coming to prominence in Detroit. Born William Francis Murphy in 1890 to Irish-American parents in what was then called Sand Beach, he chose law—his father's profession—over his mother's wish that he become a Catholic priest. He earned a law degree at the University of Michigan, then did graduate work in London and Dublin. He went overseas again during World War I, serving as an army captain in occupied Germany before accepting a position as assistant U.S. attorney in the Detroit office. There he prosecuted bootleggers, bank robbers, and other criminals, losing just one case in three years.

Murphy had shown himself to be a fearless prosecutor, but he resigned in 1922 to concentrate on the private practice that he had set up with a college friend, Edward Kemp. Kemp was a quiet and conservative counterweight to Murphy. Over the years, he accompanied Murphy throughout all his travels, remaining his closest confidante.

Murphy had long been active in Democratic politics, enjoying a reputation as an effective orator. In 1923 he was persuaded to run for Recorder's Court judge. Backed by the *Detroit Times,* which had a running feud with one of the sitting judges, Murphy outpolled all candidates to claim a seat on the municipal court. From that vantage point he saw what needed improvement and took appropriate action. He changed the bail system so poor citizens could more easily make bond and created a separate traffic court to handle the growing number of minor auto-related offenses that were clogging the docket.

The most important civil rights trials of the 1920s took place under Murphy's gaze. One September evening in 1925, a group of whites threatened a black family moving into a house at 2905 Garland on the east side. Shots rang out. One member of the mob dropped dead and another fell wounded. Eleven blacks were taken into custody, with the homeowner, Dr. Ossian Sweet, the first to stand trial for murder.

The Sweet case attracted national attention, not least because the defense brought in the country's most famous attorney, Clarence Darrow. After a jury of twelve white men could not agree on a verdict in the first trial, Murphy declared a mistrial. Sweet's brother, the only defendant to admit to firing a gun, was tried next. Thanks to Darrow's brilliant and theatrical defense, he was acquitted—a stunning victory that affirmed the right of a black man to defend his property in the face of racist threats.

Murphy's determination to give the defendants a fair trial earned him widespread praise. "It is so seldom that those of us who are trying to secure even-handed justice for Negro citizens encounter one like yourself," a member of the defense team wrote Murphy, "you may well imagine our joy when that experience does come."

Murphy liked to affect a tough-guy persona, but the wiry redhead was far from imposing. One observer described his "birdlike" mannerisms. He was an ascetic who eschewed alcohol and tobacco but occasionally binged on chocolate ice cream. An exercise fanatic, his favorite pastime was horseback riding. His distinguishing characteristic was a set of eyebrows so astonishing, they appeared to have been applied with a vaudevillian's greasepaint.

More impressive was his utter incorruptibility. Murphy, who came from a tight-knit family, was especially devoted to his siblings, George and Marguerite, who at times drew enough financial support to be listed as dependents on his tax return. Although he enjoyed a comfortable income for most of his public career, it was never near what he could have made in the private sector. "His devotion to public service was total," Lincoln said. "He was not interested in money. He could not be corrupted because he could not be tempted."

In 1930, Charles Bowles—a controversial figure with alleged ties to gangsters and the Ku Klux Klan—became the first mayor of a major U.S. city ever recalled from office. At the urging of business leaders and newspapers, Murphy ran in the special election that followed, riding the votes of the "common herd" of ordinary working-class citizens to victory.

Detroit's new mayor took over a city filled with misery as people struggled with the effects of a deepening economic depression. The once dynamic metropolis was now sadly "out of gear," euphemized commentators in the national media. Auto production fell 75 percent between 1929 and 1932, resulting in labor strife, political agitators, and newsreel images of soup lines. For many, the loss of a job represented a loss of dignity and an overpowering sense of personal failure. "It seems to me I have lost all my ability as a responsible man," an unemployed worker who refused welfare wrote to Murphy. "It seems to me I have some shortcomings somewhere."

In confronting the immense challenges of the Great Depression, Murphy was creative and proactive, "a new dealer even before there was a New Deal," observed his principal biographer, Sidney Fine. He arranged for Detroiters to plant "thrift gardens" on empty city-owned lots, convinced industrialists to turn over empty factories to be converted into boardinghouses for the homeless, and devised a plan that allowed delinquent property owners to pay their taxes over a seven-year period.

Murphy also was responsible for the apple vendors who became iconic images of Depression-era Detroit. He arranged to have unemployed men, many of whom were physically handicapped, buy apples from a local produce company at two cents apiece. The apples were then re-sold on street corners for a nickel each. At the program's peak, 650 Detroiters, most of them down-and-out World War I veterans, were supporting their families by selling apples.

An apple vendor in Detroit, circa 1931. (Walter P. Reuther Library)

Murphy's profile grew when he organized meetings of desperate mayors—first statewide, then nationally—that in 1933 officially became the U.S. Conference of Mayors. He was elected as the first president of the group, which helped convince Congress to provide direct federal aid to cash-strapped cities for the first time in the country's history. Even the *Detroit Free Press,* unfriendly to the administration, had to concede: "Frank Murphy could be elected president or emperor of any great country in the world as the Great Humanitarian." His constituency was made up of laborers, Catholics, blacks, and immigrants.

The charismatic public servant was not without his faults. He could be self-absorbed, sanctimonious, and overly ambitious. Murphy, whose favorite topic of conversation was himself and his work, took some heat for being a publicity hound. The press also questioned the size of his personal security detail—two uniformed officers and two plainclothesmen—when previous mayors had been protected by just one or two policemen. But these were minor blemishes on an otherwise outstanding

Franklin D. Roosevelt (*seated, at back left*) and Frank Murphy campaign together in Detroit during the 1932 presidential campaign. (State of Michigan Archives)

mayoral record. He easily won a second term in the 1932 election that swept Franklin D. Roosevelt into the White House. It was the first time in eighty years that Michigan, a Republican stronghold for generations, had gone for the Democratic presidential candidate.

Murphy had campaigned hard for Roosevelt, and FDR rewarded his loyalty. In April 1933, Murphy was appointed governor-general of the Philippines. Murphy saw the governorship of America's most important overseas possession as a possible stepping-stone to the presidency. While he enjoyed the emoluments of his position—the governor's palace, the servants, the yacht—he also confessed to feeling guilty about such perks. A devout Catholic, he continued to pray daily from the now-worn Bible his mother had given him on the day he went off to college.

Murphy was wedded to his job, which was guiding the Philippines' transition from a territory to a commonwealth en route to its eventual independence from the United States. "I have work to do and a short time in which to do it," he wrote to his brother.

Such single-mindedness was Murphy's stock excuse for not settling down with one of his many female friends. Throughout his long public career, the press reported on a variety of companions, including actress Ann Harding and the equally stunning Ann Parker, the latter of whom had been named the most beautiful girl at Smith College. His lifelong preference for the company of younger women caused syndicated columnist Westbrook Pegler to dub him Frank "Hubba-Hubba" Murphy. When Murphy left the Philippines in 1936, a local newspaper headlined its report: "Manila Maids Mourn Murphy's Leaving."

Murphy returned to Michigan to run for governor against the Republican incumbent, Frank Fitzgerald. Not everybody was enamored with the liberal challenger. Rural voters hated the idea of welfare, while business owners considered the New Deal to be an insidious form of communism. On November 3, 1936, thanks to overwhelming support from Detroit and Wayne County voters, Murphy squeaked through with a narrow victory.

The new governor was faced with a major crisis immediately. When he took office on the first day of 1937, autoworkers in Flint had just seized a pair of General Motors plants in an attempt to force the automaker to recognize their grievances. GM officials refused to negotiate, so the "sit-downers" barricaded themselves inside while picketers guarded the gates against police and GM henchmen.

Geraldine Blankinship of Flint is one of a dwindling number of surviving strikers and their supporters from the storied strike. "It wasn't all about money," she said. "The conditions were inhumane in the plants." Blankinship recalled the murderously hot summer of 1936, when workers laboring in triple-digit temperatures would "pass out on the line and they wouldn't even drag them away. You'd have to step over them." Terror ruled the shop floor. Workers who left the line for the restroom were followed, timed, and harassed. Those afraid of being fired urinated or defecated in their pants. Union organizers were beaten by company goons.

On January 11, 1937, police stormed the barricaded strikers, firing tear gas and bullets. Workers fought back by hurling rocks and heavy hinges and blasting water from fire hoses. At battle's end, twenty-seven people had been injured, thirteen of whom were strikers and their sympathizers

The Flint sit-down strike of 1936–1937. As governor, Frank Murphy refused to use National Guard troops to evict the strikers and instead helped mediate the historic agreement between General Motors and the United Automobile Workers. (State of Michigan Archives)

suffering from gunshot wounds. Murphy ordered National Guard troops to Flint. "When we heard that, we thought the strikers were going to get dragged out, maybe even shot down," said Blankinship, whose father was one of the sit-downers. "But the governor sent them to protect the workers. He didn't want a bloodbath."

Murphy ignored a court order to evict the strikers from the plants. While guardsmen kept the peace, he skillfully negotiated talks between the UAW and GM. Both sides gave concessions. On February 11, Murphy announced that a settlement had been reached. The biggest prize was the world's largest carmaker agreeing to recognize the UAW as the sole bargaining agent for GM workers. After forty-four days, what is generally acknowledged as the most important strike in U.S. labor history had ended peacefully, with the UAW in firm control of its destiny. From that point the UAW took off, gaining instant credibility and hundreds of thousands of new members.

Murphy was not against big business; he simply wanted employers to behave more humanely. "We have got to realize that no one is secure until all are secure," he explained, "that injustice to anyone is injustice to everyone." When strikers shut down several Detroit auto plants in 1937, he again refused to send in state troops to evict the squatters. Soon Chrysler and other large employers had no choice but to capitulate.

As governor, Murphy could boast the most reform-minded administration in decades. He did away with the spoils system among state employees and installed a civil service system. The sick, elderly, indigent, and unemployed all benefited from new legislation. When he lost his re-election bid to Fitzgerald in 1938, many thought the defeat was payback for his pro-union sympathies, though Lincoln pointed out that the incumbent was running in an off-year election without the benefit of Roosevelt's name at the top of the ticket.

Roosevelt soon found another spot for one of the Democratic Party's rising stars, this time as a U.S. attorney general. As Murphy boarded the Washington-bound train at Michigan Central Station one January day in 1939, he "seemed a little sad to be leaving Detroit because . . . he felt that it closed that whole chapter of his life," observed his sister-in-law.

Murphy's Michigan years had indeed drawn to a close, though the decade he spent in Washington was filled with the same high level of achievement. As attorney general, he cracked down on racketeering, most notably corrupt political machines in Kansas City and Philadelphia. He also created the department's first civil rights section.

Then, after just one year on the job, Roosevelt appointed him to fill a vacancy on the U.S. Supreme Court. Lincoln, hearing the news, walked into Murphy's office to offer congratulations. "Jim," he said, his head in his hands, "I don't want to do it." Murphy, who had been touted by *Time* as a potential presidential or vice-presidential candidate, knew his political career was over, Lincoln said. FDR, looking ahead to his run for an unprecedented third term, had deftly removed a rival.

Murphy donned his jurist's robe in February 1940. During his nine years as an associate justice, he stood out as the evangelist on a bench filled with legal scholars. His opinions typically were rooted more in humanism than the fine points of the law, causing a fellow justice to nickname him "the Saint." In his dissent to a 1944 decision that upheld the government's right to intern Japanese-Americans during World War II, Murphy deplored "the ugly abyss of racism"—the first use of the word "racism" in a Supreme Court opinion. It did not reappear until the court weighed in on civil rights cases in the '60s.

If the cloistered life of an associate justice meant "the end of ambition," as Murphy put it, certain rumors refused to die. There was considerable speculation that the unattached ladies' man was, in fact, gay. Among other hints, gossipers pointed to the inseparable relationship between Murphy and Edward Kemp, who shared living arrangements throughout their adult lives. Their unusually close relationship was similar to the one another prominent Washington contemporary, FBI director J. Edgar Hoover, had with his constant companion, Clyde Tolson. Roosevelt, whose son-in-law privately considered Murphy a "pansy," was aware of the gossip and urged Murphy to "get busy" about marrying.

Sidney Fine briefly addressed the question of Murphy's sexual orientation in his comprehensive three-volume biography. The respected historian later said he was "never able to find anything that could pin it down," though he did uncover a letter, written when Murphy was attorney general, "that, if the words mean what they say, refers to a homosexual encounter between Murphy and the writer." Deb Price, a Washington-based columnist on gay issues, and her life partner, journalist Joyce Murdock, dug deep into the private lives of Supreme Court justices in their well-received book, *Courting Justice*. "If I had to bet a week's salary on it," Murdock told a reviewer from *The Advocate*, "I would say yes, he was gay."

Toward the end of his life Murphy was engaged to Joan Cuddihy—the granddaughter of the publisher of *Literary Digest* and a woman half his age—though there was a noticeable lack of enthusiasm on the part of the aging bachelor to actually set a wedding date. Murphy instructed his longtime secretary, Eleanor Baumgardner, to find a house that could comfortably accommodate the engaged couple, Baumgardner, and Kemp. If Murphy was indeed gay at a time when homosexuality was a crime in most of the country and was considered career suicide for politicians, the effort in keeping such an explosive secret from the public would have added to the stress that was already slowly killing him.

Murphy's health steadily declined in his fifties. He was treated for heart and circulation problems and often was hospitalized for several weeks at a time in Washington or Detroit. He also suffered from sciatic neuralgia. Unable to sleep properly and racked by pain in his back and legs, he became hooked on Demerol and Seconal. His dependency never appeared to impair his judgment, but the seedy nature of his addiction troubled those closest to him. When doctors refused to write him any more prescriptions, he began buying the drugs from shady middlemen in hotel rooms. Murphy insisted he had the problem under control while repeatedly trying—and failing—to wean himself off his addiction.

Ignoring calls to step down because of his failing health and frequent absences, Murphy made it through the 1948–49 term. Just before the court adjourned for its summer recess, the exhausted justice flexed a bicep for a reporter. "They say I'm sick," he declared. "But feel that muscle. They can't keep a man like me down." Shortly thereafter he checked into Henry Ford Hospital. There he suffered a coronary thrombosis on the morning of July 19, 1949, his heart holding out until a priest could administer the last rites of the Catholic Church. He was fifty-nine years old.

Murphy's estate was later probated at $11,000, not quite enough to satisfy the $12,000 in debts he had left behind. For many years a simple wooden cross marked his grave at a small cemetery near Lake Huron—the terminus to what had been a remarkable journey from the quiet bean fields of Michigan's Thumb through the raucous corridors of one of the most eventful periods in American history.

"I have never deviated from the path I set out for myself when I first started in public life," he had reflected in a letter to an old friend a year before his death. "So many public servants are new-born liberals only to be sound conservatives the next day, forgetting the inarticulate and the plundered poor."

Charles A. Lindbergh in May 1927, shortly before his epochal nonstop flight from New York to Paris. (Library of Congress)

FOUR
Lucky To Have Lindy

Charles Lindbergh rose to worldwide fame in the *Spirit of St. Louis*, but his family roots were entrenched in Detroit.

Fred Smith can't always recall what he had for yesterday's breakfast, but he remembers the details of a long-ago Saturday afternoon at Navin Field about as clearly as if he were reading them off the back of a cereal box. It was May 21, 1927, in the middle innings of an entertaining contest between the Detroit Tigers and the Washington Senators, when the umpires suddenly stopped play. There was no public-address system then, and portable radios didn't exist, but the few thousand baseball fans in attendance already knew that something momentous was happening. They heard factory whistles screaming, car horns blasting, fire engines racing, and newsies hawking extras outside of the ballpark. Inside, a leather-lunged usher with a giant megaphone stepped up to each section of the grandstand and spread the word:

"Lindbergh has landed safely in Paris!"

Smith, then a twelve-year-old fan caught up in the diamond exploits of Tiger stars Heinie Manush and Harry Heilmann, was unimpressed with the news of history's first solo trans-Atlantic flight. "I was annoyed that they disturbed the ballgame even for a fraction of a minute with that announcement," he said.

At that moment Smith may have been the only miffed soul on either side of the Atlantic. Charles Lindbergh's nonstop flight from New York to Paris, May 20–21, 1927, was instantly recognized as one of the epic feats of the twentieth century, an achievement as monumental in its time as American astronauts' trip to the moon in the *Apollo XI* four decades later. Six men already had died trying to cross the Atlantic, all in aircraft more sophisticated than Lindbergh's *Spirit of St. Louis*. Squeezed into what amounted to little more than a flying gas tank, and with a greasy sack of sandwiches and a thermos of lukewarm coffee jammed under his wicker seat, the largely unknown air-mail pilot battled fog, sleet, and phantoms for thirty-three and a half hours before landing at Le Bourget airfield outside Paris. The boldface headline in the *Detroit Free Press* trumpeted his new status: LINDBERGH, IN PARIS, ACCLAIMED WORLD HERO.

The young hero was showered with countless honors, including the Distinguished Flying Cross, *Time* magazine's "Man of the Year" award, and a postage stamp that was the first to honor a living American. He received the Congressional Medal of Honor and four million pieces of mail, including ten thousand marriage proposals. "We shouted ourselves hoarse," Mary B. Mullett wrote in *American Magazine*. "Not because a man had flown across the Atlantic! Not even because he was an American! But because he was as clean in character as he was strong and fine in body; because he put his 'ethics' above any desire for wealth; because he was as modest as he was courageous; and because—as we now know, beyond any shadow of a doubt—these are the things which we honor most in life."

What made Lindbergh's triumph even sweeter in Detroiters' minds was that, like the Model T and Vernor's ginger ale, he was a homegrown product. Sure, he had been brought up primarily in Minnesota and Washington, D.C., but locals still bragged, "He's our boy!" Nearly everyone knew that, at the time of his flight, his mother was a teacher at Cass Technical High School, and his great-uncle, John C. Lodge, namesake of the freeway in Detroit, was the mayor.

Those unaware of Lindbergh's roots were enlightened when he and his mother were feted in the nation's capitol upon his return to the States. As a crowd of a quarter-million people looked on and an unprecedented national radio audience of thirty million listened, President Calvin

Coolidge began his remarks: "Twenty-five years ago there was born in Detroit, Michigan, a boy representing the best traditions of this country, of a stock known for its deeds of adventure and exploration. . . ."

Lindbergh's Motor City connections remained strong over the years before evaporating with little fanfare some three decades later. But that's getting a little ahead of the tale, because the story of one of Detroit's most celebrated native sons begins not with his birth or celebrated flight, but with his disgraced paternal grandfather.

In 1859, Ola Mansson crossed the river from Windsor into Detroit, en route to a new life in Minnesota. An unschooled dairy farmer with a large family, the fifty-one-year-old immigrant had been a member of Sweden's parliament before being convicted of embezzling—a scandal that caused him to flee the country with his mistress and their year-old baby. Once in the New World, Mansson changed his name to Karl Lindbergh (an identity fashioned from the Swedish word for mountain and the ubiquitous linden tree) and settled down on a farm near Little Falls. His son, Charles August Lindbergh—better known as C. A.—went on to earn a law degree at the University of Michigan. There the tall and handsome lawyer made the acquaintance of Evangeline Lodge Land. The headstrong schoolteacher became his wife and the mother of the future aviator.

Evangeline, who was born in 1876 on the current site of the David Whitney Building on Woodward Avenue at Grand Circus Park, descended from two prominent Detroit families. The Lodges, her mother's side of the family, had produced several physicians, while her father, Dr. Charles H. Land, pioneered the then-controversial use of porcelain in dentistry. With her blue eyes and striking figure, Evangeline had been considered the most attractive co-ed at the University of Michigan, from which she graduated in 1899 with a degree in chemistry. Resisting suggestions that she teach school in Detroit, she instead accepted a position for fifty-five dollars a month at a one-room schoolhouse in Little Falls.

On March 27, 1901, Evangeline married C. A. at her parents' house at 64 Elizabeth in Detroit. They then moved into a new house built on 120 acres of Minnesota countryside overlooking the Mississippi River.

Lindbergh's birthplace on West Forest Avenue. It later was used as a boardinghouse and fraternity house before being razed in 1973, a year before the aviator's death. (Author's Collection)

Evangeline soon became pregnant and returned to Detroit to have her baby. At 1:30 a.m. on February 4, 1902, her great-uncle, Dr. Edwin Lodge, helped deliver a nine-and-a-half-pound boy in the front bedroom of his brownstone at 258 West Forest. They named the big-footed, blue-eyed infant Charles Augustus Lindbergh, Jr.

When Charles was four years old, his father was elected to Congress. C. A. took a mistress, and the marriage soon fell apart. The estranged couple settled upon a compromise for the sake of appearances and the boy's well-being. Charles was to spend each school year in Washington and summers in Minnesota, interlarded with long layovers in Detroit to visit Evangeline's relatives. As a result of this arrangement, Lindbergh grew up a self-reliant loner, with his mother as his best friend and closest confidante.

The youngster's curiosity was nurtured in Detroit, where his doting Grandfather Land threw open the resources of his basement laboratory. Here was the ultimate playground: drills, hammers, and saws, rock samples, electrical switches, and test tubes, stacks of *National Geographic*, stuffed birds and spiders, even a human skull in a box. Grandfather "can make anything with his hands," young Charles declared. John C. Lodge described his great-nephew as "a thoughtful boy, quiet and reserved, who always saw everything and was always experimenting with something."

Lindbergh hated classrooms, but he demonstrated a keen mechanical mind. (In the 1930s he helped Dr. Alexis Carrel develop the first artificial heart.) After failing out of the engineering program at the University of Wisconsin, he learned to fly as a twenty-year-old barnstormer in Nebraska and later as a graduate of the tough army air school in Texas. Bored with hauling the mail between St. Louis and Chicago, he set his sights on the $25,000 prize awaiting the first pilot to fly nonstop between New York and Paris. The Orteig Prize had been on the table since 1919, but it wasn't until 1926 that improved technology made such an attempt truly possible.

Lindbergh had two thousand dollars saved in a Detroit bank, but he needed several times that amount to buy the right plane. "Legend has it that Lindbergh first came to Detroit to see if he could get his uncle, as mayor, to interest local aviation in financing his flight," longtime newspaperman Malcolm Bingay recalled in his memoirs. "Uncle John, as the story goes, chided the boy for risking his life in aviation, assured him there was no future in it, and urged him to settle down and get 'a good steady job.'"

Lindbergh looked elsewhere. With the backing of a group of St. Louis investors, he spent $10,580 to have a plane built to his specifications in San Diego. The silver monoplane, which under different circumstances might have been called the *Spirit of Detroit*, was christened the *Spirit of St. Louis*.

The rest is history. While better-known and better-financed pilots were delayed by accidents, equipment failures, or internal squabbling, Lindbergh took off from Long Island's soggy Roosevelt Field on the morning of Friday, May 20, 1927. Unlike his rivals, he was flying alone—a distinction that had caused the press to dub him the "Lone Eagle" and the "Flying Fool."

Lindbergh made for Paris at an average speed of about 110 miles per hour. The plane had no radio, so for much of his flight he was completely shut off from the rest of the world. He fought off sleep and the prospect of death. As the plane droned on over the gray waters of the Atlantic, his thoughts often turned to his mother, who had moved permanently to Detroit after he had taken up flying. As he later recounted in his Pulitzer Prize–winning 1953 autobiography, *The Spirit of St. Louis:* "My mother, teaching school in Detroit—she's probably been at her laboratory desk all day, wondering and worrying, and trying unsuccessfully, with chemistry experiments, to curtain off in her mind a pilot and his plane . . . I know what a message of my welfare would mean to her tonight."

The world held its collective breath. Then word came that the *Spirit of St. Louis* had been spotted over Ireland . . . then England . . . then the French coast. Finally, at 10:24 p.m. on May 21, 1927, Lindbergh completed his 3,610-mile odyssey with a perfect sideslip landing at Le Bourget airfield. All hell broke loose. Lindbergh and his plane were nearly torn to pieces by 150,000 screaming Parisians who knocked down fences and bowled over armed guards in order to get at *l'americain galant.* Lindbergh's fame, unlike that of the latest flagpole sitter or marathon dancer—both high-profile fads of the 1920s—proved to have incredible staying power. This was a tribute to his modesty, honesty, and incorruptibility. "Hell, you couldn't help but look up to the guy," said former Bloomfield Hills mayor Dominick Vettraino, who was a twelve-year-old youngster living in rural Oakland County at the time of Lindbergh's historic flight. "You'd see all about him in the newsreels. A good-looking young fella. He took off in that damned little plane. Not too many guys would've had the guts to do that."

A flood of merchandise hit store shelves, everything from sheet music and board games to straight razors and poker chips. Ed Neill of Bloomfield Hills, then a ten-year-old scout growing up in western Pennsylvania, remembered "buying everything we could" that was related to Lindy and his flight. "Kids started wearing these Lindy leather jackets and leather helmets, complete with goggles," the retired salesman recalled with a laugh. "By September, when a new school year began, it seemed like everybody was wearing them. If you'd come by our elementary school,

The Detroit Free Press

MICHIGAN'S GREATEST NEWSPAPER

WEATHER
Probably Showers

VOL. 92, NO. 237. DETROIT, MICHIGAN, SUNDAY, MAY 22, 1927.—136 PAGES PRICE: TEN CENTS

LINDBERGH, IN PARIS, ACCLAIMED WORLD HERO

ESTHER HANSEL SLATED AS CULT HEARING STAR

Testimony Expected to Outdo Previous House of David Revelations.

COURT TO TAKE RECESS EARLY IN COMING WEEK

Judge Fead Has Engagement Which Will Slightly Delay Trial.

BULLETIN

St. Johns, Newfoundland, May 21—(U.P.)—An unverified report reached here tonight that the missing French transatlantic fliers, Nungesser and Coli, had been picked up by a Grand Banks fishing schooner and brought to a south coast port. The report was entirely unconfirmed.

100-PASSENGER PLANES NEAR, FORD ASSERTS

Lindbergh Blazing Trail for Giant Commercial Ships, Detroiter Says.

G. O. P. MEETING MAY COME HERE

Detroiters Hope to Land 1928 National Convention for This City.

WORLD SPEED RECORD MADE BY SEAPLANE

Navy Flier Covers 130.93 Miles an Hour on Hampton Roads Course.

BATH BURIES 17 VICTIMS OF MAD MURDERER

Funeral Services for Twelve More Will Be Held on Sunday.

CROWDS STILL THRONG SCHOOL BLAST SCENE

Street Roped Off to Keep Back Sightseers While Hearses Pass.

DIVORCE DELAY INTERRUPTS HER WEDDING PLANS

MISS BELLE GREEN.

LOOMIS FACES TRIAL MONDAY

Judge Brennan Denies Motion to Quash Information in Slaying Case.

Auto Hits Trolley, Woman Is Killed

SHOWERS ARE FORECAST FOR MONDAY, TUESDAY

FREE PRESS TODAY.

Business Is Done In The Daytime

Free Press Want Ads Produce Best Cost Less

JOYOUS TEARS WET HER EYES; SON TRIUMPHS

Mrs. Lindbergh Weeps for First Time on Learning Boy Landed Safe.

'WHAT CAN I SAY BUT I'M HAPPY, GRATEFUL'

Tired by Long Vigil, Mother Receives Flood of Congratulations.

AIR HERO AND HIS MOTHER

MRS. EVANGELINE L. LINDBERGH AND HER SON IN FRONT OF HIS PLANE IN NEW YORK A WEEK AGO.

HE'S OUR BOY! DETROIT CRIES

City Celebrates Riotously; Plans Grand Homecoming.

FLIER'S LIFE LIKE FICTION

Public Had Come to Expect Much of Youth Before He Made "Hop."

LINDBERGH'S LOG

FIVE AIRSHIP FLIGHTS MADE PREVIOUSLY ACROSS OCEAN

AVIATOR DROPS TO SLEEP WHEN VICTORY'S WON

Lands Amid Cheering Thousands as New York-to-Paris Dash Is Completed.

MAKES EPOCHAL TRIP IN ONLY 33 1-2 HOURS

France Gives Rousing Welcome to Dauntless American, Who Wins $25,000 Prize.

Lindbergh's Fame Brings Offers of Over $300,000

DETROIT HAILS ITS "KID"

"Detroit thankful for your safety. Heartiest congratulations."

(Signed)
Thomas S. Merrill—President Detroit Board of Commerce.
Harold H. Emmons—Chairman Aviation Committee.
Harvey J. Campbell—Secretary.

"You exemplify the spirit of the National Guard in your marvelous achievement."
(Signed) Detroit Units, 32nd Division.

Ask Me Another
ON PAGE 13.

The front page of the *Detroit Free Press* proclaimed Lindbergh a "world hero" after his flight to Paris. (Detroit Free Press)

Detroiters crowd the parade route one August day in 1927 in anticipation of Lucky Lindy's return to his hometown. (Walter P. Reuther Library)

At Ford Airport in Dearborn, a pilot climbs out of the cockpit of a "flivver" monoplane to make room for Charles Lindbergh. Henry Ford stands at far left. Lindbergh gave the industrialist his first airplane ride, taking him up in the *Spirit of St. Louis*. (Walter P. Reuther Library)

you'd have thought you'd stumbled into a school for young aviators. The goggles, by the way, were great. You could pull them down during snowball fights."

Lindbergh returned in triumph to Detroit for three days in August 1927. Seventy-five thousand people greeted Lindy when he landed the *Spirit of St. Louis* at Ford Airport, and he was cheered by an even larger crowd during a motorcade to and from Northwestern Field, where he gave a speech. The next day he gave Henry and Edsel Ford their first airplane rides, then took a spin himself in Ford's experimental single-seat "flivver" plane.

Lindbergh's Paris flight "created a boom in aviation," said Tim O'Callaghan of Northville, a Ford retiree who has produced both a book and a film on Ford aviation. When Lindbergh helped establish the first transcontinental air service the following year, he stocked the airline with Henry's "Tin Goose" trimotor planes.

Thanks to the backing of many of the auto industry's top executives, the Motor City had been positioning itself to become the aviation center of the country. Ford, for one, envisioned a future in which every home would have a garage and a hangar. The Depression changed that, O'Callaghan said. "When automakers had to tighten their belts in the '30s, they decided to concentrate on what they knew best: building cars."

In 1929, the world's most eligible bachelor married Anne Morrow, a shy Smith College graduate who came from a privileged background. The new Mrs. Lindbergh developed into a bestselling author and an aviation pioneer in her own right. America's "first couple of the sky" often flew their own plane into Ford Airport or Selfridge Field in Mount Clemens, where they were good friends with base commander Tom Lanphier. They always mixed business with pleasure, visiting Evangeline and her brother Charles, an eccentric bachelor and former mining engineer, at the small house they shared at 178 Ashland.

The Lindberghs' world was shattered one winter evening in 1932 when their first-born child, two-year-old Charles Jr., was kidnapped from the second-story nursery of their Hopewell, New Jersey, estate. Because of the Lindberghs' ties to Detroit, suspicion initially fell upon the city's most notorious criminals. The Purple Gang, active in bootlegging, kidnapping, and contract murders, were known to have participated in many freelance assignments around the country, including the St. Valentine's Day Massacre in Chicago three years earlier. If members weren't actively involved in the baby's abduction, police reasoned, maybe they knew who was. Several top Purples were grilled, but nothing came of it.

Meanwhile, Charles and Anne contended with a swelling army of detectives, reporters, photographers, gawkers, and crackpots. "I should love to have the baby turn up in Detroit, in your quiet home," Anne wrote hopefully to Evangeline on April 29, 1932. "Of course, anywhere would be wonderful."

Two weeks later, the baby's badly decomposed body was discovered partially buried in the nearby woods. His skull had been fractured and his body had been half-eaten by wild animals. Three years later a German carpenter from the Bronx named Bruno Richard Hauptmann was arrested and charged with the kidnap-murder. Following the circus-like "trial of the century" and Hauptmann's execution in 1936, the traumatized Lindberghs fled to Europe.

Lindbergh, who undertook several inspection tours of Germany, returned to the States in 1939, convinced that Nazi air power would be the decisive factor in any European war. He was branded a fascist and a defeatist as he became the principal spokesman for America First, an organization that opposed U.S. intervention. In an infamous speech given in Des Moines, Iowa, in September 1941, Lindbergh identified the Jews as being among the "other peoples" who were agitating for war and warned of the growing Jewish influence in the media. The public reaction to the speech helped establish Lindbergh's reputation as an anti-Semite for years to come. Assisting his fall from grace was the medal he had naively accepted from the Nazis, which he stubbornly refused to return.

Pearl Harbor settled the issue of non-intervention. Ever the patriot despite his outspoken views, Lindbergh found himself frozen out of serving his country.

"The only person who would give him a job was Henry Ford," said Tim O'Callaghan. "He hired him as an adviser on the B-24 bomber project at Willow Run." Lindbergh served as a technical consultant and test pilot for Ford and other companies until 1944, when the War Department finally relented and allowed him to go to the Pacific to evaluate new warplanes under combat conditions.

Meanwhile, in July 1942, his family moved into a rented house at 945 Cranbrook Road in Bloomfield Hills. The wooded three-acre estate seemed ideal for Anne and the kids. After the murder of their first-born, the Lindberghs had five more children: Jon, Land, Anne, Scott, and Reeve. Scott was born in Henry Ford Hospital just days after the family moved in.

"I'd see Lindbergh every so often. He was a reserved kind of person," said Dominick Vettraino, who headed Cranbrook's security force then. "But Anne was a little more outgoing. Henry Ford gave them a trailer that they parked in the woods behind the house. Anne wrote one of her books in there. I remember helping Lindbergh push the trailer one night. They all kept a low profile. I know a couple of the kids went to Brookside Elementary. We were all quite concerned with what had happened in New Jersey, so we and the Bloomfield police kept an eye out." The new home wasn't completely without tragedy. One of the Lindberghs' dogs was killed by a passing car on Cranbrook Road. Two weeks later, their beloved German shepherd, Thor, died of old age and was buried under a hickory tree.

After a year, the Lindberghs lost their lease when the owner decided to sell. They rented a second house in the area, at 411 Goodhue Road, behind Christ Church Cranbrook.

Lindbergh's war service (he unofficially flew fifty combat missions and shot down a Japanese Zero while serving as a "technical consultant") helped restore his heroic public image. Anne, who after two years in Michigan had fallen in love with the state, was disappointed when her husband accepted a position back East. She had taken sculpting classes at the Cranbrook Academy of Art and become friends with several local artists, including sculptor Carl Milles and architect Eero Saarinen.

The Lindberghs settled permanently in Connecticut after the war but still made extended trips to Detroit, usually by train, to see the family matriarch. Evangeline had retired from teaching in 1942, just as the first signs of Parkinson's disease were becoming evident. Reeve, the youngest Lindbergh child, recalled the final mother-and-son reunion inside Evangeline's Grosse Pointe Park house shortly before Evangeline's death in September 1954. "She smiled at my father, from her bed, with lingering tenderness," Reeve wrote in her memoir, *Under a Wing*. "The look that passed between those two was so loving that even I could feel the nature of it, and was calmed."

Evangline was buried in Pine Lake Cemetery in Oakland County, joining generations of her kin. Her brother Charles, with whom she lived, had always been Lindbergh's favorite uncle and was invited to move into the Lindberghs' Connecticut estate.

Reeve remembered "moments of head-shaking exasperation" over the odd little fellow, who had entertained the Lindbergh children in his Detroit laboratory for years. "My father was especially concerned about

Charles Lindbergh's mother, Evangeline Land Lindbergh, pictured here in 1928, descended from two prominent nineteenth-century Detroit families, the Lodges and the Lands. (Author's Collection)

the inventions: toothpaste that we were forbidden to try because of its possible toxicity, car polish that took the paint off the fender of one of the family cars when Uncle applied it . . ." Then there were Uncle Charles's dirty jokes, which regularly embarrassed family members and guests. "I did not understand them," Reeve admitted, "but nonetheless knew that I was to 'overlook' Uncle's stories." Uncle Charles ultimately was sent packing to Florida, where he lived out his days.

Evangeline's passing and Uncle Charles's move marked the end of the Lindberghs' long-standing Detroit connections. There no longer was any compelling reason to visit. Lindbergh, who devoted much of the balance of his life to conservation causes, never returned to the Motor City in the twenty years following his mother's death. History's most famous aviator died of cancer on August 26, 1974, and was buried in a secluded plot on the Hawaiian island of Maui.

Today few obvious signs of Lindbergh's ties to Detroit exist. An elementary school in Dearborn—the first new school in the country to carry his name when his mother dedicated it in 1928—is still in use. And a replica of the *Spirit of St. Louis,* built for the 1957 movie of the same name starring Jimmy Stewart, hangs inside the Henry Ford Museum.

"They also display the trailer that Ford gave Lindbergh," said Ed Neill, who works as a docent at the museum. "But that's about it. Looking around town today, you'd never know that Charles Lindbergh once called Detroit home."

The Valadiers, featuring lead singer Stuart Avig (*front row, center*), was Motown's first white vocal group. (Stuart Avig Collection)

FIVE
The Flip Side

Overlooked Motown artists such as Shorty Long, the Velvelettes, and the Valadiers make up the B-side of the legendary label's story.

Amid the swirl of celebratory hype surrounding the golden anniversary of Motown Records in 2009, nobody thought to look up Stuart Avig. No Annie Leibovitz to capture his portrait for *Vanity Fair*'s special music issue. No overseas film crew to record his memories for a BBC documentary. No Parade Company designers to size his noggin for a papier-mâché head to march alongside Diana Ross's on Thanksgiving morning. The oversights were unfortunate, as Avig—still performing in his late sixties—is a finger-popping footnote of interest to anyone fascinated by the Motor City's second-greatest gift to the world. In 1959, he and three fellow members of the Valadiers became the first white vocalists to sign with Berry Gordy's fledgling record company. "It was kind of intimidating," Avig said at his Farmington Hills home. "We had white faces, but we had a black sound. Today that's pretty common, but back then it was unusual."

The quartet of teenagers rehearsed and recorded inside the now-famous Studio A at 2648 West Grand Boulevard. The two-story frame house with the sign proudly identifying itself as "Hitsville U.S.A." today serves as the Motown Museum. Avig admitted that the group "went over like a fat rat," releasing just three singles before disbanding. Despite the lack of commercial success, he is pleased to be a small part of the Motown story. "All of that crew—the Contours, the Primettes, who became the Supremes—all got there within six months of each other. We were part of history."

Although the "Motown Sound"—that unmistakable blend of "rats, roaches, soul, guts, and love" Gordy often joked about—is indelibly Detroit, the company's actual residency was surprisingly short. Just thirteen years passed from the time Motown was incorporated on January 12, 1959, until its move to Los Angeles was completed in 1972. By then Gordy himself had relocated to a new home in the Hollywood Hills, having left Detroit not long after the '67 riot.

Before Hitsville went splitsville, the studio's output "was just fantastic," said former WKNR disc jockey Paul Carnegie. As Paul Cannon, he kept favorites like "Ain't Too Proud to Beg," "Stop! In the Name of Love," and "Dancing in the Street" in heavy rotation. "For years the play list was basically the Beatles and Motown," he said. Between 1961 and 1971, a total of 110 top-10 singles, many written and produced by the team of Lamont Dozier and brothers Eddie and Brian Holland, rolled off the Motown conveyor belt. Sixty-three of them reached number one on either the pop or rhythm–and-blues (R&B) chart.

Much of the magic dissipated in the move to the coast, the result of disaffected songwriters, singers, and musicians leaving what was now called Motown Productions, as well as Gordy's growing detachment as he expanded into movies and television. By the mid-1980s, the various Motown divisions were losing money. In 1988, Gordy sold Motown Records to MCA and then shed most of his interests in the music publishing and film production divisions. The aging visionary, who for years could lay claim to running the largest black-owned business in America, later admitted that pulling his fabled record company out of Detroit had been a mistake.

Today the Motown legend revolves around Gordy and his roster of headliners and dream girls from the golden Detroit years: Marvin Gaye, Mary Wells, Stevie Wonder, the Four Tops, the Temptations, the Jackson 5, Smokey Robinson and the Miracles, Martha and the Vandellas, and Diana Ross and the Supremes. Collectively these performers account for the bulk of Hitsville's vintage song catalog. Less fixed in public

Berry Gordy outside "Hitsville U.S.A." on West Grand Boulevard. (Walter P. Reuther Library)

memory are names such as Shorty Long, Brenda Holloway, and the Velvelettes—artists who help make up the B-side of the long-playing Motown story.

> *Hey, hey, you know I miss you baby*
> *You know that-a I miss-a you baby*
>
> "Come To Me"
> —*MARV JOHNSON* (1959)

Despite having a string of hit records a half-century ago, Marv Johnson is perhaps best remembered today as the answer to the following trivia question: Who recorded the first Motown single? In early 1959, the twenty-year-old Detroiter's "Come To Me" was released on the Tamla label, one of several imprints Gordy used over the years. A simple song with simple lyrics, it showcased the singer's gospel-influenced tenor falsetto voice. A couple of instrumental elements—a tambourine and a baritone sax—were signature touches of many Motown classics. "The result," decided one writer, "was a clean R&B record that sounded as white as it did black."

At twenty-nine, Gordy was an ex-boxer who had once fought at Olympia Arena on the same card as local hero Joe Louis, former autoworker, and struggling songwriter-producer. After years of independently producing local singers, including Johnson, and then handing off distribution to the large record companies—a system that made him little money—he borrowed $800 from his family to start Motown. Because it was still a shoestring operation, Gordy had to rely on United Artists to get 45s of "Come to Me" out to the rest of the country.

The public responded, and Johnson's record settled high on the pop and R&B charts. To Gordy's displeasure, United Artists signed Johnson. Over the next couple of years the label issued several of his hits, the biggest being "You've Got What It Takes," which earned Johnson a gold record. He became a familiar figure on *American Bandstand* and at rock–and-roll shows. Gordy remained his manager but gradually quit working with him as Johnson's ego and demands grew. Still, Johnson was an important draw when Gordy launched the popular Motortown Revue in 1962.

After being dropped by United Artists in 1965, a victim of the British pop invasion, the humbled singer signed with Motown. By now Gordy's start-up had grown into the largest independent record maker in the world. Johnson released some mediocre singles at Motown, the last in 1968, and worked in the front office through the 1970s. He later cut an album in England, where his songs always did well. He never stopped performing, dying of a stroke in South Carolina in 1993.

Please Mister Postman, look and see
If there's a letter, a letter for me

"Please Mr. Postman"
—*THE MARVELETTES* (1961)

In the summer of 1961, the Marvelettes really delivered with "Please Mr. Postman." The bouncy single, written by Fred Gorman (a Motown artist whose "square" job was being a mailman), sold a million copies and became the first Motown platter to reach number one on the pop charts. The record may have saved the cash-strapped company from going under. At the time, Gordy was having trouble getting paid for an earlier single, the Miracles' "Shop Around" (Motown's first national hit and its first million-copyseller), until the orders pouring in for the Marvelettes' record gave him some leverage with delinquent distributors.

Motown's first successful girl group was originally the Marvels—five Inkster High School students (Gladys Horton, Wanda Young, Georgeanna Tillman, Juanita Cowart, and Catherine Anderson) whose performance at a talent show had earned them an audition. "That song changed our lives," said Catherine Anderson Schaffner at her Inkster home. "We weren't prepared for the response. Neither was Motown. We grew up fast. There were a lot of sharks out there in the water. My mother didn't like it, but my dad said it was a once-in-a-lifetime opportunity."

Eager to capitalize on the record's success, Gordy kept the girls touring and recording. It was an exciting but grueling pace for the teenagers,

The Marvelettes delivered Motown's first number-one pop single, "Please Mr. Postman," in 1961. (Author's Collection)

three of whom had to quit their senior year of school. "That was devastating to us," Schaffner said. "We couldn't go to the prom. There were a lot of things we missed. That's the reason why, when I had daughters of my own, I kind of overcompensated with them. I was living vicariously through them."

Despite regularly charting with songs like "Don't Mess with Bill" and "Too Many Fish in the Sea," by the middle of the 1960s the Marvelettes were completely overshadowed by the Supremes. To a degree, it was their own fault. In 1964, the struggling trio of Diana Ross, Flo Ballard, and Mary Wilson took a Holland-Dozier song that the Marvelettes had rejected—"Where Did Our Love Go"—and turned it into the first of five straight number-one hits. That streak made the Supremes America's sweethearts. Meanwhile, the Marvelettes did the best they could with what they began to regard as mediocre material, backed by skimpy production and marketing budgets. The lineup was shuffled several times, with three of the original members leaving by 1967 due to sickness or marriage. In 1970, after several years without a hit, the group decided to disband rather than follow Motown's move to Los Angeles.

Although Schaffner was one of several Motown artists who successfully sued their former employer for back royalties, she remains a proud alumna. "People will say to me, 'Oh, you used to be a Marvelette.' And I tell them, 'Oh, I beg to differ. I'm *still* a Marvelette.'"

You're in the army now
Your new life has just begun

"Greetings (This Is Uncle Sam)"
—*THE VALADIERS* (1961)

Early Motown evidently had a thing about the letter V. In addition to the Vandellas (featuring Martha Reeves) and the Velvelettes, there were the Valadiers. "I don't know what a Valadier is," confessed Stuart Avig. "I think it had something to do with being a brave warrior, brave Roman, something like that. The group was already named that when I joined it."

That was in the late '50s at Oak Park High School. According to legend, an integrated version of the group had previously approached Gordy. "Come back when you're one color," he reportedly said. They did and were signed to a contract in late 1959. Avig was only sixteen. Although a Pontiac-based instrumental group, Nick and the Jaguars, had earlier cut a single with Motown, and a handful of white vocal acts (most notably Rare Earth) came aboard in the '60s, "we can legitimately say we were the first [white vocalists]," Avig said.

The quartet—Avig, Jerry Light, Art Glasser, and Martin Coleman—blended doo-wop with early rhythm and blues. Avig, a dynamic lead singer, was influenced by such black acts as the Dells, the Flamingos, and the electrifying Jackie Wilson (a native Detroiter for whom Gordy had written several hits in pre-Motown days). "Race relations were different then," Avig said. "Detroit was a segregated city. We were copying the black sound, which didn't go over well with everyone. At Motown, people were professional, but not everybody was overly cordial or friendly."

The Valadiers' first recordings didn't make it out of the vault, but in 1961 a song about the draft, "Greetings (This Is Uncle Sam)," was a minor regional hit. Avig remembered one showstopping performance at Cleveland Arena. "The Isley Brothers were headlining. They came on after us, and we got a bigger ovation than they did." After a couple of lackluster follow-up singles, the group left Motown. Avig received his own draft notice in 1964, serving two years in the army. After his discharge, he gave music another whirl before marrying and settling into a new career in the precious metals refining business.

Today Avig performs as a member of a blue-eyed soul group called The Shades of Blue. He remains mostly upbeat about his Motown experience. "The Four Tops, the Temptations, the Supremes—they were all pushed to the hilt. As far as promoting us with as much intensity as they did black acts . . . I have no complaints. I'll be forever grateful to Berry Gordy for signing us. He didn't have to do it."

I'm getting ready for the function at the junction
And baby you'd better come right now

"Function at the Junction"
—SHORTY LONG (1966)

When Gordy acquired Tri-Phi Records in 1963, its artist roster included a performer who made up in talent and versatility what he lacked in stature. Freddy "Shorty" Long was a 5-foot-1 singer-songwriter who could play the piano, drums, organ, guitar, trumpet, and harmonica. The Alabama native had worked as a DJ and toured with the Ink Spots before moving to Detroit in 1959, where his early recordings with Tri-Phi went nowhere.

In 1964, Long co-wrote and performed the first single released on Gordy's new Soul label. "Devil with a Blue Dress On" was an unhurried, bluesy number that caused little excitement, though a couple of years later Mitch Ryder and The Detroit Wheels released a more frenzied version that has since become a rock classic. Long finally dented the national charts with his 1966 single "Function at the Junction" and 1967's "Night fo' Last." In the summer of 1968 he scored his biggest hit with "Here Comes the Judge." The song, inspired by Pigmeat Markham's popular catch phrase on *Rowan and Martin's Laugh-In,* cracked *Billboard*'s top 10 on the R&B and pop charts.

Marvin Gaye championed Long's cause. The Holland-Dozier team once brought a new song to Gaye. "Why are you going to produce me?" he demanded. "Why don't you produce Shorty Long?" One possible reason could be found on Shorty's breath. According to Motown session pianist Earl Van Dyke, Long would come into the studio loaded with liquid inspiration. "Today we ain't playing nuthin' but funk," Long would announce, pulling a bottle out of his coat. "If you don't feel funky, take a drink of this."

On Sunday June 29, 1969, Long and a friend were fishing on the Detroit River when their boat swamped and capsized. Both men drowned. At Long's funeral, Stevie Wonder played a harmonica, then placed the instrument upon the 29-year-old singer's casket. Later Gaye described Long as "this beautiful cat who had two hits, and then got ignored by Motown."

Girls, those fellas are sly, slick and shy
So don't you ever let 'em get you starry-eyed

"Needle in a Haystack"
—*THE VELVELETTES* (1964)

It's perhaps telling that in Berry Gordy's 1994 autobiography, *To Be Loved,* the Velvelettes were not mentioned once in 422 pages. Never a priority to begin with, the group felt slightly abandoned by the end of their stay at Hitsville, said lead singer Cal (Gill) Street. "We sounded just as good as the others. The focus was on the moneymakers."

The Velvelettes came to Motown in 1962 from Kalamazoo, where Betty Kelley and two pairs of sisters—Cal and Mildred Gill and Bertha and Norma Barbee—had been fixtures at local sock hops. Cal was in ninth grade; the others were in college. These five women were often placed as background singers for other Motown acts. The studio released only a half-dozen of their singles between 1963 and 1966, a minimal output that still resulted in some great dance music. Enough copies of "Needle in a Haystack" plopped onto turntables in 1964 to allow the song to reach number 45 on the *Billboard Hot 100*. The following year saw the release of "He Was Really Sayin' Something," a solid R&B hit. However, in 1964 Kelley left to join Martha and the Vandellas, and in 1967 Mildred Gill and the Barbee sisters quit to raise families. Cal, the sole remaining member, found a pair of replacements. Even so, in 1969 the group broke up.

"We didn't live to sing," Cal said. "We had other options." For her, that meant marrying Richard Street, who had replaced the troubled Paul Williams on the Temptations, and raising their son. (Williams committed suicide in 1973, just one of many Motown artists to die tragically.) The marriage ended acrimoniously. Cal, whose minister father had scolded her about "that devilish music," momentarily choked up recounting the heartaches groupies caused artists of both sexes. "If you could somehow take that element out of show business . . . ," she said.

All but one of the original Velvelettes lives in Michigan and has a profession. They occasionally re-unite on stage, not for the money, said Cal, but to thrill a crowd and maybe recapture a little of the innocence of five girls harmonizing to songs on the radio.

Well now give me money
A lot of money

"Money (That's What I Want)"
—*BARRETT STRONG* (1959)

If a singer is going to be a one-hit wonder, then the song may as well be one of the great booty-shaking singles of all time. Barrett Strong, a self-taught pianist whose family had moved to Detroit from Mississippi, co-wrote and sang "Money (That's What I Want)" over a driving boogie-woogie piano beat. He was eighteen and working at a shoe store at 12th Street and Clairmont, the future epicenter of the '67 riot. "Smokey Robinson, all of us, all doing amateur contests at theatres around town," he remembered. "Everybody tryin' to win twenty-five dollars."

Recording the song was riotous—in a good way. It was "one long party," recalled Gordy, who saw some badly needed dollars roll in as "Money"

Barrett Strong was a reluctant vocalist and talented lyricist during his time with Motown. (Author's Collection)

charged up the R&B chart in 1959, finally stopping at number 2. "We recorded everything together, the singer, the band, and the background voices. That gave it a raw, earthy feel."

Strong admits today he "wasn't crazy" about working on stage. "It's too demanding. You owe yourself to the public. I preferred to be behind the scenes." That's where the reluctant vocalist really left his mark. As a staff lyricist, he paired up with innovative producer Norman Whitfield to create songs every bit as enduring as "Money." These classics included "I Heard It Through the Grapevine" (a hit for both Marvin Gaye and Gladys Knight and the Pips), Edwin Starr's "War," and the Temptations' "psychedelic soul" tracks: "Cloud Nine" (1968), "Psychedelic Shack" (1970), and "Papa Was a Rollin' Stone" (1972). The latter earned Strong a Grammy Award.

Strong chose not to follow Motown to Los Angeles. He recorded for other labels, including a pair of albums for Capitol, and released a digital album just before suffering a stroke in 2008. Still recuperating, he doesn't care to linger too long in the past. "Talk about what I'm doing now," he said. "Yesterday's gone."

What are you gonna do when I'm gone
Whose shoulder are you gonna cry on

"When I'm Gone"
—*BRENDA HOLLOWAY* (1965)

Brenda Holloway, a stunning young singer with an ache in her voice, seemed a sure bet for stardom. After recording the pop hit "Every Little Bit Hurts" as a seventeen-year-old in the spring of 1964, there was talk of having her replace Diana Ross in the then-hitless Supremes or of teaming up with Smokey Robinson, whose duet partner, the sensational Mary Wells, had just quit Motown over a contract dispute.

Holloway grew up in the Watts neighborhood of Los Angeles and had been a back-up vocalist for local R&B groups since she was fourteen. Gordy signed her after hearing her sing Wells's "My Guy," making her the first West Coast artist to record for Motown. In the view of pop music critic Nelson George, Holloway "was the most beautiful woman ever signed to Motown. In any dress, but particularly the tight gold and silver sequined outfits she often performed in, she was a head-turner."

Holloway was a regular on such TV shows as *Shindig!;* opened for the Beatles at New York's Shea Stadium during their 1966 tour; and charted with the singles "When I'm Gone," "Operator," and "You've Made Me So Very Happy." Holloway soon grew frustrated with her stalled career. She poured out her grievances in a 1967 letter to Gordy: "As you very well know there are numerous singers that have not had a hit record or as much experience as myself working on club engagements and concerts, that are constantly touring Europe . . . also performing in Las Vegas and making good salaries and names for themselves. Again I cannot understand why I haven't had any of these opportunities."

Some think Holloway simply fell through the cracks as executives grappled with the logistics of a rapidly expanding corporation. She left in 1968 as she was working on her second album. Ironically, the disgruntled singer cashed in when Blood, Sweat & Tears covered "You've Made Me So Very Happy," which she had co-written, and that group's version sold 2 million copies. She put music on hold to concentrate on her marriage to a pastor, another union that eventually ended in an unhappy parting of ways.

Today the singer lives in New Jersey. She continues to perform. Like other artists of that era who were squeezed out of studio time and radio play by Motown's mega acts, she's a favorite in England, where the music genre is known as Northern Soul. At last look, Holloway had several hundred friends on her MySpace page. There is no booking information—just a grainy video clip showing a sultry young woman singing in soulful anguish.

THE HIT FACTORY

During Motown's stay in Detroit, the studio cranked out hits like the auto plants mass-produced Mustangs and Impalas. According to *Billboard*'s rankings, sixty-three Motown songs reached number 1 on either the pop or the rhythm and blues chart between 1961 and 1971, the period of the company's greatest commercial and artistic success. Reflecting the label's crossover appeal, nineteen singles topped both charts.

The Marvelettes
"Please Mr. Postman" (1961—Pop/R&B)

The Miracles
"Shop Around" (1961—R&B)
"You've Really Got a Hold on Me" (1962—R&B)
"I Second That Emotion" (1967—R&B)
"The Tears of a Clown" (1970—Pop/R&B)

The Contours
"Do You Love Me" (1962—R&B)

Mary Wells
"You Beat Me to the Punch" (1962—R&B)
"Two Lovers" (1963—R&B)
"My Guy" (1964—Pop)

The Four Tops in 1967. The group topped both the pop and R&B charts with "It's the Same Old Song" and "Reach Out (I'll Be There)." (Author's Collection)

Martha and the Vandellas
"Heat Wave" (1963—R&B)
"Jimmy Mack" (1967—R&B)

Stevie Wonder
"Fingertips—Part 2" (1963—Pop/R&B)
"Uptight (Everything Alright)" (1966—R&B)
"Blowin' in the Wind" (1966—R&B)
"I Was Made to Love Her" (1967—R&B)
"Shoo-Be-Doo-Be-Doo-Da-Day" (1968—R&B)
"Signed, Sealed, Delivered, I'm Yours" (1970—R&B)

The Four Tops
"It's the Same Old Song" (1965—Pop/R&B)
"Reach Out (I'll Be There)" (1966—Pop/R&B)

Junior Walker and the All Stars
"Shotgun" (1965—R&B)
"What Does It Take (To Win Your Love)" (1969—R&B)

The Temptations
"My Girl" (1965—Pop/R&B)
"Get Ready" (1966—R&B)
"Ain't Too Proud to Beg" (1966—R&B)
"Beauty Is Only Skin Deep" (1966—R&B)
"(I Know) I'm Losing You" (1966—R&B)
"I Wish It Would Rain" (1968—R&B)
"I Could Never Love Another" (1968—R&B)
"I Can't Get Next To You" (1969—Pop/R&B)
"Runaway Child, Running Wild" (1969—R&B)
"Just My Imagination" (1971—Pop/R&B)

Marvin Gaye
"I'll Be Doggone" (1965—R&B)
"Ain't That Peculiar" (1965—R&B)
"One More Heartache" (1966—R&B)
"I Heard It Through the Grapevine" (1968—Pop/R&B)
"Too Busy Thinking About My Baby" (1969—R&B)
"What's Going On" (1971—R&B)
"Mercy Mercy Me (the Ecology)" (1971—R&B)
"Inner City Blues (Make Me Wanna Holler)" (1971—R&B)

Marvin Gaye and Tammi Terrell
"Ain't Nothing Like the Real Thing" (1968—R&B)
"You're All I Need to Get By" (1968—R&B)

Gladys Knight and the Pips
"I Heard It Through the Grapevine" (1967—R&B)
"If I Were Your Woman" (1970—R&B)

The Supremes
"Where Did Our Love Go" (1964—Pop)
"Baby Love" (1964—Pop)
"Come See About Me" (1964—Pop)
"Stop! In the Name of Love" (1965—Pop)
"Back In My Arms Again" (1965—Pop/R&B)
"I Hear a Symphony" (1965—Pop)
"You Can't Hurry Love" (1966—Pop/R&B)
"You Keep Me Hanging On" (1966—Pop/R&B)
"Love Is Here and Now You're Gone" (1967—Pop/R&B)
"The Happening" (1967—Pop)
"Love Child" (1968—Pop)
"Someday We'll Be Together" (1970—Pop/R&B)
"Stoned Love" (1970—R&B)

Diana Ross
"Ain't No Mountain High Enough" (1970—Pop/R&B)

Originals
"Baby, I'm for Real" (1969—R&B)

Edwin Starr
"War" (1970—Pop)

Jackson Five
"I Want You Back" (1969—Pop/R&B)
"ABC" (1970—Pop/R&B)
"The Love You Save" (1970—Pop/R&B)
"I'll Be There" (1971—Pop/R&B)
"Never Can Say Goodbye" (1971—R&B)

SIX
Dark Days of the Black Legion

The most infamous white supremacist group of the Great Depression was brought down by one of its own victims.

White supremacists of the 1930s maintained that there was one sure way to identify a fellow member of the "master race": blushing. It was thought that only a true pure-blood Aryan was capable of displaying a noticeable change of color in the skin, marking an episode of shyness, shame, or modesty. That Charley Poole was a non-Aryan was not the real issue for the Black Legion, which saw to it that his cheeks were eternally blanched for a different and more powerful reason: the sanctity of Protestant womanhood. On the night of May 12, 1936, the young unemployed autoworker was taken into the countryside west of Detroit and shot five times at point-blank range. The honor killing was the latest in a long string of atrocities committed by the black-robed vigilantes.

"Nobody could hate Charley," cried Becky Poole, after being told by detectives that her husband's body had been found near Gulley Road in what is now Dearborn Heights. "He never hurt anyone in his whole life."

That wasn't what the local chapter of the Legion—which included Becky's brother-in-law, Lowell Rushing—believed. Rushing had gotten wind of Charley's occasional arguments with Becky and reported back to his friends at the Wolverine Republican Club, one of various fronts the Legion used to mask its activities. He exaggerated the Pooles' dis-

Becky Poole and her daughter Nancy, who was born shortly after Poole's husband was murdered by members of the Black Legion. (Walter P. Reuther Library)

cord, which typically centered on Charley's inability to find a steady job. At a secret meeting held inside a rented hall, "Colonel" Harvey Davis helped stir Legionnaires into a frenzy by describing Charley as an abusive husband who had beaten his pregnant wife so badly that she had miscarried. "What shall we do about such a man?" Davis asked. "Whip him!" members yelled. "Kill him!"

The following evening, as Becky lay in her bed at Detroit's Herman Kiefer Hospital, where she had given birth to Nancy, Rushing lured Charley into a car filled with Legion members. Charley, a talented sandlot ballplayer, thought he had been invited to the organizational meeting of a factory baseball team, which would have assured him a job at the sponsoring plant. But, in the hard-boiled vernacular of the day, this was a one-way ride. "You've beaten your wife for the last time," he was told before being shot and dumped into a ditch.

As unremarkable as Poole's life had been up to that point, in death he wound up extracting an extraordinary price from his killers. His murder caused the previously unknown Black Legion to explode into the headlines, resulting in most of its leaders being sent to prison and exposing the clandestine brotherhood of bullies to ridicule. "Hooey may look like romance and adventure in the moonlight," the *Detroit News* editorialized toward the end of the Legion's brief but spectacular appearance on the public stage, "but it always looks like hooey when you bring it out in the daylight."

Despite its similarities to the Ku Klux Klan, the Black Legion wasn't a direct descendent of that right-wing organization; rather, it was more like a sinister stepbrother. Many Legionnaires were former or concurrent members of the Klan, originally a vigilante group active in the former Confederacy for several years following the Civil War. In 1915, the Klan was jolted out of its decades-long dormancy by D. W. Griffith's controversial film *The Birth of a Nation*. Hollywood's first blockbuster sentimentalized the KKK and provided a new generation of extremists with a template for ritualistic terrorism, right down to the cross burnings and standardized white costumes—dramatic devices that Griffith had invented for the movie. The flood of immigrants and Southern blacks to America's big cities were made-to-order targets, allowing the resurgent Klan to expand from its rural Southern roots to become a truly national political movement, agitating for such reforms as immigration control. The "Invisible Empire" soon controlled state governments in Indiana, Colorado, and Oregon.

Longtime Detroit mayor Coleman Young never forgot his first glimpse of the Ku Klux Klan when he was a youngster in Huntsville, Alabama, in the early 1920s. "As my mother was walking me to the restaurant one night," Young recalled in his autobiography, *Hard Stuff*, "we crossed a street and all of a sudden a car came wheeling around the corner with men standing on the running boards wearing sheets. What made the scene so vivid to me was my mother's reaction. I sensed immediately that she was terrified."

Ironically, Young's family was in the process of moving from one Klan hotbed to another. They arrived in Detroit in 1923, not long after the first Kleagle (recruiter), Ira Stout, set up shop in the city. That year the Klan burned a six-foot-high cross in front of city hall on Christmas Eve. In 1924, Detroit's Klansmen numbered 35,000 members, many of whom were signed up at spectacular nighttime rallies. Only the decision by the election commission to toss out 17,000 illegible ballots kept a Klan-backed candidate, Charles Bowles, from defeating John W. Smith in that year's mayoral race.

During the 1920s, the KKK's heyday, Michigan reportedly had more Klansmen than any state in the country—as many as 800,000, according to some estimates, though historians today believe a figure in the range of 80,000 to 120,000 is more plausible. Roughly half lived in metro Detroit. Prospective members—many of whom were white factory workers originally from the South—had to swear to be a "native born, true and loyal citizen . . . a white male Gentile person . . . a believer in the tenets of the Christian religion, the maintenance of White Supremacy, and principles of pure Americanism."

In 1925, the Klan movement was stopped dead in its tracks by a sensational sex scandal involving its most prominent leader. David Curtis Stephenson, the Grand Wizard of Indiana and twenty-two other states, including Michigan, was convicted of rape and murder in the case of a woman whose body bore so many bite marks that she was described by a witness as looking as if she had been "chewed by a cannibal." Distraught at receiving neither clemency nor a commutation of his life sentence from the Klan-backed governor of Indiana, the vengeful Stephenson took several public officials down with him. The high-profile series of exposés caused a drastic decline in membership, from an estimated peak of 6 million in the mid-1920s to only about 30,000 a few years later.

During this period, a small-town physician in Bellaire, Ohio, named William Shepard—a former Grand Cyclops in the Klan—fiddled with the Klan's formula and came up with his own version of hooded Americanism. He called the secret fraternity the Black Legion. (An alternative account says the Legion was originally formed as the Black Guards in about 1925 to provide security for officers of the Ohio KKK.) Shepard's followers wore black silk robes sporting a skull-and-crossbones insignia; a black hood topped by a high-horned headpiece bearing the same mark as the robe completed the ensemble.

As Protestant nativists who were convinced that "their" country was slowly being taken over by "aliens," the Legion's professed enemies were the same as the Klan's: Catholics, Jews, immigrants, blacks, communists, and labor activists. Unlike the Klan, however, the Legion eschewed publicity. They operated in deep secrecy, with any member foolish enough to mention the Legion's existence to an outsider subject to a bullwhipping. During the day, "Dr. Billy" made house calls with a .45-caliber pistol packed inside his satchel; at night, he presided over elaborate initiation ceremonies and the occasional tar and feathering of an unlucky local deemed to be "un-American."

The Black Legion expanded and grew lethal after another ex-Klansman, Virgil Effinger, an electrician from Lima, Ohio, assumed leadership in the early 1930s. Effinger, described as a "dour, humorless fanatic," recruited large numbers of members in Michigan. He was capably assisted by Isaac "Peg Leg" White, an ex-Detroit cop. Ultimately Michigan was home to tens of thousands of members. While many of them regarded the Legion as a secret lodge and an outlet for mild adventure, a fanatical few used it as an excuse for night riding that often was more personal than ideological in nature. Their victims may have included the father of a famous black-nationalist leader.

One evening in 1931, Earl Little was run over by a streetcar in Lansing. Local authorities considered the outspoken preacher's death either an accident or, improbably, a suicide; however, Little's young son, Malcolm, grew up believing that it had been an execution—a chilling message delivered by the Black Legion to intimidate "uppity" blacks. Malcolm Little, who later changed his name to Malcolm X as he rose to prominence with the Nation of Islam, doubted that his father could "bash himself in the head, then get down across the streetcar tracks to be run over."

Other beatings, bombings, and murders of left-wing political and labor organizations occurred over the years, but authorities never seemed able to solve them. Then came the killing of Charley Poole.

The twenty-two-year-old Poole was a slightly built, pleasant looking man of French heritage, with slicked-back hair and a pencil mustache. A Catholic who had been chased out of Kentucky by the local Klan, he had been married for three years to Becky, an attractive, blonde-haired Baptist. In the spring of 1936, she was pregnant with their second child. Charley had been approached about joining the Legion but refused. His mildly disparaging comments about the group annoyed Lowell Rushing, a young Legionnaire whose brother was married to Becky's sister. Rushing fabricated a story about Charley beating Becky, knowing full well the Legion's likely response. Some people later suggested that Rushing was infatuated with Becky and wanted to remove Charley from the scene. Whatever his motive, the result was murder.

Detroiters were shocked at newspaper stories describing Poole's killing, with page-one photos of the young family producing a blend of outrage and sympathy. Within days, several of the victim's friends stepped forward and described three men who visited Poole's house on the day of the killing. Harvey Davis, a thirty-eight-year-old employee of Detroit's public lighting department, was the first to be taken in for questioning.

Davis had a commanding presence: tall, with graying close-cropped hair, bushy eyebrows, and a perpetually sullen expression. In a Southern accent, he talked in a roundabout way of "something sinister and gigantic, a threat to the peace of the nation itself." Fascinated detectives were hearing of the Black Legion for the first time. Every person of interest Davis named was quickly tracked down and brought in. Search warrants were executed, and soon an arsenal of pistols, rifles, ammunition, knives, blackjacks, whips, and leather-bladed bludgeons was stockpiled on desktops for the photographers. Some detectives donned robes for the cameras. On May 22, nine days after Poole's body was found, Detroit's three dailies screamed front-page news about "a fantastic tale of terrorism . . . straight from the heart of the Deep South of Carpetbag days."

Among the earliest of those arrested and charged in the Poole case was the chief triggerman. Dayton Dean worked with Davis in the public lighting department and was a "major" in the Legion. A short, thickset navy veteran with oddly spaced eyes, the thirty-six-year-old grade-school dropout admitted he had fired the first shots—but only because he had feared being plugged by Davis if he didn't obey his command. Dean had once been tied to a tree and flogged by his fellow Legionnaires for some transgression, and that memory was still fresh.

Dean was shocked to learn from detectives that Becky Poole had actually given birth to the baby she had supposedly miscarried (a girl

Detroit detectives display robes, hoods, and weapons confiscated from Black Legionnaires. (Walter P. Reuther Library)

Harvey Davis, an employee of the Detroit Lighting Department and a colonel in the Black Legion, has his mug shot taken. (Walter P. Reuther Library)

she named Nancy) and claimed to have never been mistreated by her husband. "A horrible mistake," Dean said. "But I was just following the orders of my superiors." To the delight of his interrogators, the shaken suspect abandoned the blood oath he had made to keep the inner workings of the Legion a secret unto death. He started talking—and kept talking for days. In the view of Charles T. Haun, who covered the case for the *Detroit Free Press,* "somewhere in that peculiar mind there was a sense of fair play, a willingness to be a good boy after having been such a very bad one. It made police a little afraid of what he had to tell, but most of his stories turned out to be true ones."

The second murder Dean detailed, after Poole's, was the racially motivated "thrill killing" of Silas Coleman. One May evening in 1935, the forty-two-year-old army veteran was taken out into the marshes near

Pinckney and forced to run for his life before finally being gunned down. The ringleader was Davis, who had simply wanted to "see how it felt to shoot a Negro," Dean said. On another occasion, a carload of Legionnaires, frustrated that they'd not found their targeted prey, randomly shot and wounded a black man walking down an Ecorse street.

More revelations poured forth—of murders and attempted murders, of firebombings and floggings, of spooky rituals and ominous-sounding oaths. Dean told of failed Legion plots to kill the publisher of a Highland Park newspaper, who was running for office against a Legion candidate, and the mayor of Ecorse, who had hired too many Negroes for the Legion's taste. He described the initiation ceremony, in which new members knelt with a loaded pistol aimed at the backs of their heads and swore: "In the name of God and the devil, one to reward and the other to punish, and by the powers of light and darkness, goodness and evil, here under the black arch of heaven's avenging symbol, I pledge and consecrate my heart, my brain, my body, and limbs; and swear by all the powers of heaven and hell, to devote my life to the obedience of my superiors that I will exert every possible means in my power for the extermination of the antichrist, Communist, the Roman hierarchy, and their abettors."

Caught up in the excitement of this newfound threat, the press published unsubstantiated claims of the Legion's size and its body count of victims. The Legion was said to be responsible for as many as fifty deaths, many of them staged suicides, stated the *Free Press,* while the *Detroit News* reported ten thousand Legionnaires in Wayne County alone. The Associated Press wrote of "vague stories of a plot to establish a Fascist dictatorship with 6 million armed men taking part in a coup." This involved issuing the Legion's ultimate password, "Lixto," which, when sounded at a prearranged time, would call members to take over government buildings, arsenals, and power plants.

Just how insidious was the Black Legion? In Oakland County, circuit judge George Hartrick conducted a one-man grand jury investigation. He estimated that the Legion had between 2,200 and 4,500 members countywide. In addition to scores of policemen in Pontiac and Royal Oak, their ranks included eighty-six public officials, among them the county prosecutor, a state legislator, and the police chief of Royal Oak. In Wayne County, the city halls of Ecorse and Highland Park were found to be riddled with "black knights" in positions of power, while Detroit's police chief was widely suspected of being a Legionnaire. These kinds of ties helped explain why certain crimes committed by the Legion before Poole's murder were unenthusiastically investigated.

Among the most shocking developments—though it didn't come to light until after the trials of Poole's killers were completed—was Wayne County prosecutor Duncan McCrea's admission that he had "accidentally" signed a membership card. Legion defendants testified that McCrea had actually gone through the initiation ceremony and attended several secret meetings; however, McCrea's past affiliation with the Legion didn't prevent him from vigorously prosecuting the Poole case.

Each new revelation ramped up the hysteria. At the time, the public was absorbing newspaper reports and newsreel images of fascism on the march throughout Europe. Could a homegrown movement topple the U.S. government? The ongoing depression of the 1930s provided the perfect ingredients for revolution: fear, desperation, confusion, and hate. Two national embodiments of intolerance stood right in Detroit's own backyard as automaker Henry Ford and "radio priest" Father Charles Coughlin shook their fists at Jewish bankers and Bolshevik union organizers. In such an environment, it was easy to over-reckon the power and reach of this strange new group.

However, as investigators dug deeper, it became apparent that the Legion was not a tightly controlled national paramilitary organization of ideologically driven acolytes prepared to move in lockstep at a moment's notice. Instead investigators found an uncoordinated collection of cells comprised of poorly educated blue-collar workers, centered principally in Michigan and Ohio, with a scattering of members in Indiana and Illinois. According to historians who have studied the Legion, its membership rolls numbered no more than between 60,000 and 100,000 overall.

As exemplars of the model Christian behavior they demanded of others, local Legion leaders fell far short. Davis was revealed to have been a petty criminal in Kentucky, where he served time for grand larceny and impersonation, before moving to Detroit. Dean hardly qualified as anyone's choice to defend the flower of Protestant womanhood. After his first wife divorced him for cruelty, his common-law wife—with whom he'd had two children—left him after he was found taking "indecent liberties" with the woman's fourteen-year-old daughter. The woman said she dropped sexual assault charges against Dean after his Legion friends threatened to "dump me in a ditch."

Jack Carlisle, the veteran crime reporter of the *Detroit News,* visited the Legion's founder, Dr. Shepard, in Ohio. "To the substantial and solid citizens of Bellaire, like his cronies in the luncheon club, Shepard is a 'harmless old coot' who was always joining something and talking a lot of sentimental twaddle about the old South and white supremacy," Carlisle wrote. "They heard he was a Klansman, and then they learned he wore a black robe with a skull and cross bones, and sat on the hillsides near town at midnight. But the solid folks just thought that was 'Dr. Billy's way.'

"To others, like the mill workers and the steel men, Dr. Shepard was a messiah, who stood for mystery and adventure, who sent out the 'Lixto Call' for the hillside meetings and gave the secret password from the old South. They called him chief, and they said they were ready to die for him, but Dr. Billy confided 'they only got drunk instead.'" Shepard was no Hitler or Mussolini. He told Carlisle that he had never been to Michigan, did not know or approve of any of the Legion's crimes committed there, and said that any member found guilty of murder should be executed.

By mid-June, the *Free Press* was criticizing the wave of overreaction (to which the newspaper itself had contributed), saying that the "exposure of the Black Legion's activities in Detroit has been used by certain newspapers to whip up a wave of hysteria out of all proportion to that dark organization's power or importance." The paper dismissed estimates of the Legion's strength as 5 million members nationally, including 100,000 in Michigan, as "just so much poppy cock." The FBI, whose agents had been following Legion activities for a year, found no evidence of a federal crime and thus declined to get involved. In a memo to director J. Edgar Hoover, one special agent described the Legion as "a bunch of low-type hillbillies who have come out of the mountains of Kentucky and Tennessee . . . it is easy to see how they would kill with impunity just on the violation of a woman."

Nonetheless, individuals targeted by the Legion, notably civil rights attorney Maurice Sugar, were convinced that the group was an immense threat. Sugar and Homer Martin, the latter of whom was president of the fledgling United Automobile Workers, believed that the Legion's reach extended into the factories of local automakers like Hudson and Packard, where members were given jobs and special privileges in exchange for sabotaging the efforts of union organizers. They insisted that Legion members had infiltrated union ranks as management spies while others worked for the Dawn Patrol Detective Agency, a private security force that guarded factories. Eventually three unsolved murders of labor activists, one of whom was hanged, turned out to be Legion handiwork. There almost assuredly were more, but Dean could only attest to those crimes of which he had firsthand knowledge. Other implicated Legionnaires kept their mouths shut.

Sugar had a deeply personal interest in bringing down the Legion: they had marked him for assassination. Dean confirmed a couple of botched attempts to kill Sugar the previous year when the liberal lawyer had been running in elections for city council and Recorder's Court judge. Sugar spent months investigating the Legion for a book he never wrote. One of the most chilling plots he uncovered was the plan to release cyanide gas in local synagogues during Hanukkah. Another unrealized scheme involved "Major General" Arthur Lupp of Highland Park, an investigator for the Detroit Board of Health and the Legion's buffoonish state commander. Lupp, who was not charged in the Poole murder, allegedly experimented with methods of injecting typhoid germs into dairy products sold in Jewish neighborhoods.

Psychologists studied Legion members in custody. They found that most such members were Southern transplants with few industrial skills who were nagged by a feeling of alienation in an urban environment that seemed to increasingly favor foreigners, minorities, and Catholics at the expense of the old-stock Protestants who had settled the nation. Detroit, one of the largest ethnic and racial melting pots in the country, was particularly threatening to these men. The Legion offered mem-

Black Legion defendants on May 26, 1936: (*Standing, from left*) Dayton Dean, Urban Lipps, and Harvey Davis; (*sitting, from left*) Ervin Lee, Lowell Rushing, Herschell Gill, and John Vincent. (Walter P. Reuther Library)

bers fraternity in a city of strangers and provided simple solutions in a complex, uncertain world.

On June 29, 1936, Dean pleaded guilty to his role in the Poole and Coleman slayings. He was sentenced to life in prison with no parole. In September, he testified in the trials of a dozen fellow Legionnaires. All but one of the defendants were convicted of first-degree or second-degree murder. During a break in the proceedings, Becky Poole approached the prosecution's star witness, cradling an infant in her arms. "This is Mary Lou, my oldest girl," she said. "I have another baby at home, too." Dean stared at her and said nothing. After the verdicts were read, she strode up to Lowell Rushing. "I hope you never come out alive," she told her brother-in-law. She got her wish. Rushing was handed a life sentence.

The most notorious fascist group of 1930s America vanished as suddenly as it had appeared. *The New York Times,* for example, which published eighty-four stories about the Legion in 1936, ran only ten the following year. Although much of the Legion's suspected criminal activity proved to be impossible to prosecute due to lack of witnesses and informants, within three years of Poole's killing, nearly fifty members were in prison for murder and other crimes. Thirteen of them were serving life terms. Many others, their identities exposed in various grand jury investigations and newspaper reports, managed to keep their freedom but lost their public-service jobs. The Black Legion was permanently broken, its bizarre story briefly living on in pop culture. By 1940, it had inspired at least one novel, two films (one starring Humphrey Bogart), and an episode of the radio crime drama *The Shadow* (which featured the voice of Orson Welles).

Charley Poole's clandestine killers went to their graves not knowing Becky Poole's own little secret. The fair-skinned blonde's ancestors included an African-American great-grandmother—a revelation that would have flushed the cheeks of her wayward Aryan defenders.

HOLLYWOOD AND THE BLACK LEGION

In Hollywood's best ripped-from-the-headlines style, studios capitalized on public fascination with the Black Legion by rushing into theatres over the winter of 1936–1937 a pair of films based on the black-hooded mob. First out of the blocks was Columbia Pictures' *Legion of Terror.* The low-budget, action-packed B movie featured Bruce Cabot as a postal inspector who uncovers the secret group behind a series of deadly mail bombings; before he can blow the whistle on the vigilantes, however, they kill his girlfriend's brother. The film came out in late 1936, just as the hysteria surrounding the real Legion had faded and anticipation for Warner Bros.' own robes-and-torches exposé was building. *Black Legion,* a fast-paced melodrama released one month after *Legion of Terror,* starred Humphrey Bogart as Detroit factory worker Frank Taylor. Upset about losing a promotion to foreman and coworker Joe Dombrowski, Taylor joins a secret "All American" organization that drives the hardworking Polish immigrant and his family out of their home. Taylor becomes

Humphrey Bogart starred in a 1936 film based on the notorious white supremacist group known as the Black Legion. (Author's Collection)

deeply involved in the Legion, but its violent ways soon cause him to fall into a downward spiral of heavy drinking and self-loathing. After losing his marriage and his job and betraying a friend who is then marked for execution, the soul-sick Taylor finally stands up to Legion leaders. While Warner Bros. maintained that the organization, characters, and events depicted in *Black Legion* were strictly fictional, one group of white supremacists was not satisfied. The Ku Klux Klan sued the studio for copyright infringement.

SEVEN

The Bomber That Fell From the Sky

On October 24, 1958, a British jet crashed into a Detroit neighborhood—a quickly forgotten footnote to the Cold War Era. This is the story of that frightful day and of the airmen who perished.

It was a rainy Friday afternoon when the crippled jet bomber came howling out of nowhere, rattling windows, lifting rooftops, and blowing birds out of trees. "It looked like a huge gray bat, something quite fast," said a lady who had been shaking out drapes on her second-story dust porch. "It had a sharp point in front and sort of tapered back. It looked like it was going to land on me. I started to scream . . ." Moments later, before startled residents of Detroit's lower east side had a chance to fully comprehend the disaster rushing their way, the delta-winged Vulcan aircraft smacked nose-first into Ashland Street like an eighty-ton lawn dart tossed from the heavens, burrowing itself deep into the spongy ground and exploding into thousands of little pieces.

Seven blocks away in Grosse Pointe Park, one man was sitting on the upper terrace of his home when he was rocked by the thunderclap. He saw flames shoot into the sky, followed by a mushroom cloud of dirt, smoke, and debris—"just like an atomic bomb." A group of schoolchildren dropped to the ground and huddled near a fence, fearing it was the Russian nuclear attack they had been preparing for via civil defense drills and government films for as long as any of them could remember.

A British Vulcan jet bomber, the same make as the one that crashed into an eastside Detroit neighborhood in 1958. (Author's Collection)

Thirteen-year-old Fred Schwartz, just home from Guyton Elementary, was changing clothes when the suction from the blast six blocks away ripped open his bedroom's crank-style windows. "There was this huge ball of fire," remembered Schwartz, who hopped on his bicycle and pedaled, accompanied by the sound of sirens, to where his father, a battalion chief, commanded the first firefighters on the scene.

The youngster came upon an astonishing sight. Thick smoke and flames poured out of a giant crater where, moments before, two houses had stood. Dazed neighbors wandered out of their blast-shattered homes and through streets littered with smoking wreckage and body parts. Some were crying or screaming for help. Trees were on fire. Flames shot up from a broken gas main under the buckled sidewalks. Nearby canals were littered with debris. A utility pole stuck through the roof of a cabin cruiser. In what could only be described as a true miracle, nobody on the ground was killed. But there had been six British airmen onboard the stricken jet, and nobody who heard the crash or saw the devastation doubted their fate. Nearly every newspaper report and sidewalk conversation that followed used the same expression: the crew had been "blown to bits."

Among the ghoulish finds turned over to authorities was a finger with a ring attached to it, a discovery that inspired a prank a few days before Halloween. "Some kids came to school the next week and showed this teacher a finger they said came from the crash," Schwartz said. "One of them had cut a hole in the bottom of a small jewelry box and poked his finger through it, then packed cotton around it. It was a gag, but she just about fell over."

Schwartz followed his father into the Detroit Fire Department, retiring as a senior chief. Although his recollections of the crash have remained vivid over the past half-century, he admits: "I've never really thought about the fellows who were in that plane."

The crew that climbed into the Vulcan XA908 at Goose Bay, Labrador, on October 24, 1958, was a plucky band of cold warriors. The four-engine jet—developed for the Royal Air Force by the venerable British aircraft manufacturer Avro in the early 1950s—was an integral part of Britain's nuclear deterrent, designed to deliver an atomic payload against the Soviet Union in the years before intercontinental missiles made this form of delivery obsolete. Flight Lieutenant John Willoughby-Moore and other Vulcan pilots were told that in a first-wave attack on Moscow, more than half of them wouldn't return.

Willoughby-Moore, the thirty-four-year-old father of two young children, Nigel and Judith, wasn't dissuaded by such a grim prospect. As the captain of the aircraft, he fully enjoyed flying the "tin triangle," though his wife, Julia, sometimes grew nervous. The aircraft was sleek, powerful, and menacing, painted a brilliant "anti-flash" white to reflect thermal radiation from a nuclear explosion. With its uniquely shaped wings measuring nearly a hundred feet across, the Vulcan was as large as an airliner but surprisingly nimble. It soon became a popular symbol of British might and was later featured in the James Bond film *Thunderball*.

The captain and his copilot, twenty-seven-year-old Flight Lieutenant Brian Peacock, were perched in the windowed "blister" above the Vulcan's nose. The flight deck was so crowded with gauges, switches, throttles, hoses, wires, and other equipment that the pilots used "fighter-style" control sticks instead of the conventional handlebar found on large aircraft.

Squeezed into the drop-down section behind the cockpit were three officers: navigator Harvey Skull, thirty-five; radar navigator Jim Watson, thirty-four; and electronics officer Tony Baker, twenty-three. They sat shoulder to shoulder, facing backward, with their work area four feet below the flight deck. Like some tribe of atomic-age cave dwellers, the "rear crew" inhabited a clammy, claustrophobic world of glowing dials, quivering needles, and jammed chart tables. Their only view of the outside was through a pair of small portholes located high above them. Even their method of escape was primitive when compared to the pilots' ejector seats. In an emergency, they were expected to force open a floor hatch and then slide down the door into the slipstream, at which point a static line would pull open their parachutes. The hatch was located directly in front of the main wheel; if the main wheel was not retracted, an exiting crew member risked being blown straight into it.

The crew had been together since September 1957, when the XA908 was delivered to Squadron No. 83 at the RAF base at Waddington, just outside Lincoln, England. Since then they had visited such exotic stations as Tripoli, Entebbe, Bulawayo, and Embakasi, where they helped ceremoniously open Nairobi's new airport prior to embarking on a goodwill tour of Rhodesia.

Crews were social units whose bonds grew tighter on "ranger" missions—overseas flights that separated a plane from the rest of the squadron for several days of training and public relations. On Thursday, October 23, 1958, the XA908 embarked on its first "western ranger" to the United States. The bomber was scheduled to fly from Waddington to the Offutt Air Force Base near Lincoln, Nebraska, home to the Strategic Air Command. They were to return home the following Monday.

The first leg of the trip was an uneventful transatlantic flight to the air base at Goose Bay. After an overnight stay for rest, refueling, and a buying spree at the commissary, the following day it was on to Nebraska, where the crew planned to surprise Lincoln's mayor with a "best wishes" letter and package from his English counterpart.

"Taff" Evison, crew chief of the doomed Vulcan, stands at far right, next to Charles Bland. (Tony Regan Collection)

On ranger flights the normal five-man crew grew by one with the addition of a crew chief, whose duties ranged from overseeing all ground maintenance to ensuring that sausages, ale, and contraband were stowed safely on board. The crew chief on this particular flight was an old hand: thirty-nine-year-old Edward "Taff" Evison, who had joined the RAF in 1937.

Evison had the dry, absurd wit that many Brits appreciate. Charles Bland, a retired RAF crew chief who boarded with Evison when they were training at the Avro works, remembered his roommate merrily waving to perfect strangers as they drove past on their way to class. "The first time he did it, I asked who it was he was waving to," said Bland. "Taff's reply was, 'I have no idea, but he will go to work wondering all day who was in the car that waved to him this morning.'" In the evenings, Evison enjoyed a pint and a tall tale at the local pub. "Taff used to concoct the most fantastic stories. We went from being nuclear scientists to secret agents. He would always warn people not to repeat what he had told them. It was all very serious. He liked the idea of somebody going home and saying he had just met with some very special chaps, but that he was not to breathe a word about it."

Wearing their flight suits and "bone domes" (flying helmets), Evison and his adopted crew left Goose Bay in the XA908. The tremendous roar from its four turbojet motors built into a throbbing crescendo as the bomber quickly climbed through the gray Canadian sky before leveling off some nine miles above the earth. The Vulcan—designed to carry one thermonuclear warhead or twenty-one conventional thousand-pound bombs—was unarmed, though its tanks held some nine thousand imperial gallons of aviation fuel.

For the first couple of hours, the flight was routine. Evison sat among the rear crew in a small pull-down seat; all were hooked up to oxygen hoses. The Vulcan whisked along at subsonic speed, covering one mile every six seconds in the thin, freezing reaches of the bright blue stratosphere. The plane was due to arrive in Nebraska at 5:23 p.m., Detroit time. At 3:18, Willoughby-Moore matter-of-factly reported to a ground station in Erie, Pennsylvania, that he was flying on instruments at 47,000 feet. He expected to be over Flint's Bishop Airport a half-hour later.

There were no more transmissions until 3:40 p.m., when the cry of "Mayday! Mayday!"—the international distress call—was picked up by a radio operator at Cleveland's municipal airport. Willoughby-Moore reported that he was flying at 35,000 feet over Dresden, Ontario, about fifty miles northeast of Detroit. He requested an emergency "steer" to Kellogg Field in Battle Creek. Before the operator could respond, the pilot anxiously asked for directions to any airport.

Investigators later determined that a short circuit in the Vulcan's electrical system had caused all four generators to shut down. The emergency battery was intended to provide auxiliary power for twenty minutes, enough time to find an airfield at which to land; however, the back-up battery quickly failed. This locked the flying controls in neutral—and the Vulcan helplessly rolled over and fell into a steep dive. "The plane had a total electrical failure," Bland said, "and as all the controls were electro-hydraulic, it did not stand a chance. It had no gliding ability at all. It just went straight down."

According to Tony Regan, a former Vulcan crew chief who lives in Devon, England, evacuation was out of the question for the rear crew. As the bomber plunged at a 70-degree angle, the immense pressure exerted by the rushing air on the hatch "made it impossible for them to leave the airplane." With the jet flipped over on its back, the pilots would have had a brief, baleful view of Detroit's topography rushing up to meet them. At some point the canopy blew off. Willoughby-Moore "may have ordered Peacock to eject," Regan said. "We will never know." By the time a score of witnesses looked up and saw the Vulcan tearing out of the soggy sky, the men on board had only seconds to live.

The Kurshildgens' home at 477 Ashland was part of a neighborhood of narrow lots, crowded boatyards, and winding canals in the vicinity of Harbor Island and Windmill Pointe. Four-year-old Curt Kurshildgen and his mother were inside the kitchen when some mighty, unseen force suddenly gripped the two-story dwelling. Fifty years later, Kurshildgen can still see the growing look of terror on his mother's face. "The sound overhead kept getting louder and louder," he recalled. "The windows were rattling and the dishes were shaking inside the glass cabinets. The engines were so loud and screaming that I could feel them rumbling right through me."

The frightened youngster jumped into his mother's arms just as the shuddering roar became a thunderous boom. "The explosion shook the house so badly—it was like an earthquake. My mother ran with me to the bedroom, yanked a blanket off the bed, and covered us with it as she ran out of the house with me in her arms. I remember peeking out and seeing nothing but flames and smoke down the street, this before she covered my eyes."

The free-falling Vulcan was traveling at tremendous speed at the moment of impact. It tore through treetops before burying itself among houses on Ashland, near Scripps Street, leaving behind a trench a hundred feet long and forty feet wide. Inside 179 Ashland, Otto Ewald, a seventy-seven-year-old retired patternmaker, was watching television while his sixty-five-year-old wife, Emily, was ironing. "Then—BLOOM!" Ewald later told a reporter. "Everything seemed to be afire all at once—

An aerial view of the crash site shortly after the XA908 hit Ashland Street on the afternoon of October 24, 1958. (Jeanne Haber Collection)

carpets, walls, furniture, everything. Flames went shooting all through the house."

Emily came rushing out of the kitchen, screaming, "I'm on fire!" Otto tried breaking through the buckled front door, but it wasn't until a couple of neighbors heard their cries for help that the elderly couple were able to escape the burning house. Moments later the roof fell in, and the porch collapsed. Meanwhile, the family collie, Lassie, jumped into the canal behind the house, her hindquarters ablaze.

The house next door, 175 Ashland, was flattened. "The only things I could recognize were a bathtub and a sink laying in the middle of the street," said a neighbor. Fortuitously, the homeowners were at the music shop they operated on John R. Street. Later that afternoon, Ivan and Florence Kay received a call from Otto Ewald. "Come see what's left of your house," he said.

Mud, red-hot debris, and squirting jet fuel rained down on Harbor Island, the one-street island directly across the canal from Ashland. Splintered boards and timbers from the shattered seawall flew like giant matchsticks. "A car got blown from the foot of Ashland across the canal," Schwartz said. "The transmission was stuck in the seawall." C. C. Gallagher rushed out with a garden hose to battle the flames licking at his boatyard.

Pieces of the plane and the crew were scattered over a seven-block area. A six-foot wing section landed on a porch. A one-pound fitting hit the back of a terrified paperboy running home, knocking him down. For blocks around, the force of the explosion cracked plaster walls, blew out windows, and ripped at least one garage door off its hinges.

The first alarms went out at 3:40 p.m., a minute before the Vulcan hit the ground. More than two hundred Detroit policemen and firefighters were quickly on the scene, as well as three fire trucks from Grosse Pointe Park. Thousands of spectators flocked to the site, snarling traffic. Priests and nuns from nearby St. Ambrose hurried to the scene. "The Gallaghers' roof was covered with small body parts," Schwartz said. Father Tom McWilliams "administered the last rites to remnants of one of the plane crew," reported the *Grosse Pointe News*. Meanwhile, Grosse Pointe Park police "gathered fragments of burnt flesh and bones and twisted metal in a bushel basket, taking them to their station, where the grim remains were tagged . . . and later turned over to Selfridge Air Force authorities."

Aviation experts, including a panel of British investigators who arrived several hours later, set up shop at the air base near Mount Clemens. There they tried to reconstruct the plane and the accident.

Over the next few days, military police and Detroit policemen roped off the crash site, allowing only residents with identification tags to enter and leave the area. Search teams sifted through the wreckage. Authorities asked souvenir hunters to turn in anything they had picked up. Inside the heated garage used as a collection center, Schwartz saw "the end of a flight shoe with a couple toes," among other items. A hearse was parked outside, but the county medical examiner said the fragments were too small to help him identify the airmen. "I don't know how they ever sorted out what few remains they did find," Schwartz said. "There was

These snapshots taken by schoolboy Fred Schwartz and a friend minutes after the crash show the houses on Ashland Street on fire and the canal between Ashland and Harbor Island filled with debris. (Fred Schwartz Collection)

no DNA testing back then, so there must've been a lot of guesswork." The crash crater, flooded because of the shattered seawall, had to be pumped before the twisted remnants of two engines could be pulled out. A power shovel dug seventy feet deep into the muddy ground in a futile attempt to find the cockpit or identifiable remains of the pilots. The coast guard searched Lake St. Clair as far north as Harsens Island on reports that an airman may have parachuted into the water. A chute was found tangled in a boat propeller, but no body was found.

When the first calls went out, many casualties were assumed. Emergency staff were on standby at all area hospitals awaiting a flood of victims that, to everybody's surprise and relief, never arrived. Several people on Harbor Island were slightly injured by the blast, but seventy-three-year-old Victoria Ozelski was the only one who agreed to go to a hospital; she was treated for minor cuts and soon released. Emily Ewald was the most seriously injured. She was taken to Bon Secours Hospital and treated for third-degree burns on her face and upper body. She survived, as did the Ewalds' scorched collie, Lassie.

Over the following weeks, residents slowly rebuilt their ruined homes and interrupted lives. All told, five houses were either destroyed outright or were later torn down. Scores of additional residences were damaged, most of them in an area bounded by Manistique, Alter, Scripps, and the Detroit River. Several boats had also been lost or damaged.

In time, investigators issued their report. Upon their findings, the electrical systems in all Vulcans were modified; however, escape procedures for the rear crew remained unchanged. The final Vulcan squadron was phased out of service in 1984. By then Charles Bland had been retired from the RAF for several years.

Now living in Lincoln, England, Bland recently did some housecleaning. "I have got rid of a lot of old photos because my kids will not be interested," he explained, "and at my time of life most of the people are dead and gone anyway."

One memory is impossible to discard. Not long before the accident, he crossed paths with Evison at Goose Bay. Evison was on his way back to England after a six-week assignment while Bland was working on a Vulcan with a failed engine. British Bomber Command asked Evison to stay and

The day following the crash, a crane was used to lift wreckage out of the deep crater created by the jet's impact. (Fred Schwartz Collection)

assist. But Bland told his homesick friend—a "real family man" with a wife and son waiting for him—that he could manage on his own.

"That was the last time I saw Taff," Bland said. "He had not been home long when he went off in XA908. I have often wondered that, had he stayed with me, he would not have been in the plane that day. But fate deals out all sorts of hands."

The day the bomber fell out of the sky was a quickly forgotten footnote to Detroit's Cold War Era. The injuries and damage, while considerable, were not nearly as catastrophic as they could have been. "Can you imagine if that plane had come in on a flatter angle?" Schwartz said.

The six Royal Air Force servicemen who died aboard the XA908 rest at Oak Ridge Cemetery in Flat Rock. (Walter P. Reuther Library)

"It would've wiped out an entire block or two." Guyton Elementary was only two blocks away while the U.S. Public Health Service Hospital at the foot of Alter Road was just a thousand yards south of the crash site. "The death toll could have been tremendous," more than one official on the scene was quoted as saying.

Fortunately no citizens were killed. The injured recovered, the ruined houses were rebuilt, and more than a hundred claimants had their property losses covered by private or government insurers. The airmen's deaths were tragic, of course, but as faceless flyovers with no connections to the city, their loss failed to truly resonate with the public or media. Moreover, mere hours after the crash another major event with far greater local implications pushed the Vulcan out of the headlines. Cardinal Edward Mooney—the longtime spiritual leader of Detroit's one million Catholics—unexpectedly died in Rome while participating in the election of a new pope. Special coverage was accorded the cardinal's life, death, and funeral as his body was brought back to Detroit. Meanwhile, developments in the bomber crash received short shrift.

The following spring, the body of Lieutenant Peacock was recovered from the Detroit River, said Schwartz. The only nonswimmer in the crew was found still strapped into his ejector seat.

British military tradition calls for service members to be buried in the country where they fall. The crew of XA908 was laid to rest at Oak Ridge Cemetery, joining the eleven British airmen killed in training accidents at nearby Grosse Ile during World War II. Each Memorial Day, small Union Jacks are planted at this corner of a distant graveyard that lies in Flat Rock but is forever England.

The hellish roar of the doomed Vulcan still resonates in Kurshildgen's mind. "I was haunted by the memory for a long time," he confesses. "I could never stay in a room when I heard an airplane flying near. I always covered my ears or wanted to go outside. My nightmares were always of airplanes crashing."

Ironically, the former Detroiter learned to fly a helicopter and now works in corporate aviation in Texas. "I became less phobic about loud approaching noises. But to this day, I still pause and listen to make sure aircraft engines sound normal as they fly overhead."

EIGHT
Dead of Summer

In June 1968, six vacationing members of the Robison family were murdered at their secluded cottage in the northern Michigan village of Good Hart—an unsolved mystery as dark and inscrutable as the surrounding woods.

An adopted child of Michigan's north country, Carolyn Sutherland talks freely about Good Hart in the dead of winter. How the interminable snow is always whiter than the stuff downstate. How there's no salt on the roads and no dampness in the air. How the only really bad time is mud season, those ugly months of November and April when Old Man Winter can't decide whether he's coming or going. "That's when I head for Florida," said the saucy sexagenarian, who grew up in Huntington Woods. "I have my drinks poolside."

What sets the proprietor of the village's general goods store apart from other locals is that she's equally glib about the dead of summer in Good Hart—the dead of the summer of 1968, to be precise. "People come into the store and they all want to know about the murders. I'm a walking encyclopedia, so I tell 'em."

It was a crime that gripped the state and placed an unwelcome microscope on this stretch of wooded bluffs hugging the Lake Michigan shore. The murders took place in an isolated cottage just two miles up the road from the Good Hart General Store. On July 22, 1968, a caretaker investigating complaints of an overpowering stench pried open the door to the

The Robisons of Lathrup Village. *Top row, from left*: Gary, Randy, and Richard Jr. *Bottom row, from left*: Shirley, Susan, and Richard Sr. (Author's Collection)

cottage. He walked into what one investigator later described as "a wall of flies." Inside were the badly decomposed bodies of six members of a vacationing Lathrup Village family: advertising executive Richard Robison; his wife, Shirley; and their four children. Shirley had evidently been raped; the youngest child, seven-year-old Susan, had been bludgeoned with a hammer. All had been shot. They had been dead a month.

"The sheer mad violence of those killings burned into my mind," recalled Tom DeLisle, then a young reporter for the *Detroit Free Press*. "It's disturbing to this day."

Some thought the slayings were entirely random—perhaps a drifter, a cult, or a motorcycle gang had stumbled across the cottage. Many longtime residents still believe it was revenge by an unhinged local builder over an imagined slight. DeLisle chased down rumors connecting the murders to the infamous "Co-ed Killer," John Norman Collins. Ultimately, detectives closest to the case came to the conclusion that

The Robisons' cottage near Good Hart, site of one of the most gruesome mass murders in state history. (Walter P. Reuther Library)

Robison's business partner was the probable killer—a determination that doesn't sit well with everyone.

"I don't think you can tie it up into a nice package and put a ribbon on it," said a former neighbor, pointing out that the case remains officially unsolved. "You have to keep an open mind."

There is an intemporal quality to Good Hart, borne of ancient rocks, mature mixed forests, enduring Ottawa tribal legends, and the turquoise waters of Little Traverse Bay. The unincorporated village in lightly populated Emmet County is intersected by Lake Shore Drive (M-119), the famously picturesque "tunnel of trees" that connects the wealthy resort town of Harbor Springs thirteen miles to the south with Cross Village eight miles to the north. The Robisons called their secluded waterfront cottage Summerset. It stood at the end of a private drive nestled in the lower reaches of the Blisswood Resort. The subdivision of widely scattered log-and-stone cabins was developed by the Bliss family, which also maintained the thickly wooded property.

The Robisons could have stepped right out of *The Donna Reed Show* or some other faux-family TV program of the era. Richard C. "Dick" Robison was the handsome, cultured forty-two-year-old breadwinner. He operated a small ad agency, R. C. Robison & Associates, and published an arts magazine called *Impresario* out of his one-story office building at 28081 Southfield Road in Southfield. He enjoyed attending the theatre with Shirley, his stylish and pretty wife of twenty years, painting the occasional watercolor, and flying his private plane. The churchgoing couple didn't smoke, drink, or gamble and had no known enemies.

The children were bright and mannerly. Ritchie was a nineteen-year-old student at Eastern Michigan University. Gary, seventeen, attended Southfield-Lathrup High School and played in a garage band. Randy, twelve, was friends with Tom Mair, who lived a couple doors down from the Robisons' brick ranch in Lathrup Village. "We did normal things together—ride bikes, work on our stamp collections," said Mair, today a movie-house manager in Traverse City. "They were just a typical suburban family." Susan, a quiet little girl with big blue eyes, dreamed of having a pony.

Before the family left for a summerlong vacation on Sunday, June 16, 1968, Robison had dropped hints about a "big deal" that was going to make him a "tycoon." It apparently involved a certain "Mr. Roberts" who was to fly into Pellston on his personal Lear jet, spend a little time at the cottage, and then take the family on a trip south. Robison was looking to buy a horse farm in Kentucky and a beachfront condo in Florida.

Based on phone records and the recollections of tree trimmers working around the cottage, police determined that the murders occurred on the evening of Tuesday, June 25. Earlier that day, Robison had called his bank to see if an expected $200,000 deposit had been made in the agency's account. A bank official said it hadn't and then inquired about the surprisingly low balance.

The only other person with access to the account was Robison's partner, Joe Scolaro, who had been running the business for three months while Robison traveled around the country, working on his secret venture. Several calls were made between the cottage and the Southfield office. The receptionist later testified that Robison sounded angry. At 10:30 a.m. on June 25th, Scolaro left the office and didn't return. The family was last seen alive by the tree trimmers, who stopped work for the day at 4 p.m.

Forensics experts reconstructed what happened a few hours later. In their scenario, the killer (or killers) came out of the woods at twilight, approaching a window near the front door. Several shots from a .22-caliber rifle were fired into the living room. Dick Robison was struck in the chest as he relaxed in an easy chair. Stunned family members had only moments to grasp what had happened before the assailant burst through the door, gunning down Randy and Shirley and then shooting Susan as she tried to run for cover. The two oldest boys were playing cards at a table. As Ritchie and Gary raced for the rear bedroom, trying to reach a rifle stored in the closet, the assailant shot down each in turn. The killer returned to Susan, striking her in the head with a claw hammer. As a *coup de grâce,* each victim was shot in the head.

Such commotion might ordinarily have alerted neighbors, but the owners of the nearest cabin, which was a hundred yards away, were not home. A couple living a quarter-mile away later said they had heard some gunfire and the shouts of two men and a woman coming from the direction of the Robisons' cottage but decided against going to see if anything was amiss. "We just heard a series of shots . . . one with a little short pause . . . and then three or four others after that," one recalled. "It was still light out, so we thought that somebody was shooting gulls on the beach."

Before leaving, the killer threw a blanket over Shirley, dragged Dick, Susan, and Randy into an interior hallway so they couldn't be seen from outside, drew the curtains, turned up the heat, locked the cottage, and placed cardboard over the shattered windowpane. Taped to it was a note: "WILL BE BACK—ROBISON."

For the next twenty-seven days the bodies lay in the heated cabin. Dust and twigs settled on the family's two parked cars. A sickening smell wafted over Blisswood, ruining one cottager's annual bridge party. Nonetheless, the community of vacationers assumed that the Robisons were on the out-of-town trip they had talked about. Finally, caretaker Monnie Bliss and a helper approached the Robisons' cabin to remove what they figured was a dead raccoon rotting in the crawl space. A few minutes later, the phone rang at the Emmet County Sheriff's Department in Petoskey. "There's a body inside one of our cottages," Bliss said.

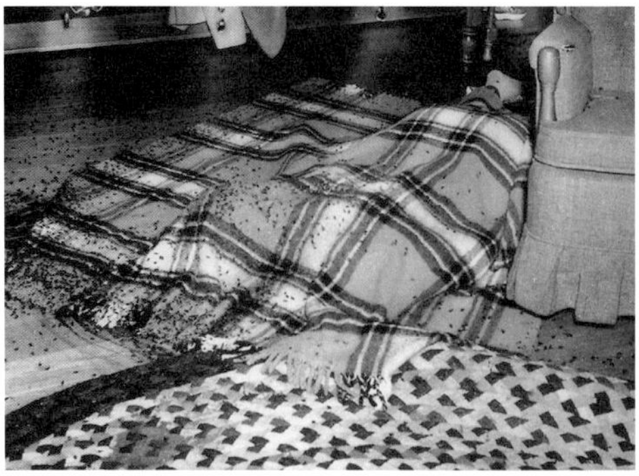

Shirley Robison's body lies under a blanket covered with flies. (Michigan State Police Archives)

Investigators at the crime scene were forced to wear gas masks because of the stench and flies. (Michigan State Police Archives)

Deputies encountered a grim tableau. Swaths of congealed blood and armies of dead flies covered the plank floors. The victims were dressed as if going on a trip, and deputies found a partially packed suitcase on a bed. Shirley's skirt had been hiked up, and her undergarments had been pulled down to her ankles. The medical examiner could not determine if she had been raped, but seven stab-like perforations were found in her sanitary napkin. The bodies were in such a wretched condition that the hospital in Petoskey refused to accept them. Instead, autopsies were performed inside a chicken coop at the local fairgrounds.

Investigators wearing gas masks went over the crime scene. Fifteen shell casings were found: eleven from a .22-caliber rifle and four from a .25-caliber handgun. An expensive ring and some cash were missing, but the killer left most valuables behind. There was one bloody boot print. The initial theory was that a maniacal gunman was on the loose.

Seven-year-old Mardi Link was in the backseat of the family Ford, on her way to a relative's cottage, when WJR interrupted a ballgame with breaking news of the grisly discovery. Link, who now lives in Traverse City, is the author of *When Evil Came to Good Hart,* the first nonfiction account of the murders. "I guess I was struck by the fact that Susie and I were the same age," she said. "I was always intrigued by the case. Who would kill an entire family? And why?"

Police asked those same questions. Within a few weeks all persons of interest around Good Hart, from transients and summer people to "mentals," had been cleared. "We now believe the killer was familiar with the cabin, that he knew the family and they knew him," the county sheriff said. The focus of the investigation shifted 275 miles south to Detroit.

Joseph Scolaro III had spent three years in the army and a year at Harvard before joining Robison's firm in 1965. He was a stocky six-footer with a high I.Q. and an interest in guns, said Link. Scolaro was a competitive trapshooter used to hitting fast-moving targets. The bookish-looking Scolaro "had no history of violence. But detectives determined he had embezzled about $60,000 over a couple years from the company and Robison had just found out about it. There was the motive."

Lloyd Stearns and John Flis were the veteran state police detectives assigned to the case. They grilled Scolaro about his activities on June 25, and much of what he said didn't match up. He said he had gone to a plumbing convention at Cobo Hall, then had a drink at the Salamander Bar before doing a little shopping and then driving home in a rainstorm. Not a single person could be found to corroborate Scolaro's whereabouts in the ten to eleven hours after he had left the agency that morning.

Stearns and Flis learned that Scolaro had owned two model AR-7 .22-caliber rifles, the type of weapon determined to have been used in the murders. One was recovered from a friend in Chicago, but the other, supposedly given to his brother-in-law, was never found. The detectives visited a private range where Scolaro was known to have fired the missing AR-7. Flis dug some old cartridge casings out of the mud; a crime lab identified them as coming from the same gun used to kill the Robisons. Moreover, in early 1968 Scolaro had bought two matching .25-caliber

Joseph Scolaro was Robison's business partner and the chief suspect in the murders. (Michigan State Police Archives)

Beretta pistols. He said he kept one and gave the other to Robison, who brought it to the cottage. Based on the rare type of ammunition the pistols used, police concluded that Robison's Beretta—also missing—was the second murder weapon.

In all, Scolaro took—and flunked—three polygraphs. "We interviewed him a dozen times," said Stearns, now retired and living on a farm near Greenville. "Not once did we ever walk away thinking, 'This guy is innocent.'"

Doubts remain. The drive between Detroit and Good Hart takes five to six hours. Witnesses heard shots about 9 p.m. on the night of the murders, yet Scolaro's wife said he was home in Birmingham about 11 that evening. One also has to believe that a composed white-collar criminal like Scolaro could metamorphize into somebody capable of *Helter Skelter*-style monstrosities, a leap not everyone is comfortable making. "You come across guys like Scolaro all the time," countered Stearns.

"People say, 'We never suspected him.' But out of fear of exposure, they're capable of doing these things."

Even if Scolaro was determined to kill the Robisons, skeptics say it would have been nearly impossible to do it within an eleven-hour time frame. And arranging a contract killing on such short notice seems improbable.

Dick Robison's own secrets began to emerge after his murder. A little spadework revealed that he had cheated on his wife. Among his quirks was the habit of inviting a secretary into his office after work and then asking her to lift her skirt while he admired her legs. No sex was involved, but sometimes the ogling and fondling lasted as long as an hour.

Worse, word leaked out that the solid citizen whom newspapers had initially described as "the man without a vice" had swindled clients out of as much as $50,000 over a three-year period, billing them for ads he either didn't run or didn't pay for. He'd also published full-page airline ads without permission in his own magazine, making it appear more successful than it was.

The choice of ads was telling. Robison envisioned *Impresario* as a marketing tool for his quixotic scheme to create an international network of giant computerized warehouses. According to his plans, each would be based at an airport and would feature a fly-in cultural center.

Robison aimed to raise $100 million from investors known as the "Superior Table." In documents he'd left behind, he described the Table as a "world-wide organization" dedicated to "complete peace and unity among all countries on Earth." Its chairman was a mysterious figure named "Roebert," who presided over other investors with names like Mr. Thomas and Mr. Peters. The cryptic references to Roebert included an engraved St. Christopher medal that police found around the neck of Robison's corpse. The inscription ran: "Richard—To my chosen son and heir—God bless you—Roebert." No surviving family members could ever recall seeing or hearing of such a medal, which led to speculation that it may have been placed there by the killer.

Was Roebert the "Mr. Roberts" expected on the night of the murders? If so, no such person ever arrived at the Pellston airport nor inquired about the family afterward. Detectives learned that Robison had spent three days at the Metro Airport Hotel just before the family left for Good Hart—which was not the first time that he had checked into an airport hotel while telling his family he was away on a business trip. Scolaro, who claimed to have little idea of what the secretive Robison was up to in the months preceding his death, said the hotel was probably being used as a headquarters for the new venture. But detectives said Robison evidently never left his room, saw any visitors, or placed any unusual phone calls. What, if anything, did these clandestine activities have to do with the murders? Were Roebert and other members of the Superior Table real or part of some elaborate fantasy? To this day, nobody knows.

As the investigation moved along, the search for another mass murderer had already seized the public's imagination. Between August 1967 and July 1969, the mutilated bodies of seven young women were found dumped around Ann Arbor. Some anxious citizens began to think the rape-killings had to be related somehow to the equally horrific murders in Good Hart. A clean-cut college student named John Norman Collins—who coincidentally had attended Eastern Michigan University with the oldest Robison boy in 1967 and may even have roomed with him during a week of orientation—finally was arrested for the last of the murders. Collins was convicted in 1970, but not before various agencies had shared information and decided that he was not a suspect in the Robison case.

In early 1970, an intriguing lead emerged from Leavenworth penitentiary in Kansas. Alexander Bloxom, a career criminal who had recently been locked up for bank robbery, told detectives that in 1968 he had lived in a Detroit halfway house at the same time as a fellow parolee named Mark Warren Brock. One day he drove Brock to a meeting at a Flint restaurant with a dark, heavyset man he remembered as "Scollata." Brock next went to Toledo to pick up some guns, then headed up north with a man named Robert Matthews in a borrowed blue Dodge. Bloxom was left behind because "there weren't no colored men up in Good Hart." Brock returned two days after the murders.

Bloxom's story was remarkably detailed. He described a briefcase of Robison's that Brock had brought back and later destroyed, as well as plans for the victim's new venture that few people had ever seen. Brock produced a sealed black suitcase, whose heft suggested to Bloxom that the murder weapons were inside, and a manila envelope containing a Robison family photo, canceled checks, and other material to be saved for possible blackmail purposes against "Scollata." At Brock's direction, Bloxom disposed of the suitcase at a salvage yard during a trip to Alabama and hid the envelope at the home of an unsuspecting relative. Despite a rigorous search by the detectives, neither item was ever found.

Bloxom paraphrased Brock's account of the murders: "We went to the cottage and knocked on the door and I faked a heart attack. While I was lying on the floor and Mr. Robison was trying to help me, Matthews came in and started shooting. The wife was the first one down and then one of the kids tried to run so we took him down too. Then, we just kilt 'em all."

Brock, thin but tough, had spent most of his life behind bars. Back in prison for the same armed heist that put Bloxom away, Brock verified nearly every detail of his ex-partner's story. He admitted that he would consider carrying out a multiple murder if the price was right—say, $5,000. But, no, he did not kill the Robisons.

An alibi witness had Mathews, the alleged accomplice, buying guns in Toledo at the time of the murders. Mathews passed his polygraph. Brock, however, refused to be hooked up. "I'm not going to tell you anything I might know about the murder of that family. If I ever change my mind, I'll let my parole officer know, but it ain't too likely you'll be hearing from me."

Bloxom welcomed his "liar's test"—and flunked it. Inconsistencies in his story, coupled with the lack of further cooperation from Brock and Mathews, caused the once promising lead to dry up. However, Link said, Mathews did volunteer that "Brock was ruthless enough to kill the family and Bloxom was too dumb to make up such a story."

Behind the scenes, friction had developed between Emmet County, which was handling its first homicide case in a decade, and downstate agencies. The county's professionalism took an early hit when a deputy at the crime scene held up the bloody hammer for a photographer, obliterating any possible fingerprints.

Emmet County had jurisdiction over the case. Despite the mounting evidence against Scolaro, prosecutors resisted filing murder charges in the hope that accomplices, eyewitnesses, or the weapons would turn up. "We could've gone to trial and gotten a conviction based on circumstantial evidence alone," Stearns said. "Most cases, especially murder, are circumstantial. There just was no experience up there." Oakland County authorities met with frustrated state police detectives and decided to build their own case. By early 1973, prosecutor L. Brooks Patterson was close to charging Scolaro with conspiracy to commit murder. But someone tipped off Scolaro's mother that a warrant was imminent, and she in turn told her son.

Scolaro was already chin-deep in woe. He had bought Robison's business interests and driven them into the ground. He was being hounded by detectives and creditors and was, at last, reduced to having his mother serve as his unpaid secretary. His new venture, the high-sounding Dimensional Research Inc., was nothing more than a check-kiting scheme. Each day on his way to work he drove past Acacia Park Cemetery, where the Robisons were buried.

On the afternoon of March 8, 1973, two men entered Scolaro's office looking to collect a $730 debt. They discovered Scolaro in his chair, a bullet from his Beretta through his brain. On his desk was a suicide note: "Mother—where do I start . . . I am a liar-cheat-phony. Any check that any of the people have with your signature isn't any good, because I forged your name to it to get them off my back . . . I know I'm sick, but seeking help isn't going to help the people I've hurt." He added a postscript: "I had nothing to do with the Robisons—I'm a cheat but not a murderer."

Some point to Scolaro's note as proof that he didn't commit the murders. Others believe he carried his untruths into the next world. "My personal theory is he was so tied to his mother, he just couldn't bear to hurt her by admitting that he did it," Link said. Stearns added: "Remember, practically the first words in his suicide note were, 'I am a liar . . .' In other words, 'From this point on don't believe anything I've written.'" Scolaro, thirty-eight, left behind a wife and two young sons, none of whom knew what to believe.

Al Koski covered the crime beat for various media outlets during his long journalism career. Now semi-retired and living in Royal Oak, the vinegary octogenarian has spent half his life pondering all aspects of the case. He believes the evidence points to Scolaro. "He had the motive and the weapons, so you have to figure he's the guy."

But there are other roads of inquiry that Koski likes to meander down. One of Robison's ex-secretaries later married a rich and powerful manufacturing tycoon with rumored ties to organized crime in Cleveland. About the time of the murders, the woman had a miscarriage, and there were whispers that the baby was Robison's and not her seventy-year-old husband's. Also, the family of one of the companies Robison swindled was thought to be associated with the mob. Had either jealousy or embezzlement led to a bloody reprisal?

The theory of an underworld connection "certainly has some merit," said Link. The AR-7 used in the murders was a "novelty weapon" much preferred by Mafia hit men of the era. In 1968, the press reported an informant saying that Robison owed the mob $12,000 a month but was seriously delinquent in his payments. The informant quoted a colleague: "If he hadn't held back on us like he did, we wouldn't have wiped out the whole family."

The case stalled after Scolaro's death. Then, in February 1974, a state trooper from the Romeo post made a routine search of a blue 1965 Chevrolet with Ohio license plates that had been found deserted by the side of M-14 and then impounded at a local auto repair yard. Inside the glove box was a luggage tag bearing this inscription: "Shirley L. Robison, 18790 Dolores, Lathrup Village, Michigan."

What was such an item doing inside an abandoned car six years after the murders and two hundred miles from the crime scene? Detectives combed the car for clues but found nothing. A title search showed that the car had been purchased new off a Toledo lot in 1966. Between that time and its abandonment several years later, any number of people could have driven it, legally and illegally. Every registered owner was tracked down. Nobody could recall ever seeing the tag or had any idea how it had gotten there. The forsaken Chevy and derelict luggage tag added up to just one more baffling dead end.

Carolyn Sutherland, who runs the general goods store in Good Hart, has no doubt who murdered the Robisons: "People around here know who did the killings, but they politely keep their lips zipped."

That's more than Monnie Bliss, the man who helped build the Robisons' cottage and discovered their bodies, ever did. "Bliss was an oddball," Link said. "He was a motor-mouth, constantly talking to himself, and he had a quick temper. A lot of people were afraid of him." Bliss and his father, who built scores of distinctly styled cabins beginning in the 1930s, were famous for their craftsmanship. The "Bliss homes," still highly coveted today, feature lacquered logs on a stone foundation and such artistic touches as hand-forged hardware.

Bliss died in 1980 at age sixty-nine, but family members still live in the area, making longtime residents reluctant to talk. However, one person who arrived shortly after the murders happened agreed to be quoted pseudonymously. "You think Good Hart is rugged now, you should have seen it forty years ago," said "Pat," a big-city transplant. "I couldn't believe the mentality of this place—guns, superstitions, vigilante justice."

According to local lore, Bliss inexplicably held the Robisons responsible for his eighteen-year-old son's death. Norman Bliss, a friend of the Robison boys, crashed his motorcycle while driving home drunk one night from the Legs Inn in Cross Village. Bliss found his son's lifeless body crumpled at the base of a tree. On the day before the funeral, Dick Robison stopped by to offer condolences and regrets that his family could not attend. He gave Bliss's wife twenty dollars for flowers. Bliss supposedly was insulted by the gesture. On the following evening, the Robisons were murdered.

Pat points to the overzealous manner in which the two female victims were killed. "To me that says this was someone who was half-crazy, that it was some kind of revenge-style murder." While conceding that the brutality could have been a ploy to make police think they were dealing with a psychotic, Pat mentioned the claw hammer—just the type of weapon a builder would have handy. Talk circulated after the killings that one of Bliss's hammers was missing from his tool chest, though

Monnie Bliss (*far left*) was considered a suspect by some. (Michigan State Police Archives)

police eventually decided it was a rumor hatched by some locals over beers at the Legs Inn.

Bliss was cleared as a suspect. Afterward his behavior grew more bizarre. He began wandering the woods at night, chatting nonstop with equally restless Indian spirits and his dead son. "He had the keys to all the houses he built," Pat said. "You'd get up at four in the morning and find him in your kitchen, frying eggs." Locals suspected Bliss of setting several fires, including a mysterious blaze in which one unlucky fellow was found tied to the bed, roasted. Some defended Bliss as a harmless eccentric, but he didn't help his cause by occasionally blurting out, "The Robisons had it coming," or saying he had killed the family during one of his rambling monologues.

Despite the compelling small-town gossip, few outsiders pin the killings on Bliss. "That poor sumbitch was a nut case," Koski said. "But he wasn't a murderer."

Stearns once told Scolaro: "You killed the Robisons. And if you didn't, then you know who pulled the trigger." That remains the position of the state police and Emmet County Sheriff's Department to this day, though proving it to the satisfaction of a court is another matter.

In 2003, evidence was brought out of storage and underwent DNA analysis. There were hopes that a match could be made with a known suspect or someone cataloged in national criminal databases. However, the evidence was too degraded to yield any conclusive results. Occasionally there has been talk of a renewed effort to have prosecutors finally put cold case No. 7471 to rest. "We owe it to the memory of the victims," Mair said.

Outside of some stray chimney stones, nothing remains of Summerset today. Due to the lingering stench, the decision was made to level and burn the cottage a year or so after the murders. "It was impossible to clean the wood," Koski said. "It was saturated with body fluids." Even the top foot of sand beneath the foundation had to be replaced. Pines eventually were planted on the spot.

To the dismay of subsequent owners, strangers occasionally traipse through the property. They are drawn by the site's macabre history and struck by the timeless tranquility. Lake Michigan laps the rocky shore as languidly as a puppy cleaning its paw. Birdsong fills the scented air. Trespassers who dare to linger are chased off—like the Robisons, premature departures from the blessed calm.

THE COLLINS CONNECTION

John Norman Collins, the infamous "Co-ed Killer," is thought to be responsible for brutally torturing and murdering as many as fifteen young women in Michigan and California between 1967 and 1969. His spree stopped after he raised the suspicions of his uncle, David Leik, a state police corporal. Collins used Leik's Ypsilanti home to kill eighteen-year-old Karen Sue Beineman, a student at Eastern Michigan University, while Leik was vacationing in Canada.

"Co-ed Killer" John Norman Collins also was a suspect in the Robisons' murders. (Author's Collection)

Coincidentally, Collins and the Robisons' oldest son, Ritchie, attended EMU together. It was even rumored that the two had belonged to the same fraternity. Police investigating the Robison murders kept their eyes on Collins but eventually eliminated him as a suspect in their case.

The most persistent advocate of a possible Collins connection is Tom Mair of Traverse City. He knew the Robisons and has long been active in various crime-stopper programs. He insists that Collins met Ritchie Robison during a week of orientation at EMU—a scenario police rejected but which true-crime author Mardi Link considers very likely, considering the small size of the group. Mair suggests that Collins may have visited the cottage before the murders. "There's no proof anywhere of that," Link said.

Mair also hinted that Leik, who later commanded the state police post in Petoskey, may have impeded any subsequent investigation of ties between his nephew and the Robisons. To Link, that made no sense. "Why would Leik turn in Collins for Beineman's murder but then obstruct a look into any possible involvement with the Robisons?"

A few years ago, a CNN report featuring Mair gave the dubious Collins theory a certain legitimacy. It gained more traction with the publication in 2004 of Judith Guest's fictionalized account of the murders, *The Tarnished Eye*. Guest, a former Royal Oak schoolteacher best known for her breakout novel, *Ordinary People,* took tremendous liberties with the lives of some of the principal characters, going so far as to describe an affair between Collins and Shirley Robison.

Veteran crime reporter Al Koski, who covered both the Collins and Robison cases, is galled by this kind of creative license. He even confronted Guest during a chance meeting in Oscoda, where the Minnesota-based novelist maintains a summer cottage. "She told me, 'It's fiction, Al.' But this is how the public starts believing such bullshit. They get their 'facts' from people like her and Mair and it just muddies the water."

Mair maintains that he's not necessarily saying Collins committed the Robison murders; he's only suggesting that authorities shouldn't be so quick to reject the possibility. "They've never even interviewed him about it."

Collins, who changed his name to John Chapman in prison, is currently serving a life sentence in Marquette. He has always steadfastly maintained his innocence. (In 2004, DNA evidence cleared Collins of one of the murders long attributed to him.) In his last public interview, he admitted that it was bothersome being called a serial killer. "It's bad enough being convicted of one thing," he said in 1988, "without being labeled for other things you haven't done."

NINE
Arms in the Arctic

The First World War was over, but confused Michigan soldiers continued fighting in the frozen reaches of post-Czarist Russia.

It's Sunday morning at Troy's White Chapel Cemetery. A large marble monument looms in the milky mist. Carved in the image of an arctic polar bear, with a hubcap helmet of the archetypal doughboy near its paw, it appears sullen and indomitable as its unblinking eyes survey a handful of visitors.

The monument commemorates a footnote in the war that idealists maintained would "make the world safe for democracy." The inscription on its base states that it was raised "In memory of the North Russian Expeditionary Force, 1918–1919." Erected in 1930, and surrounded by the grave markers of many of those who fell in the campaign, it served as a vivid reminder to their surviving comrades who thought they would be fighting Germany and inexplicably found themselves plunged into the chaos of post-Czarist Russia.

The first American blows against Soviet Russia were struck by men who hailed principally from Michigan. On November 11, 1918, as the rest of the world was wildly celebrating the armistice that had brought four years of unprecedented bloodletting to a halt, members of the expeditionary force were engaged in a fierce struggle at Toulgas, near the Arctic Circle. In three days of intense infantry combat, more than a hundred Allied soldiers and three hundred Bolsheviks were killed. Reports of the

The Polar Bear monument at Troy's White Chapel Cemetery. (Author's Collection)

fighting and the deaths in an undeclared war in the middle of nowhere made little sense to anxious family members. In the days and months that followed, letters from home increasingly asked "What are you doing in Russia?" and "When are you coming home?"

The First World War began in the summer of 1914, but the United States didn't formally enter the European conflict until April 6, 1917, when Congress declared war on Germany. A draft was instituted, but plenty of volunteers were anxious to get into uniform and get "Over There," as a popular song of the period put it.

"In those days you had to be twenty-one in order to enlist," recalled Joe Taube, a dapper and slightly built Detroiter. "If you walked in underage, the recruiting sergeant would tell you, 'Take a walk around the block and come back when you remember your *real* age.'" Many young men, miraculously aged by a few minutes' walk, were thus able to sneak in on their second try. Age wasn't Taube's problem, though. "I was old enough, but I got rejected because I was underweight. I felt very bad about it at the time."

One successful enlistee was Donald Shand, a young Detroit man just a year out of high school. Shand, who described himself at the time as "pretty patriotic," enlisted in the Army Medical Corps with several friends. They were assigned to the 337th Ambulance Company, then forming at Camp Custer in Battle Creek. Other men waited to be drafted. Ivan Gibbs of Shelby, whose grandfather had served with the camp's namesake, General George Armstrong Custer, as a Michigan cavalryman during the Civil War, was finishing college in Kalamazoo when he was called.

"I received my diploma on a Tuesday," Gibbs said, "and the following Monday I was drilling at Camp Custer." Several high school classmates, including a fellow named Stillman Jenks who lived down the road from the Gibbs' farm, were also drafted. Meanwhile, a jubilant, if somewhat skinny, Joe Taube was called. Both Gibbs and Taube were assigned to the 339th Infantry Regiment, a unit soon to become known as "Detroit's Own" for the large number of Detroiters in its ranks. Together with Shand and about five thousand other soldiers training at Camp Custer, two-thirds of whom were from Michigan, they soon found themselves fighting for their lives in a bewildering war at the top of the world.

In addition to the 339th Infantry Regiment and the 337th Ambulance Company, the expeditionary force also included the 337th Field Hospital Company and a battalion of the 310th Engineers. "We were all part of the 85th Division," said Shand. "We were all sent over to England in the summer of 1918. From there we expected to be sent to France to fight the Germans. Instead, we wound up in Russia." The Americans "were never really told why we were there," the ex-orderly said in the tiny room of a Wayne nursing home. "Some of the men thought it was to guard some supplies there in Archangel. Others thought it was to train the White Russians against the Bolsheviks. We were just there and did as we were told."

The reason for their presence was complicated. Germany was the enemy in the popular mind as Ford, Packard, and other Detroit manufacturers re-tooled for war production. Anti-German sentiment reached

Members of the 339th Infantry Regiment in Russia in 1919. The unit was known as "Detroit's Own" for the large number of Detroiters in its ranks. (Author's Collection)

feverish heights, transforming sauerkraut into "Liberty cabbage" and prompting the little community of Berlin, near Grand Rapids, to change its name. But the dismantling of Czarist Russia presented the United States and its allies with a new threat. After a popular revolt shockingly toppled the old regime in April 1917, war-weary Russian soldiers started deserting their positions on the Eastern Front against the Germans. Anarchy reigned in Russia. Following the Bolshevik Revolution in November of that year, civil war broke out between the Red (Bolshevik) and White (anti-Bolshevik) Russians.

To the horror of the French and British, who were barely holding their own on the Western Front against the Germans, the Bolsheviks signed a separate peace treaty with Germany. This freed hundreds of thousands of German troops for duty in the west. The Allies envisioned a human steamroller that would push them across Flanders and into the English Channel, thus winning the war for the hated "Huns" before America could fully flex its industrial and military might. To prevent this scenario, the Allies deemed it imperative to intervene in Russia. Such intervention would not only help re-open the Eastern Front, thus relieving some of the pressure that was already building in the west, but it also would present an opportunity, as Winston Churchill put it, to "strangle Bolshevism in the cradle."

The geopolitics of their situation were lost on the Americans who clambered down the gangplank into Archangel—a city of lively wharves and picturesque churches that was the chief seaport of medieval Russia—in early September 1918 to join a force of British, Canadian, and French troops already stationed there. From that point on, these Allied forces were engaged in a war against two enemies: the Bolsheviks and the 330,000 square miles of tundra, swamps, and thick fir forests that the "Bolos" inhabited. It was the gloomiest and most inhospitable place any of the American men had ever seen; nothing back home in Michigan compared to it. It also was lethal—a reality brutally driven home just days after the new arrivals had fanned out in positions around Archangel.

Ignacy Kwasniewski and Anthony Soczkoski, a pair of Polish-Americans from Detroit, were among the three members of the 339th Infantry killed on September 16. They were the first Americans to fall in combat. "They were buried beneath wooden crosses at Obozerskaya," wrote historian E. M. Halliday, "two boys from Detroit and one from Pittsburgh who had come a long way to die, for reasons that were by no means clear."

Four days later, another Detroit man, Corporal Morris Foley, evidently had a premonition of what was waiting for him. Shortly before going into action against a fortified village, he shared a can of bully beef with his good friend, Private Bill Henkleman.

"Hey, Morris, let's save enough for after while," Henklemen suggested.

"There might not be no 'after while,'" Foley responded.

During their subsequent charge through a rye paddy, Foley and several others were cut down by machine-gun fire. After the village was taken, Henklemen returned to find Foley shredded, "half his face and neck gone." He helped bring his friend's body back to camp. "I just wondered, so there was no 'after while' for him," Henklemen later wrote.

When the snow came, it covered all of northern Russia like a giant blanket of white cotton. In many places, the powdery drifts reached the roofs of the log dwellings that the Americans either built or shared with Russian peasant families.

Corporal Ivan Gibbs of A Company spent his winter near the far-flung advance base at Shenkursk on the Dvina River, some 200 miles south of Archangel. The winter was bitterly cold, he recalled, with temperatures frequently plummeting to 40 degrees below zero. To lose a mitten was to risk losing a hand, he said; to touch bare skin to metal was like gripping a red-hot poker. The rivers and sea froze over, locking the Americans in Russia until the spring thaw. The low temperatures often froze the oil in Gibbs' machine gun, rendering it useless.

Gibbs billeted with a Russian family in a log house. All of the peasants' homes were similar: warm, if unattractive, with a giant stove dominating the living quarters. Russians kept their livestock indoors, separated from the main room by a thin wall. The smell took some getting used to, as did the thousands of cockroaches and other vermin that swarmed over the ceiling and walls. All in all, the stoic Russians and their *Amerikanski* guests got along well enough (eight Americans took Russian wives home with them), though Gibbs concedes, "If somebody armed with a rifle decided to invite himself into your house, I guess you'd be rather hospitable yourself."

Because the fighting fronts were, on average, less than three degrees of latitude below the Arctic Circle, days in January and February consisted of less than four hours of sunlight, which was little more than a pale half-light. Gibbs frequently found himself alone on guard duty at some desolate forward post, the sun slung low over the horizon, with nothing but the shapeless snow and the eerie elongated shadows of fir trees everywhere he looked.

Accentuating the surreal air of the campaign was the use of double-runner sleighs called *drahskis*. The Russian sleighs, which proved invaluable in transporting men and supplies across the heavy snow and frozen rivers, were drawn by ponies as well as reindeer. It was oddly romantic to watch a team of reindeer pull a *drahski* across the winter landscape like something out of a Currier & Ives print; only

Corporal Joe Taube, circa 1919. (Author's Collection)

the inevitability of an armed soldier disturbed its idyllic aura as one glided by.

"Everybody who talks about Russia remembers the snow and the cold," said Taube. "And it's true. But my experiences are of a different nature. What I remember is the rain and the mud."

Corporal Taube of K Company took part in a futile attempt in late September to seize a section of the Trans-Siberian Railroad, a single-track railway that ran two thousand miles across Russia. Strung out far down that track was a large group of Czechoslovak soldiers who at one time had been allied with the czar's troops but were now trying to battle their way through the Bolshevik army. The British general in charge of the Allied troops envisioned a combined mission with the Czechs that would help renew the fight against the Germans. It was a fantastic plan, but its poor planning and sorry execution were emblematic of the entire campaign in the desolate land.

Rain prevailed for two or three days, Taube said. "At one point, we had to cross the Emsta River in icy water up to our chests. The ground was so mucky we couldn't pitch tents. We scattered tree limbs over the mud and slept on top of that." On September 27, the day before Taube's birthday, his unit was near the village of Kodish when a sentry accidentally discharged his rifle.

"I guess the Bolsheviks thought we were attacking them," said Taube. "It was very confusing. Anyway, I found cover. I was on the ground with my commanding officer, Lieutenant Chappel, on my left, and this young boy named Wojta on my right. There was machine gun fire, and I could see Lieutenant Chappel get hit. I could see he was dead.

"This young fellow, Wojta, kind of stood up, and he was preparing to say something. I was looking right at him . . ." At this point Taube broke into a sob as he recounted the tale. "I was looking at him when he got hit right there in the throat." He paused for a long moment before continuing. "I don't know what religion you are, but as he was going down he blessed himself with the sign of the cross. I tried to get to him, but I had to wait for the shooting to stop. When I finally reached him, he was dead.

"I never knew his name. Just Wojta. I don't know if they ever brought his body back to the States. When I got back home I wanted to find his parents, to tell them what a fine boy they had raised, tell them how proud they should be of him. . . . But I never did. I should have. It's haunted me all through these years . . ."

Morale eventually fell as low as the temperature. The sea froze over, locking the men in until spring thaw. There didn't seem to be any cohesive strategy. Men fought small and disparate actions on several fronts. "When I got home and people asked me what I was fighting for in Russia," said Gibbs, "I told them, 'I was fighting to save my neck.'"

Some French troops actually mutinied. Dissatisfaction in the American ranks never quite reached that point, though there were more and more cases of self-inflicted wounds, and one sergeant ended his despondency by putting a revolver to his head. Meanwhile, families, organizations, and newspapers clamored for the Americans' return home. Citizens at a mass meeting in Detroit demanded that politicians do something immediately to rescue their stranded sons and fathers. One telegram read:

With flags waving and flowers strewn in their path, surviving Polar Bears return to Detroit on July 4, 1919. (Walter P. Reuther Library)

"For heaven's sake get action on the 339th Infantry rescue in Russia, cut the red tape, smash the ice, and get the boys out."

In late February 1919, word came that the Americans would leave Russia once the ice in Archangel's harbor had melted. President Woodrow Wilson had decided that the Russians had the right to self-determination after all, at least as far as the United States was concerned. The departing Americans were to be replaced by a contingent of eight thousand British troops, whose government remained doggedly determined to crush Bolshevism.

Taube, Gibbs, Shand, and their comrades found themselves in a form of limbo. While now assured of going back home to the farms and shops they had left behind in Michigan, they had to wait several weeks before they could leave. They continued to fight and die. Gibbs was one of the last Americans wounded.

"It was in March, in the village of Vistafka," he recalled, seated inside his small Ferndale home. "The Bolsheviks had hit the village with artillery, and it was pretty much every man out for himself. A Russian

The parents of Private Andrew Skocelas, a young Detroiter killed in Russia, receive his recovered remains in a ceremony at White Chapel Cemetery in 1930. (Walter P. Reuther Library)

shot me in the back." Gibbs reached over to the end table and proudly produced the bullet that a surgeon dug out of him. "It missed my spine by a half-inch." In a scene straight out of *Dr. Zhivago,* Gibbs rode over a hundred miles nonstop in a *drahski* to get treatment in Archangel.

Others weren't as lucky. As the combat melted away with the snow in April, and all the Americans were either in or near Archangel awaiting departure, the casualty lists were compiled. At least 195 Americans had died; 85 of the total came from drownings or disease. Another 41 were missing in action or prisoners of war. There were 305 wounded, and many more had been hospitalized with influenza. Most poignantly, when the self-anointed "Polar Bears" finally left Russia in June 1919, they did so without more than 125 of their fallen comrades whose bodies were buried in ground that the Bolsheviks had recaptured.

The Polar Bears returned to a thunderous homecoming in Detroit on July 4, 1919. The soldiers were treated to a full day of dancing and picnicking on Belle Isle and were each awarded a check equal to fifteen dollars per month of service in Russia. Among those not present to enjoy the festivities was Stillman Jenks, Gibbs' neighbor back in Shelby. Private First Class Jenks was one of seventeen members of A Company reported missing in action on January 19, 1919, the day the Bolsheviks overwhelmed the American-held village of Nijni Gora in a major surprise assault.

"Mr. Jenks kept on coming over to the house and asking about his son," Gibbs said. "He'd come over and ask questions about him. It got to where I didn't want to see him. I was sorry, but I couldn't give him any encouragement." A decade later, a Veterans of Foreign Wars committee obtained permission to enter Russia and search for American graves. They returned with eighty-six of the missing dead. Jenks was not among them. He remains buried somewhere in the iron Russian tundra.

The Holcombe and Alvord Studio on Woodward placed the portrait of an unknown Detroit cyclist, circa 1885, inside the wheel of his "bone-shaker." (Burton Historical Collection)

TEN

Hot Wheels

Nothing captured the imagination of nineteenth-century Detroiters like the bicycle, an invention that was as much a social revolution as a free-wheeling means to see the world.

Henry Ford was looking for a new and better way of exploring the city and the countryside. He'd never liked horses, which were expensive and messy. Trains and trolleys didn't offer the kind of individual mobility that would allow someone to satisfy wanderlust at a moment's whim. Then one day in 1893, the man destined to become the world's most famous automaker brought home what countless enthusiasts were touting as the perfect mode of personal locomotion: a bicycle.

During the Gay '90s, Detroit was a city on wheels—but not the variety of wheels that one day earned it the distinction of being the motorcar capital of the world. "Cass Avenue was so crowded with wheels after dark that the street twinkled with the tiny headlights and the air was filled with the clanging of bicycle bells," Florence Marsh, one of Ford's contemporaries, later wrote of the two-wheel mania of the late nineteenth century. Pedestrians on Cass, Lafayette, and other popular cycling thoroughfares "waited in vain for a chance to cross the road."

Bicycling was the first national fad, setting free millions of men, women, and children and popularizing such terms as "face-plant" and "scorcher." It was as much a social movement as a pastime. Cyclists championed the fight for better roads, helped advance the cause of female emancipation, and prepped the world for the coming automobile.

Bicycles came of age in Europe in the middle 1800s. The first regular sightings of "bone-shakers" on Detroit's streets occurred in the years following the 1876 Centennial Exposition in Philadelphia. These were giraffe-high contraptions with the pedals attached directly to an oversize front wheel. The rider, who needed a short stepladder or horse block to mount, sat almost five feet off the ground. The comical contrast between the front and rear wheels caused the British to call them "penny-farthings," after their largest and smallest coins, though the style was more commonly referred to as the "ordinary." They were as expensive as they were dangerous, making bicycling the pastime of a select few. In the spring of 1879, the Detroit Bicycle Club was formed. In a city of nearly 120,000 people, it had no more than twenty members and no clubhouse.

The sport blossomed with the invention of the "safety" bicycle, which by 1886 resembled the bike we know today. Pedals powered the chain-driven rear wheel, which was now of equal diameter to the front. Tires, which had previously been solid rubber, were now pneumatic. These design changes made control and braking much easier (though many die-hards continued to ride ordinaries). That summer, a state meet sponsored by local bicyclists of Detroit was held in that city. Membership grew, and a clubhouse was rented. In 1890, two rival groups—the Detroit and Star bicycle clubs—reorganized as the Detroit chapter of the League of American Wheelmen, an influential national group lobbying hard for improved roads for its members to ride on.

Modern motorists who grumble about their car disappearing into a yawning pothole have no idea how abysmal road conditions were in their great-grandparents' day. Detroit's streets were a hodgepodge of cedar block and cobblestone construction veined with trolley tracks, making for a jolting ride that left a cyclist's jaw aching, spine screaming, and kidneys feeling as if they'd been whacked with a shovel. Even so, city streets were an improvement over unpaved country roads, which were either dirt or gravel and often a challenge to traverse in either case. Because mud, dust, ruts, and chuckholes weren't the obstacles to horses that they

Bicycle clubs gather on the steps of Detroit City Hall in the 1890s, when the cycling craze was at its peak. (Burton Historical Collection)

were to cyclists, property owners felt no urgency to do something about the sorry road conditions. Over time, cyclists were able to see a fraction of America's 2.1 million miles of rural roads paved and identified with signposts, though the greatest benefits of the "good roads" movement they initiated was not realized for another generation, when local road commissions and the federal government took over responsibility.

In 1890, Jefferson, Lafayette, Cass, and Second became the first Detroit streets to be paved with asphalt. That summer, a group of Detroit Wheelmen garbed in knickers and visor caps rode to Niagara Falls and back, a three-hundred-mile adventure that helped gain Detroit the national body's convention the following year. The city became a cycling hotbed, with the Wheelmen and other clubs sponsoring meets and excursions to communities both near and far. Each time after completing a "century run"—one hundred miles within eighteen hours—earned the "centurion" an impressive-looking badge from the Century Road Club of America. "Uphill and downhill on dirt roads, it was not a trip for the short-winded," one reporter said of one such run to Port Huron, "and even the long-winded were content to return by steamer, which they always did."

Beer gardens and rustic resorts catered to cyclists at the end of a hard day of pedaling. In 1889, the first bridge to Belle Isle was built, opening up the island playground to cyclists. Beller's Garden, near the bridge, did a land-rush business. "As early as 7 o'clock each clear summer evening, Jefferson Avenue was thronged with cyclists heading for the bridge, nearly half of them female," Don Lochbiler wrote years later in the *Detroit News*. "Many stopped at Beller's for refreshment, and two long racks were provided for wheels. Under the elms large tents were decorated with Chinese lanterns and a family of musicians . . . entertained on zithers and mandolins."

On holidays prize races were held on Belle Isle, with winners receiving everything from a concert piano to a shaving mug with the champ's initials etched in large gold letters. Bicycle racing was a professional sport decades before football and basketball, with fans avidly following the exploits of cyclists such as Eddie "Cannonball" Bald and Charles "Mile-A-Minute" Murphy through sporting journals and tobacco cards. Local favorites included Tom Cooper of the Detroit Wheelmen and his good friend and fellow "fast speed freak," Barney Oldfield, who hailed from Ohio. Speed demons, both on and off the track, were known as "scorchers."

What most Detroiters liked best about the new pastime of cycling was the opportunity it gave them to enjoy a leisurely street-level view of their city. "Washington Avenue is one of the widest and prettiest avenues that Detroit can boast of," cycling enthusiast P. N. Jacobsen wrote in an 1891 issue of *Outing*, a premier national sporting magazine. "On one side of the walk is a wide boulevard and on the other well-kept private lawns. A triple row of trees lines the avenue on each side. Ancient maples along the edge of the boulevard almost join their wide-spreading branches over the centre of the street and the walk is completely shaded in summer. The many pretty flowery lawns, together with the absence of all fences, add greatly to the general effect."

This country lane in western Michigan was typical of most roads of the late 19th century. The rutted lanes and loose rocks played havoc with a cyclist's progress. (Burton Historical Collection)

By 1896, the bicycling craze was approaching its peak. That year the Wheelmen—characterized by one observer as "the new bon tons of Detroit's smart set"—built a clubhouse for its four hundred and fifty members at 53–55 East Adams (a site now occupied by Comerica Park). The ornate three-story stone-and-brick structure, which cost an estimated forty thousand dollars to build, featured an auditorium, library, kitchen, dining room, baths, billiard and whist tables, and a bowling alley. A long wrought-iron bike rack ran along the front of the building. The club became the scene of dances, banquets, and other social events.

The pastime's exclusivity faded as more and more people discovered its joys. Prices fell to a point at which most members of the middle class could afford a new or used bike. The cost of the cheapest model in the Sears catalog dropped from $55.95 in 1894 to $17.85 four years later. Although this still was a significant expenditure at a time when the average workingman made about fifty dollars a month, stores offered credit payments of one or two dollars a week. According to Jacobsen, local thoroughfares

The introduction of the safety bicycle, with its pneumatic tires and brakes, helped emancipate a generation of women, including the unidentified Detroit ladies pictured here. (Burton Historical Collection)

became "daily thronged with wheelmen," the most reckless of whom weaved in and out of traffic as teamsters swore at them and streetcar conductors shook their fists. Pedestrians and dogs were at risk. Minor accidents—a skinned knee, a bent wheel—were common. Looking to curb the number of nighttime mishaps, a city ordinance required riders to use a small kerosene-lit brass lamp when cycling after dark.

The Detroit Police Department's "scorcher squad" of bicycle cops had its handlebars full controlling sidewalk cyclists and chasing scofflaws down city streets, sometimes in freewheeling Keystone-Kop fashion. As far as is known, their tactics didn't include using a portable slingshot-like device to fire small lead balls at a scorcher's wheels in hopes of breaking the spokes and disabling his machine—a practice reportedly used by Chicago's finest. But more than one madly pedaling offender was "brought to grief" by a tenacious "wheelcop" whose speed and lung capacity surprised the object of his pursuit. "It was one of those cyclized policemen," noted a local historian, "who gained nameless immortality a few years later when he wrote the first violation ticket for a speeder in one of those new-fangled automobiles."

Obnoxious cyclists didn't confine their antics to city streets. Taunting farmers and kicking up dust were considered good fun by some scorching through the countryside, and even the most conscientious riders found it hard to avoid spooking cows and terrifying poultry as they rode past in search of a bucolic picnic spot. Country folks responded by pelting cyclists with eggs, stones, and horse droppings, setting dogs loose on them, and planting rocks in their path. Farmers around Milford began stringing wire across the roads abutting their property. Enterprising cyclists fought back by welding vertical rods to the forks of their bikes to avoid possible decapitation.

For ladies, the bicycle was a liberating invention. Victorian women were second-class citizens, their lives as restrictive as the corsets that encased them. The tenor of the times can be gleaned from an 1897 item in the *Detroit Free Press* describing a certain Mr. Wilkins, who was sitting by the cracker barrel one day when a man rushed into the general store with terrible news. "Your wife's just met with an accident, Wilkins," he announced. "She ran over a dog while riding her bicycle, and they've carried her to the hospital."

Wilkins was visibly distraught. His "face turned pale" and his voice trembled. "Did you notice," he asked, "whether it was a liver colored dog with two white spots on his fore shoulder?"

Women cyclists got the last laugh, shucking their corsets and long trailing dresses for the more comfortable ensemble of shirtwaist blouse, leggings, low shoes, and—most shocking—a divided skirt, bloomers, or knickers. Once homebound and dependent on men for getting around, they were now free to explore the same far-off vistas on their own. They ignored warnings that riding would harm their reproductive organs or cause them to follow pathways to immorality and damnation. Girls just wanted to have fun. In the process, they struck an early and significant blow for the feminist movement. Susan B. Anthony, the country's leading suffragist, declared in 1896: "The bicycle has done more for the emancipation of women than anything else in the world." Historians estimate one of every three cyclists was a woman.

Like all fads, the cycling craze was bound to end. By 1900, the bicycle—once a novelty item and a symbol of conspicuous consumption—was so ubiquitous that a used model could be bought for five dollars. With the dawning of a new century, two-wheeling gave way to a new sensation: "automobubbling" in one's motorized buggy. Soon automobiles, be they electric- or gasoline-powered, were too fast for the swiftest bicycle cop. In 1908, Detroit bought the country's first Harley-Davidson police motorcycle in order to keep up with a new generation of scorchers.

Several of Detroit's biking aficionados made their mark in the automobile age. The Dodge brothers, Horace and John, shifted from building bikes to cars while Edward Hines, a charter member of the Wheelmen, became one of the great innovators in highway development, numbering the traffic dividing line and the world's first stretch of concrete highway among his accomplishments. Henry Ford turned to a pair of bicycling daredevils, Tom Cooper and Barney Oldfield, to jump-start his faltering automaking career.

In 1902, Cooper financed Ford's construction of a ten-foot-long behemoth called the "999." It was too powerful a machine for even a speed maniac like Cooper to handle, so Oldfield—who had never driven the car before—was asked to take the wheel in a well-publicized challenge race in Grosse Pointe. Before his world's record run, one that made household names out of him and Ford, the former champion cyclist displayed the bravado of a true scorcher. "Well, this chariot may kill me," he told reporters, "but they'll say afterward I was going like hell when she took me over the bank."

ELEVEN

Oh! What A Pal Was Sophie

It was an adventuresome journey from rogue to reformer for Sophie Lyons, legendary "Queen of the Underworld" and Detroit philanthropist.

Sophie Lyons spent the last several years of her life preaching that crime doesn't pay, but those sifting through the contents of her safe-deposit box shortly after she passed away in the spring of 1924 were hard-pressed to believe it. Trustees of her estate found a royal stash of brooches, rings, watches, earrings, stickpins, and assorted pieces of jewelry—all encrusted with rubies, pearls, emeralds, and other gems fit for a monarch's crown. Included in the cache were a giant starburst brooch with an eight-carat stone in the center, a twelve-carat diamond ring, and a blazing diamond cross. It was said that the reformed "Queen of the Underworld" had amassed as much as a million dollars through her activities, both legal and otherwise.

Hers had been a life of big scores and narrow escapes, of fleecing the gullible and outwitting authorities on two continents. She had charmed wealthy men out of their pants and their fortunes, smuggled pearls across the Atlantic, and broken out of Sing Sing. A local reporter who interviewed Sophie in her later years felt he "had been listening to the highly colored yarns . . . detective story writers had been telling for ages." As striking as her criminal exploits was her moral transformation. At the Detroit House of Correction, where she spoke to prisoners of the redemptive powers of the Bible, appreciative inmates tweaked the lyrics

Sophie Lyons, circa 1885. (Author's Collection)

to a popular song of the day titled "Oh! What A Gal Was Mary," singing, "Oh! what a gal is Sophie / Oh! what a pal is she."

Sophie's streetwise ministry never gained the scope she wished. But before joining that Great Rogues Gallery in the Sky, she was a dependable benefactor to numerous criminally inclined men and women who, like herself, had strayed down the wrong path and were now desperate to chart a new course.

During the 1800s, America's growing urban centers were a breeding ground for criminals of all types, including an underclass of street urchins whose schooling came at the knee of experienced adult malefactors. In the case of Sophie Levy, born December 24, 1848, in New York City, the tutor was her own stepmother, an accomplished thief. Little Sophie was only six years old when she stole her first pocketbook. "I was very happy because I was petted and rewarded," she recalled. "My wretched stepmother patted my curly head, gave me a bag of candy, and said I was a 'good girl.'"

However, when the engaging youngster failed to come home with the requisite number of pocketbooks, she was beaten. Once her arm was burned as punishment. Sophie never attended a real school, and she didn't learn to read or write until she was twenty-five years old. By then she had graduated from petty crime to more sophisticated ruses.

During the 1860s and '70s she was part of an elite inner ring of thieves and confidence women headed by Fredrika "Marm" Mandelbaum, a fat Prussian-born society matron who acted as a patron and fence to many underworld characters. Among the guests at Mandelbaum's lavish dinner parties were Margaret Brown, an elderly Irish immigrant and incorrigible pickpocket known as "Old Mother Hubbard;" the diminutive Christene Mayer, dubbed "Kid Glove Rosey" for her shoplifting skills; and "Black Lena" Kleinschmidt, who was sent to prison several times for larceny.

Sophie did not have the hard looks of these notorious women. She was "beautiful when young, and the traces never quite rubbed off," recalled a contemporary. "Her features were regular and chiseled into a well-shaped oval face. Her eyes were an indeterminate gray-blue, and her almost blond hair was piled on top of her head. She was a consummate actress, could be demure when it best fitted the circumstances, or she could assume the grand and lofty manner. She could weep or smile, as she chose." In addition to her pleasant features and skilled deportment, she wore fine dresses elaborately trimmed in laces and rich embroideries.

Sophie's beauty, charm, and natural intelligence made her irresistible to men. She was married four times, first and most famously to Ned Lyons. As one of the country's most notorious bank burglars, Lyons was a good provider; however, Sophie's "mania for stealing was so strong that when in Ned's company she plied her vocation unknown to him, and would surprise him with watches, etc., which she had stolen," New York police inspector Thomas Byrnes wrote in *Professional Criminals of America,* the classic compendium of nineteenth-century scofflaws published in 1886. After Sophie gave birth to their first child, Ned provided her with a farm on Long Island, "thinking her maternal instinct would restrain her monomania; yet within six months she returned to New York, placed her child out to nurse, and began her operations again, finally being detected and sentenced to Blackwell's Island."

Ned and Sophie spent the next several years alternating between pulling off bank capers and pulling on prison stripes. Both were sentenced to Sing Sing, with Ned busting out first and then returning to arrange Sophie's escape. One night just before Christmas 1872, he and an accomplice drove a sleigh through a blizzard up to the prison entrance. They rang the bell and announced that they were delivering fruit for a sick prisoner. As a guard reached for the basket, Sophie ran through the open gate and jumped into the sleigh, which then disappeared into the blinding snow.

After a productive spell in Paris, Sophie was re-arrested for picking pockets in 1876 and was returned to Sing Sing, where she served out her term. Shortly after her release, she charmed a wealthy merchant out of his clothes inside a Boston hotel room—and then held on to them as she demanded a check for ten thousand dollars. Sophie and her accomplice were caught attempting to cash it, but the embarrassed victim refused to testify, allowing the blackmailers to go free. "His money was saved," Byrnes wrote, "but his character was ruined, and the result was the breaking up of a happy home."

Around this time Sophie shifted her base of operations to Detroit. During the nineteenth century, the city drew more than its fair share of grifters, shoplifters, card cheats, bank sneaks, forgers, burglars, blackmailers, safecrackers, window smashers, hotel thieves, pickpockets, pimps, prostitutes, mystics, medicine men, and murderers. Chased out of one town after another, shadowy career criminals bearing such colorful aliases as Big Rice, Hungry Joe, Bottle Sam, Gentleman George, and The Red Headed Jew eventually tried their luck in Detroit— usually more than once. A big part of the city's attraction was its close proximity to Canada, which at the time did not have an extradition treaty with the United States. "In that era, Detroit was a haven for the polite crooks of the nation," newspapermen Norman Beasley and George W. Stark wrote in *Made in Detroit*. "They enjoyed immunity as long as they behaved themselves. Thus, if the mysterious underworld grapevine brought word of an impending arrest, the flight to Canada was easily arranged. All that was needed was darkness, a rowboat, and a pair of oars."

Sophie's local activities included trying to blackmail a prominent Grand Rapids citizen who had sampled her charms. She would appear in front of his home daily in hopes of embarrassing him into writing her a large check to get out of his life. This fellow was a rare bird. Not only did he refuse to be intimidated, but he dowsed Sophie with a garden hose and pummeled "an unfortunate theatrical agent who espoused her cause," Byrnes wrote.

On February 6, 1883, Sophie was sentenced to three years in the Detroit House of Correction for larceny. The facility, opened in 1861, sprawled over three acres at Russell and Alfred streets, near Eastern Market. It was unusual in many respects: progressive, self-supporting, and, though a municipal jail, housing many prisoners from other jurisdictions, including federal prisoners from the western territories. Sophie's term overlapped with that of the celebrated outlaw Belle Starr. If the two lady bandits rubbed shoulders, it probably was in the woodworking shop, where the few hundred prisoners labored ten hours a day building furniture. Inmates cranked out 310,790 chairs, 5,715 beds, and 1,353 cradles in Sophie's first year alone.

The Detroit House of Corrections in the 1880s, when Sophie Lyons was an inmate. (Burton Historical Collection)

The administration deemed a busy mind as important as busy hands. Thus prisoners with sentences longer than ninety days were required to attend evening classes. "Candles are provided," a contemporary noted, "that they may pursue their studies in their cells." The environment was more humane and supportive than any Sophie had ever known. She was released in 1886. She later called the House of Correction the nicest institution she had been incarcerated at.

By the time she was released, Sophie was in her forties. She had spent a quarter of her life behind bars. Crime was a family affair, with her stepmother, husband, and two oldest sons in and out of prison. She had placed two daughters in Ontario convents prior to entering jail. Their cold receptions when she visited them stung her. She continued her criminal ways. She knew no other lifestyle. Byrnes reported that she had acquired a taste for opium.

Her notoriety grew on both sides of the Atlantic. She was involved in any number of scams, from "goldbricking" (passing off gold-plated lead bars as solid gold ingots) to cheating smitten young bloods at cards. She was credited with a variety of firsts. As a young woman she was the first to employ the kleptomaniac defense, getting a charge dismissed by tearfully explaining to a New York court that her compulsive stealing was something she had no control over because of her upbringing. It was also said that she invented the "sliding drawer panel" trick, whereby a victim lured to her room would place jewelry into a dresser drawer for safekeeping only to discover long after Sophie had excused herself that she had previously cut a hole in the wall of the adjoining room, allowing her to slide open the panel, reach into the drawer, remove the goods, and be on her way before her victim was the wiser. She may have not been the first to hollow out her heels or use false trunk bottoms to smuggle jewelry from Amsterdam to New York, but she was one of the best.

By midlife Sophie had given up on Ned Lyons, a medical marvel who had been shot several times and had his left ear chewed off in battles with the law and fellow miscreants. She went through two more husbands before marrying Billy Burke, a noted burglar.

Modern criminologists would probably classify Sophie as an adrenaline junkie, an adventuress who craved crime as much for the challenging rush as for the actual monetary rewards. But as she moved through her middle years, the rush slowed to a crawl. There appears to have been no grand epiphany, just a gradual realization that a life of sensation in New York, London, and Paris had brought her little true happiness. Her taste for criminal escapades diminished as she focused her energies on real estate, taking advantage of Detroit's rapid growth to make a tidy profit. The core of her investments was several rental properties on the city's developing west side. Meanwhile, she worked on a book that she hoped would disprove the old adage "Once a thief, always a thief." On its pages she offered her own reformed life as proof.

In 1913, a New York publisher came out with *Why Crime Does Not Pay,* a cautionary tale that described the life of "the cleverest crook in the world" as one ultimately devoid of purpose or true reward. The author told reporters gathered inside her Detroit home that she was now dedicating her life to helping other criminals, especially first offenders. "You know how hard it is for a man or woman to secure permanent work after leaving a prison?" she said, citing her own experiences of being shunned upon her discharge from the House of Correction years earlier. "I am going to help some of these. They will find a friend in Sophie Lyons."

And they did. "There was never a friendless girl who came to my grandmother and did not receive a welcome, there was never a tenant who was out of work who was asked for his rent," claimed Sophie's granddaughter, Esther Bower. Sophie spent thousands of dollars on shoes, clothes, and groceries for desperate families and found them lodging as well. She provided holiday meals to jails and helped struggling ex-prisoners get back on their feet. Sophie admitted that her biggest project was Burke, a classic recidivist who "couldn't keep his fingers off a dishonest dollar." The latest stop for her "weak and easily tempted" husband was a prison in Stockholm, Sweden. Upon his release he moved in with Sophie, who kept a close eye on him.

In this new phase of her life, Sophie moved among the same kind of shady characters she had as a crook. A lifetime of flimflam enabled her to separate the charlatans from those who sincerely desired her help in going straight, but her vulnerability was a worry. She made little effort to hide her wealth, freely wearing her jewelry even as she lived in an unimposing weather-beaten frame cottage on 23rd Street, between Savoy and Lafayette. Rumor had it that cash and gems were stashed inside the walls and attic. Burke's presence was somewhat of a deterrent, but after he died in 1919 Sophie was the only occupant, although later she hired a live-in housekeeper.

Perhaps inevitably, the elderly evangelist became a crime victim herself, being robbed at least twice. Once bandits took ten thousand dollars in cash from her as she shopped in a neighborhood grocery store. The second time, she returned from a July 4th outing to find that thieves had broken into her home. "Look," she told reporters, "the fools loaded themselves up with a lot of useless bric-a-brac, but they overlooked that gold-headed umbrella in the corner there. That is very valuable. It's solid gold, and it was given to me by my late husband, Mr. Burke." Published comments like these seemed an open invitation to robbery.

Despite the recognition Sophie received for her good works, some questioned her sincerity. Cynics said she found the righteous path only after she "got hers." While she may have made honest profits in real estate, they said, the seed money had come through larcenous means. And for all her contributions to children's charities, the truth was that Sophie had been a horrible mother. Her two oldest sons were career felons; her firstborn, George, died in prison. She admitted to having had nine children overall; it appears that most, if not all, had at one time or another been placed in orphanages or convents. They were scattered across at least four countries. One daughter, Lotta, had grown up to be an opera singer in Paris. Another lived in London. Her favorite child was Carleton, a Spanish-American War veteran who, ironically, worked for the Internal Revenue Service in Seattle before dying in 1922.

The only one of Sophie's offspring to live in Detroit was Florence, who as a young girl entrusted to the care of nuns had changed her name in shame over her mother's notoriety. Florence had since made a new life of her own but then had fallen on hard times after her husband died. She was reduced to begging on downtown corners. Sophie once passed her impoverished daughter on the street, ignoring her completely. Still, it was a sign of Sophie's mercurial morality that the estranged Florence wound up a major beneficiary of her will. Guilt is a powerful engine. Years earlier, Sophie had sent a check to a down-on-her-luck actress to reimburse the woman for the jewelry that Sophie had stolen from her when times were flush.

Sophie's many imperfections gave her what most other reformers lacked—street credentials—while her energy and unbreakable spirit endeared her to the petty criminals to whom she spoke. She would visit them, an old woman with a Bible in her gnarled, knotty hands and a black shawl thrown over her hunched shoulders, "preaching the doctrine of goodness." Sophie became involved with a welfare organization called the Pathfinders. Inspired by their work in prison reform, she announced plans for a home in which children too young for school could stay while their parents were in jail. To that end she intended to donate land worth thirty-five thousand dollars.

All of Sophie's plans and good intentions came to an immediate halt on May 7, 1924. On that day, the seventy-five-year-old philanthropist was found comatose on the floor inside her home. She was taken to Grace Hospital, where she died without regaining consciousness.

The circumstances surrounding her passing were cloudy. The autopsy revealed death due to a cerebral hemorrhage, but did her demise have anything to do with the trio of underworld types who had reportedly been alone with her earlier that day? According to the *Free Press,* "hold-up men she had befriended and tried to reform, but whose names she always kept secret, had threatened to 'get' her after accusing her of 'squealing' to the police." Someone had heard the shout, "Quit, don't do it." However, other papers reported that the visitors had been discussing legitimate real estate business with Sophie and that one of them had summoned help when she suddenly collapsed.

While allegations of foul play were soon dismissed, it's possible that certain closemouthed types in her circle of criminal acquaintances knew more than they ever let on. A few weeks earlier, three men had accosted Sophie inside a restaurant, roughing her up and throwing her under a table as they robbed the place. Some suggested the robbery was a smoke screen, that the brazen treatment of the old woman had been a "message." One detail not in dispute was that a copy of *Why Crime Does Not Pay* was on the table next to her hospital bed when she died.

Sophie Lyons was cremated, and her ashes were placed in her son Carleton's grave at Woodmere Cemetery. After several years of wrangling, her estate was finally settled in early 1929. Among her bequests was a thousand dollars for the purchase of a piano for the new House of Correction being built in Plymouth. Perhaps the repentant Queen of the Underworld imagined future generations of the misguided gathered around it, singing the praises of their big-hearted benefactor with the reworked chorus of a favorite parlor song:

Though she is gone
Love lingers on
For Sophie
Old pal of mine.

THE LADY WAS A SCAMP

One of the more fascinating itinerant rogues to pass through Detroit a century ago was the mysterious Madame Ann O'Delia Diss Debar, whose exploits and aliases filled newspapers and police blotters in several countries. According to an Atlanta daily, "nobody knew from whence she came and nobody knew whither she departed when she did depart. But while she was here the people saw and heard a great deal of her." When Diss Debar wasn't claiming to be Princess Editha, the illegitimate child of King Ludwig of Bavaria, she was insisting she was the reincarnation of the famous spiritualist Madame Blavatsky. However, records indicate that her real name may have been Edith Salomen or Della Ann Sullivan and that she probably was born in Kentucky in 1848 or 1851. Whatever her true identity, she was "one of the most extraordinary fake mediums and mystery swindlers the world has ever known," said master magician Harry Houdini, who was also a leading paranormal skeptic.

A striking brunette in her prime, Madame Diss Debar was married at least four times. She was incarcerated on several occasions and spent time in an insane asylum. Like many female criminals, her unsavory lifestyle caused her children to be taken away by authorities. Her most notorious exploit came to light in 1901. As Swami Laura Horos, she helped her husband at that time (trumpeted as "Christ returned to earth, and the only perfect man in the world") procure young women to service wealthy members of the Purity League they had established in London. Following a sensational trial involving charges of fraud, rape, and buggery, Diss Debar spent the next five years in prison.

After brief stays selling occult cures in South Africa and Florida, Diss Debar arrived in Detroit in early 1907. Identifying herself as Mrs. Elinor L. Mason, she took over the local chapter of the House of Israel, a cult alternately known as the Flying Rollers. Assisted by her "son" and "secretary"—a thirty-five-year-old hypnotist named David Mackay—"Mother Elinor" worked psychic swindles on both sides of the Detroit River. When the "Queen of the Flying Rollers" and her accomplice left

Madame Ann O'Delia Diss Debar, who in 1907 worked psychic swindles on both sides of the Detroit River before hastily leaving town. (Library of Congress)

town that summer, it was with customary haste and somebody else's jewelry.

The fugitive spiritualist resurfaced as A-Diva Veed-Ya at the School of the Mahatmas in New York, dispensing flapdoodle from her throne while dressed in a flowing white robe. Quickly exposed by the press, she stuck around just long enough to tell her side of the story. She denied fleeing Detroit. Referring to the angry Flying Rollers she had left in her wake, she said: "They have it in for me because I made them take baths when I went there to take charge. Some of them hadn't taken baths in six months. I called in the authorities. I forced them to do it. That's why they [slander] me when my back is turned."

Madame Diss Debar was soon off to another town. Her last known stop was Cincinnati in 1909, after which the "spook priestess" vanished—this time apparently for good.

TWELVE

Albert Kahn's Blueprint for Detroit

A color-blind Jewish immigrant with no formal education, "A. K." conquered many obstacles en route to becoming one of the great architects of the twentieth century.

Many decades after Albert Kahn last pulled a jackknife out of his vest pocket to whittle the business end of a drafting pencil, his standing as one of history's great architects remains as solid and enduring as any of the more than two thousand buildings he and his firm created during his lifetime.

Kahn, who is respected today as one of the fathers of modernism, is principally remembered as the man who built Henry Ford's factories; however, this sawed-off, bespectacled steam engine of a man also was responsible for some of metro Detroit's most distinctive non-industrial landmarks. They include such architectural gems as the Fisher Building, Police Headquarters, the Belle Isle Casino, General Motors Headquarters, the Detroit Athletic Club, and the Edsel and Eleanor Ford House. Not that the modest old master ever got carried away with the "artsy" aspects of his classical masterpieces. "Architecture," he liked to say, "is ninety percent business and ten percent art."

Kahn's emergence was complicated by his lack of a formal education as well as his Jewish heritage in a virulently anti-Semitic world. "The prejudice was particularly strong in the auto industry," said his nephew, Bill Kahn. "It was very rare for a Jew to advance far."

Albert Kahn at work. (Albert Kahn Associates)

As imposing as these obstacles were, it was a simple inability to distinguish between certain colors that threatened to put the brakes on his career before it had a chance to take off. In about 1885, the teenaged Kahn was tracing and drafting at the office of Mason & Rice, one of Detroit's leading architectural firms. An associate suspected that the apprentice was color-blind—a fatal handicap for a fledgling architect—and marched him into the office of George Mason. The youngster, facing dismissal, was asked to identify the colors in an area rug.

Some colors came easier than others. Finally, Kahn had to guess between green and brown. With his future hanging in the balance, he mentally flipped a coin and chose green. "If I had guessed brown," he later reflected, "I might be a butcher today."

Albert Kahn was born in Germany on March 21, 1869. His father, an itinerant rabbi, soon left Westphalia for America. It wasn't until 1880 that eleven-year-old Albert, the oldest of six children, shepherded the brood across the Atlantic to join their father in Baltimore. Four years later, the entire family moved to Detroit.

As a youngster, Albert demonstrated promise in art and music. "But his mother decided that being a concert pianist wouldn't do," recalled Kahn's daughter, Rosalie Kahn Butzel of Seattle. "There were not enough opportunities in the field. But he loved listening to classical music until the day he died."

Albert was fired from an early job as an office boy with the firm of John Scott & Co. Legend has it that the city's premier sculptor, Julius Melchers, found the boy crying on a downtown street corner and took him under his wing. It was Melchers who recommended him to Mason & Rice.

Narrowly surviving the rug color test at Mason & Rice, Kahn impressed his bosses with his dedication. "Every spare moment of the day and evening . . . Albert would spend reading our collection of architectural books," Mason remembered. "Hours meant nothing to him when he was absorbed in his work." When he was eighteen, the promising apprentice was given his first commission: designing the porch of the Grand Hotel, the luxury resort hotel then being built on Mackinac Island. At some 660 feet, the porch reportedly is the longest in the world.

Kahn designed the Belle Isle Aquarium with a curved, green-tiled ceiling to suggest the sensation of being underwater. The aquarium opened in 1904 and closed in 2005. (Albert Kahn Associates)

In 1890 Kahn won a traveling scholarship to Europe from *American Architect* magazine. The prize required him to regularly submit drawings and accompanying articles for publication. His traveling companion was artist Henry Bacon, the future designer of the Lincoln Memorial. Kahn, already a fast and accurate sketch artist, learned a great deal about drawing from Bacon but nothing about writing. "Never mind the articles," his editor finally wired. "Send more sketches."

In 1896, the same year the first experimental automobiles appeared on Detroit's streets, Kahn married Ernestine Krolik. The petite University of Michigan graduate was "the power behind the throne," said Rosalie. "She was quiet, sophisticated, and graceful, and ran a very good household. She was a great gardener and talented interior designer. She advised my father on color and design and fabric. They complemented each other wonderfully."

Albert had started his own firm with two partners the year before, so the newlyweds lived with Ernestine's parents until the business became established. One of the company's first commissions was Children's Hospital, followed by such varied jobs as a library for *Detroit News* founder James Scripps and a pneumatic hammer factory. By 1901, the firm of Nettleton, Kahn & Trowbridge had become Albert Kahn, Architect, Ernest Wilby, Associate, and Kahn's brothers Julius and Louis.

"Uncle Albert was one of the first architects to recognize that an industrial building was worthy of a competent architect's work," said Bill Kahn, Louis's son and a retired engineer. "Prior to him, industrial assignments commonly were given to apprentices."

Kahn and the automobile industry came of age together. In 1903 he designed a series of buildings for the Packard Motor Car Company. His tenth building for Packard, built in 1905, broke new ground. Previous factories had been dark, cramped mills with creaking, oil-soaked wooden floors. Kahn replaced the traditional fire hazard with a building made of reinforced concrete that featured wider floor space and acres of extra glass to allow for more natural light and ventilation. Building No. 10 was so advanced, it became a tourist attraction.

Kahn's reputation soared after he collaborated with Henry Ford to design his most famous building, the Model T plant in Highland Park. Ford envisioned a moving assembly line in order for workers to build his cars from start to finish—with the entire production process housed under one roof. "I thought he was crazy," Kahn later admitted. But the resulting factory, opened in 1909, made possible the mass production of the American dream. In 1917 alone, more than 700,000 Tin Lizzies were assembled at the heavily glassed "Crystal Palace."

All told, Kahn was responsible for more than a thousand Ford buildings, including the sprawling Rouge complex. Kahn's clients also included the Dodge brothers, Walter Chrysler, and the Soviet government. (He designed 521 buildings between 1929 and 1931 for the Soviet government alone.) In addition, he designed many of the buildings on the University of Michigan campus in Ann Arbor.

Kahn was an Old World autocrat, always working in vest, shirt, and tie and tolerating no challenges to his authority. Sheldon Marsten spent the bulk of his professional life with Albert Kahn Associates, retiring in 1967 as the executive vice president. "I joined the firm in 1923 as an assistant superintendent of construction for the Michigan Stamping Plant on Mack Avenue," said Marsten, recalling "A. K." in his prime. "Mr. Kahn liked to put the responsibility on your shoulders. If you did your job, you were all right with him. If you didn't, you probably wouldn't last long." There never was any doubt as to who was in charge, said Marsten, who once dared to correct his boss on a certain minor manner and got "a good bawling out" for his trouble.

Kahn's energy was legendary. Twelve- and fourteen-hour days were the norm. He was known to grab a catnap by stretching out his five-foot-four-inch frame on a drafting table. Re-energized, he might decide to drive to a job site—a dangerous proposition.

"He had a hard time distinguishing between red and green," said Bill Kahn, "which made it a little difficult driving in the city. He knew that red was on top and green was on the bottom. But if the lights were changing, he was in trouble." Added to this, "He was always in a hurry. Consequently, a lot of people in the office wouldn't get in the car if he was going to drive."

Albert and Ernestine had four children: Edgar, Lydia, Ruth, and Rosalie. Edgar, who shunned the family business, captained the University of Michigan's hockey team and became a noted surgeon, accomplishments in which his father took great pride. The family lived in a mansion that Kahn had designed on Mack Avenue; today it's home to the Detroit Urban League.

"He was a strong disciplinarian when it was needed," said Rosalie, who recalled once accidentally melting some of her father's beloved opera records on a radiator. "He didn't spank us. His voice was all it took. It wasn't raised, just very firm."

The exactitude that marked his work sometimes could be exasperating in a domestic situation. When one of his children used the phrase "that guy," Kahn issued an immediate reprimand. "'That guy?' We don't speak that way."

On those rare occasions when Kahn allowed himself to relax, he did so inside an opera house or museum on either side of the Atlantic. He also was an avid baseball fan, enjoyed playing bridge with members of

Right: The Kahn-designed Belle Isle Casino opened in 1908. (Burton Historical Collection)

Below: The Highland Park assembly plant was one of more than a thousand buildings Kahn designed for Ford. (Author's Collection)

The auditorium of the Kahn-designed Temple Beth El at 8801 Woodward Avenue, built in 1921–1922. (Albert Kahn Associates)

his extended family, and escaped the heat of the city at a five-bedroom summer house he built on Walnut Lake.

"For the most part, though," said Bill Kahn, "his life was his work."

Kahn always considered himself a Jew—an *American* Jew. He belonged to Temple Beth-El (which he designed) and an exclusive Jewish club, the Phoenix Social Club. He gave generously to Jewish causes. But he was criticized in some quarters for not taking a more visible role in local Jewish affairs. Like most of Detroit's old-line German Jews, a group that tended to be more cultured and better educated than the Eastern European Jews who began arriving in the early 1900s, he favored assimilation over such ritualistic practices as bar mitzvahs and Passover seders.

For all of his status and desire to be Americanized, Kahn encountered anti-Semitism on a regular basis. The exclusive Detroit Athletic Club, which opened in 1915 on Madison Avenue, was one of his creations. The club, normally off-limits to Jews, offered Kahn a token membership, but he quietly rejected it.

Henry Ford's infamous anti-Semitic tirades in the *Dearborn Independent* put "a major strain on the relationship" between tycoon and architect, Bill Kahn said. Displaying the same kind of hardheaded practicality that characterized his buildings, A. K. swallowed his bile and continued to build for Ford. "Let's be reasonable," his nephew said in Kahn's defense. "You wouldn't turn down a commission for an entire firm because your nose was out of joint." Kahn's compromise was not to meet personally with Ford after the 1920s.

Even so, Kahn's last great project was for Ford. With American industry re-tooling to fight World War II, he built the massive Willow Run plant to produce the bombers that ultimately turned the land of his birth into a nation of rubble.

Kahn's phenomenal pace finally caught up with him when he suffered a heart attack that confined him to bed for the last month of his life. He was a terrible patient, continuing to conduct business in his pajamas. On the morning of December 8, 1942, he phoned Rosalie to wish her a happy thirtieth birthday. An hour later he was dead.

"He really died with his boots on," is Rosalie's assessment of her father's remarkably productive seventy-three years. "He kept going all the time, all the way."

Albert Kahn Associates continues to be one of the country's largest and most respected architectural firms, though none of today's hundreds of employees has any personal memories of the company's namesake. Even Bill Kahn admitted that, after all this time, thoughts of Uncle Albert pop up only infrequently. "Principally it's when I go down to the Fisher Theatre, or I'm in Ann Arbor and I see buildings that I know were his personal favorites—the Clements Library or Hill Auditorium."

And exactly what is it that goes through his mind on these occasions? Kahn deliberated a few moments before answering. "I'm thinking: 'I am very damn proud.'"

Daniel West: "He was a man who played many roles," said his attorney. (Walter P. Reuther Library)

THIRTEEN
The Mysterious Daniel West

One of the greatest con men ever to hold public office in Michigan capped his legislative career with a disappearing act that continues to baffle.

Everybody who knew Daniel West agreed that he was some guy. Exactly which guy, however, didn't become clear until December 5, 1964. That snowy Saturday, news broke that the distinguished looking fifty-five-year-old Detroit Democrat, a man with one of the most impressive résumés in the State House of Representatives, had assumed the identity and professional credentials of a dead New York lawyer by the same name.

It was an astonishing exposé, even by the standards of big-city politics, but there was more. The laid-back legislator with the pencil mustache, who had just been elected to a second term in Lansing, was charged with hiding an extensive criminal past, engaging in voter fraud, and bilking the government out of a cool $250,000 by filing bogus income tax returns. As the national media spotlight shone on Detroit, friends and fellow House members said they would suspend judgment until Representative West gave his version of events.

They're still waiting. West has been unavailable for comment for more than forty years, ever since he disappeared on the eve of his federal trial for tax fraud.

"He was a man who played many roles," said his friend and defense attorney, Peter P. Cobbs of Detroit. "He was always involved in something fascinating." This is a charitable way of saying that his client, arguably the greatest scam artist ever to hold public office in Michigan, spent his entire adult life keeping one step ahead of the bloodhounds.

Daniel Harvey Laverne Wilson West—a name he used in various combinations, depending on where he was incarcerated—was born in 1909. Exactly where remains a mystery. On various documents he listed locations in four different states as his birthplace.

West settled in Detroit (where, by some of his accounts, he was also born) sometime in the 1940s and married a local clerk, Susan Fikes, in 1953. Fikes later admitted she wasn't sure how many times he'd been married before, nor could she describe exactly what he did for a living. He worked as a bookkeeper for a couple of nursing homes ("sort of a manager," she said) before drifting into "real estate." While he may actually have managed properties, it's worth noting that numbers racketeers often used the term as a cover for their activities.

During the 1950s West became a familiar figure at local Democratic clubs. His quietly confident air impressed people, though some privately wondered why this well-dressed Phi Beta Kappa graduate of Swarthmore College and Yale's law school was running a dingy hardware store on the west side of Detroit. "I came to doubt that he really was who he said he was," admitted Cobbs, who nonetheless enjoyed listening to West's stories about his experiences as a black attorney in the South. "But he was very cunning, a great impersonator, right down to the school rings he wore."

In 1962 those rings, along with the photo of him and John F. Kennedy that he kept in his store window (ostensibly taken at the 1960 Democratic Convention), helped get West elected to the Michigan legislature as representative of the 6th District. Voters evidently were impressed by the credentials of Daniel W. West, the name that appeared on affidavits filed with election commissions. In addition to his lofty academic record, his credentials seemed to show that he was a retired attorney licensed to practice law in New York and Tennessee who also had held elected office in the Virgin Islands and the District of Columbia. This biography was reprinted in the 1963–64 edition of the *Michigan Manual,* the official compilation of data for all state officials.

Belying his august background, during his two years in Lansing, West did little but sit tight-lipped in the back of the chambers. He didn't pal around with his colleagues. The only legislation he introduced—a bewildering, badly worded bill aimed at motorists who drove with one arm around a girl—was met with embarrassed chuckles. Civic Searchlight, a nonpartisan organization that evaluated political candidates, listed "No rating" next to West's name when he ran for reelection in 1964. This was tantamount to being called unqualified, said William O'Brien, the Detroit attorney who served as executive director of Civic Searchlight.

"I interviewed West. He was a pretty sharp guy," said O'Brien. He recalled that West had once been asked in a questionnaire to describe specific improvements he would promote, if elected. The prison system needed reform, he had responded authoritatively.

It was Thomas O'Hara, an autoworker defeated by West in the 1964 Democratic primary, who set West's downfall in motion. Because of legislative reapportionment, West ran for re-election from the new 24th District rather than the old 6th District. Checking voter registration cards, O'Hara discovered fourteen families from outside the 24th District who claimed to live at the same sparsely furnished apartment that West listed as his residence. When confronted by police investigators, all admitted that West had encouraged them to falsify registrations in order to vote for him. This misdemeanor offense, to which West pled innocent when arraigned in Recorder's Court two weeks after the primary, did not affect his overwhelming victory over the Republican candidate in the November election; however, the Internal Revenue Service and veteran *Detroit News* reporter Jack Carlisle were concluding investigations of their own at that time.

For several years West had been working as a tax consultant, filing returns for people who were encouraged to sign blank forms and let him fill in the details. He would typically prepare two separate forms. On one he would show the client receiving no refund. On the other he would add fictitious dependents and other bogus deductions and have the refund check sent to his address. The IRS estimated that he had swindled about fifteen hundred people and defrauded the government of $250,000 in phony refund claims.

At the same time that the IRS was building its case, Carlisle, tipped off by O'Hara, was trying to resolve the many discrepancies in West's biography. He found out that a Daniel W. West had indeed graduated from Swarthmore and Yale. Further digging revealed that that particular West had been a white attorney who had died at age thirty-six in Larchmont, New York. As incredible as it seemed, Representative Daniel West, a felon whose higher education consisted of a mail-order diploma from a Chicago correspondence school, had assumed the brilliant attorney's background.

The news of West's outrageous hoaxes was a bombshell. As the national media picked up the details of the legislator's extraordinary double life, he remained unruffled and declined comment. On the Monday following the revelations, he was arrested by the FBI and arraigned on 117 counts of income tax fraud. West was released three days later on a $10,000 bond. The uproar cost him none of his characteristic chutzpah. When the House, following its own investigation, refused to seat him, he filed to run in the special election to fill his vacancy. When the time came to cast ballots, however, Detroiters had been made aware of new details of his past, thanks to an FBI comparison of fingerprint records.

In 1928 in Minneapolis, an eighteen-year-old "bishop" claiming to be a descendent of Daniel Boone was sentenced to six months in prison for stealing a watch and some clothes from his "parishioners." Soon after his release, the dubious prelate was given an eighteen-month sentence after pleading guilty to burglary. Having served time for two felony convictions, he was then picked up for creating a disturbance inside a whorehouse. The judge, who didn't buy the man's story about conducting an undercover investigation for the mayor of Minneapolis, gave him forty-five days.

The same glib fellow appeared in New York in 1935 and attached himself to Harlem's famous Father Divine. There he was identified in the preacher's publications as a member of the Minnesota state legislature and the personal emissary of the governor. Over the next six years, the self-described "overseer of young people of the Church of God in Christ for Minnesota, South Dakota, and Montana" was arrested for larceny in New Jersey, did time in a Virginia reformatory for housebreaking, and was sentenced to serve fifteen years in the Iowa State Penitentiary for forgery.

Needless to say, these revelations were hardly a boost to West's campaign to win back his seat. He finished fifteenth among seventeen candidates.

Meanwhile, the world was closing in. According to Fikes, after her husband was exposed, "he didn't know what to do." Nobody would give him a job. He couldn't pay his lawyers. His car was repossessed. He was facing a maximum sentence of 755 years in federal prison and $864,000 in fines. Beyond that were the misdemeanor charges for voter fraud and subornation of witnesses, as well as the inevitable lawsuits from the hundreds of taxpayers he had swindled. Feeling the pressure, the normally jaunty West broke down and "cried like a baby," she said.

Then, on July 5, 1965, the day before his trial was to begin, he simply vanished. He left behind a wife and two sons.

"I don't know where he is," Fikes told the press, "but I know he's a good man. From what I know about him I'm sure he will turn himself in soon. He has everything to live for and we had everything to be happy about."

Her optimism, like the ink on the feds' fugitive warrant, gradually faded. "He completely disappeared," Cobbs said. "I knew some people who knew him well, and they never heard from him again."

Authorities have always assumed that West fled to Canada, a convenient refuge. In addition to its proximity, the country's extradition treaties do not cover the crimes with which he was charged, meaning he could not be forced to return to the United States to stand trial.

After all these years, West is most likely dead. Cobbs provided an epitaph of sorts for the chameleonic con man, who skipped town owing him money. "Daniel West actually had great integrity," he insisted. "But he had a great imagination, too."

Frank Gaca holds a photo of his daughter, Barbara, fifty years after she disappeared while walking to school. (Matthew Moore Collection)

FOURTEEN
Who Killed Barbara Gaca?

In 1955, the abduction and slaying of a seven-year-old schoolgirl gripped Detroit. Several decades later, the identity of the perpetrator continues to baffle police.

On that damp, bleak Thursday when little Barbara Gaca (pronounced GAHT-za) skipped off to school and never returned, she had been settled into a routine as comfortably predictable as the route her father, Frank, followed every day for thirty-eight years as a Detroit mail carrier. Every morning she dressed in her blue-and-white school uniform and black strap shoes, kissed her mother good-bye, and walked the six blocks from the frame house at 14102 Faircrest to Assumption Grotto, one of the city's largest Catholic parishes. The second grader attended Mass and ate breakfast at her desk before beginning a long day of study under the watchful eyes of the nuns. Noon provided a welcome break for Barbara and her younger siblings, Gloria and Robert, who weren't allowed to watch television until Barbara came home and personally clicked it on. Then they all had lunch with Soupy Sales.

However, on March 24, 1955, Barbara didn't come home for lunch. Her mother called the school office. Barbara hadn't shown up at school today, Rita Gaca was told. Wasn't she home sick?

"Mom was anxious, then angry, then anger turned to despair," remembered Robert Gaca, who was five years old at the time. "It didn't take long for her to fall apart."

Police issued a bulletin for the lost youngster. Frank Gaca left work to join friends and relatives in searching the neighborhood around Gratiot and McNichols. As darkness fell, more and more police were sent out to look for the slender brown-eyed girl in the blue snowsuit and print babushka. By the following day, thousands of concerned Detroiters turned the city upside down. "Knock on every door," police and volunteers were told. "Look under every car. Check everywhere a little girl possibly could be."

Garages, confessionals, garbage cans, and abandoned refrigerators were scoured. The nuns and eleven hundred students at Assumption said rosaries. On Friday night, Frank Gaca made a televised appeal, asking whoever had his daughter to set her free. A snowfall didn't deter three thousand Boy Scouts from combing a ninety-square-mile area the next day. Meanwhile, police rounded up every known pervert and contended with a flurry of tips, rumors, and hoaxes.

On March 31, the largest search in local memory ended when a railroad worker came across Barbara's body wrapped inside an army blanket. She had been raped, strangled, stabbed, then discarded like so much trash at an Oakland County dump site twenty-five miles from her home. Detroit Mayor Albert Cobo was so upset by the news, he broke down and wept in public. "What are we going to do?" he cried. "What can we do! A little girl like this—it just seems we have to build a chain around our children!"

As Holy Week began, fifteen thousand people stood in block-long lines to view the little girl laid out in the white dress she had been planning to wear at her upcoming First Holy Communion. The funeral was held on April 5, five days before Easter. The cortege that accompanied Barbara to Mount Olivet Cemetery was so long, motorists caught at traffic crossings had to wait nearly an hour for it to pass through. The United Casket Company donated the casket, and Mount Olivet donated the plot.

In the years since, society has grown inured to crimes involving children, even homicide. National crime statistics reveal that on a per capita basis, Detroit today is easily the deadliest big city for youngsters, with eighty children murdered between 1999 and 2001 alone. There have been no mayoral meltdowns over their loss, no truly communal outpourings of grief. In 1955, however, the murder of a seven-year-old schoolgirl was enough of an aberration to send a city of nearly two million citizens into a state of collective revulsion. The abduction and murder caused a popular crime magazine to ask, "When are the kids going to be safe in Detroit?" After all, *Real Detective* pointed out, Barbara Gaca was the sixth child to have been murdered in Detroit in the last eight years. "Detroit," it declared, "is a kid-killer's town."

Who killed Barbara Gaca? It's a question that has baffled police for well over a half-century. Over the last few years, old suspects have been dusted off and promising new leads pursued—all in what amounts to a last push to solve one of Detroit's most infamous murders while there still is somebody left who cared for Barbara Gaca.

Despite several heart operations, Frank Gaca is a trim and robust octogenarian. With a trace of a Polish accent, he talks about his daughter. "She was a happy kid," he said one morning inside his White Lake Township home. "She made friends very easily. She'd talk to everybody, though she shied away from a lot of grown-ups. Once, she refused to get into a car with her grandfather until he got out and she recognized him."

Such reticence caused investigators to speculate that Barbara must have known her killer, that she would not have been lured into a stranger's car. Friends and relatives were interviewed and cleared. Who else was there? One boy said he spoke to Barbara at the corner of Linnhurst and Gratiot, four blocks from school. She told him she was waiting for a friend. A neighborhood girl said she saw somebody being pulled into a car.

"It had to have been a random pickup," Gaca said, his voice trailing off. "Some pervert . . ."

Police were puzzled. Plucking a girl off a sidewalk was one thing, but how could her abductor then drive twenty-five miles in daylight, through populous sections of Detroit and the suburbs, without Barbara attracting somebody's attention? Two witnesses reported seeing a 1954 green Hudson at a gas station at 10 Mile and Groesbeck that morning. The driver was described as a 40- to 45-year-old man, about 5-feet-6 inches and 150 pounds. A girl matching Barbara's description was inside the car as an attendant pumped gas. The girl looked frightened, he said.

The wooded hollow where Barbara's body was found was two hundred feet off Halstead Road, between Walnut Lake Road and Pontiac Trail. Evidence established that the rape and murder occurred within two to four hours of her abduction and that both happened inside a clean car or room. Police focused on three clues found at the crime scene: the bloodstained army blanket, footprints made by large shoes, and fresh tire tracks leading from fifty feet beyond Barbara's body to the rutted dirt lane that connected to Halstead.

Detectives discovered that for the last two summers, the Gacas, along with relatives and friends, had often picnicked at Pleasant Lake in Waterford. The speculation ran that the killer not only knew the area but also may have known the family or was stalking them.

After the body was found, a half-dozen witnesses came forward with a new clue. All said that on the day of Barbara's abduction, they had spotted a new Buick with a cream-colored top parked at the dump site between 10:30 and 11 a.m. The trunk had been open, though they saw nobody around. Some said the car was green, others said maroon. Another person reported seeing a tall, thin man in the area at about the same time.

Police investigated hundreds of suspects, checking out their shoes, cars, blankets, and whereabouts. A fifty-three-year-old Redford man named Paul Hassell came under close scrutiny when a female friend turned him in as a child molester. The woman said Hassell had taken her for rides through Oakland County in his green Chevrolet and once offered to show her the place where Barbara's body had been found. He was familiar with the site, he told her, because he often hunted rabbits in the area.

Hassell was a serial predator. His police record included convictions for child molestation in 1940 and indecent exposure in 1953. There had also been many other complaints for which he had not been prosecuted. A search of his home revealed several dolls used to lure girls. A few were three feet tall—just a few inches shorter than Barbara. Several incriminating items—candy, Vaseline, and an army blanket—were found inside his car.

Hassell had started his new job at the Ford tank plant in Plymouth just three days before Barbara's disappearance. On the morning of March

24, witnesses confirmed that he had punched out at 7:20 a.m. But would he—*could* he—have driven all the way to the east side of Detroit to randomly snatch Barbara by 8 a.m., the approximate time she had vanished? Police had their doubts, especially after Hassell submitted to six polygraph tests and all proved inconclusive.

Other suspects emerged. They included an Oakland County mailman, a known pervert, who had missed work the day of the murder, and a soldier who was caught molesting a six-year-old girl in his barracks. There was a gangly "cowboy" named Charlie, who was spotted in a rural area of Wayne County with a girl whom a witness said resembled Barbara. Charlie happened to have a green car whose interior had been freshly scrubbed; moreover, a bag of candy was found on the floor. These and other promising leads went nowhere.

At one point sixty detectives were assigned to work overtime on the case, but by 1957 the investigation had lost much of its steam. After two years, police had chased down 1,974 tips, looked at 850 suspects, and still were no closer to solving the mystery.

The Gacas got on with life the best they could. Frank and Rita, responding to their physician's suggestion that they "replace" their lost daughter, had two more children. They bought the cottage in White Lake Township, which they expanded and moved to permanently after Frank retired. Today its paneled walls are crowded with dozens of framed family photographs, including an oversize portrait of Barbara painted by a relative. All the while, the close-knit family has put up with prank calls, most made on the anniversary of the crime. "We never changed our number," Gaca said. "We always thought someday, somebody who knew something would call."

The dormant case was reopened in 1965 when a twenty-nine-year-old autoworker already serving time on a manslaughter conviction became a suspect in an earlier slaying of a fourteen-year-old girl. Certain evidence seemed to link him to Barbara's killing, but in the end police eliminated him as a suspect.

Then, in 1967, an old suspect re-emerged when a neighbor complained of Paul Hassell's inappropriate behavior with two little girls. State police picked him up for questioning, then scheduled a polygraph test in

Pontiac prior to his arraignment on child molestation charges. Hassell conferred with his lawyer, at which point he confessed to having killed Barbara. He then went home, put a shotgun to his head, and pulled the trigger.

Despite the damning evidence against Hassell, Gaca agrees with the conclusion of state police detectives. They determined that the distance Hassell needed to travel from his workplace to the area in which Barbara was abducted was impossible to cover in the time available. "You have to remember, in 1955 there wasn't a freeway to get you from that part of town to the other," he said. It was all surface streets and stoplights in rush-hour traffic. Why did Hassell confess? Nobody can say for sure, though criminologists know that bogus admissions of guilt, for whatever reason, are not unusual among the deranged. Neither are suicides.

In retrospect, Gaca wishes detectives had more closely examined a visiting priest who had been brought in to assist Assumption clergy during the Lenten season. According to Gaca, the priest had been interviewed by police and "shipped to a parish in Nova Scotia immediately afterwards"—a transfer by church officials that aroused little suspicion in 1955. Gaca lets out a short, rueful laugh. "At that time, who would ever think a priest could do something like that to a child?"

Captain Tim Sheridan of the West Bloomfield Township Police Department was brought up in St. Raymond's Parish, near Assumption. "I was only three years old when Barbara was murdered," he said, "but I grew up hearing about it from my older sisters."

Seated inside a conference room, the polished-looking veteran detective admits that the case hits home—not only because of the crime's connection to the old neighborhood, or his and the Gacas' shared faith, but because he's a father himself. "What happened to Barbara," he said, "is every parent's nightmare."

That characterization is underscored by the files he has brought along. Crime scene and autopsy photos show a ponytailed girl in almost angelic repose—knees drawn up, eyes and mouth closed—but with her frail torso punctured by fifteen stab wounds. A 1955 memo from the autopsy report refers to the presence of chocolate-coated peppermint candy in her stomach: "She died shortly after eating the candy and was emotionally upset after eating the candy. It was only partially digested."

Although Detroit and state police were far better equipped to handle the original investigation, West Bloomfield Township has maintained official jurisdiction over the case from the start. The community has only two unsolved murders on its books. Barbara Gaca is one of them. Despite a full caseload, Sheridan started "nosing around." In 1996, he submitted a detailed report to the FBI's Violent Criminal Apprehension System (VICAP), a national computer database that collects and analyzes the unique aspects of violent crimes. Patterns can be detected and leads provided to local law-enforcement agencies. VICAP came back with the name of William Henry Redmond, an itinerant carnival worker who had died in 1992 while awaiting trial for the rape and strangulation of an eight-year-old Philadelphia girl in 1951. Redmond, who had a long record of convictions for sex offenses, also was linked to the rape-murders of girls in Ohio and New York. "They may have me on this one," Redmond had reportedly told an inmate while in jail, "but not the other three."

Authorities connected Redmond to only three murders, not four. Was Barbara the fourth victim he was referring to? With some difficulty, Sheridan pieced together Redmond's job history. He finally determined that Redmond had been working for a railroad in New Mexico at the time of Barbara's murder.

Another suspect whom Sheridan subsequently identified is still alive—and, according to Sheridan, acting suspiciously. Today the middle-aged man runs a business in Detroit, has a stable family life, and, despite three convictions for minor crimes as a young man, no record of sex offenses. In 1955, however, he was a thirteen-year-old runaway from a troubled family. Two days before Barbara's body was discovered, he had been arrested in a stolen car at Faircrest and Chalmers, just one block from the Gacas' house. Detectives from the Youth Bureau interviewed him at the juvenile home, and he had directed them to an abandoned car where he had been sleeping. Inside police found blankets and fourteen "skin" magazines, which the boy admitted he had stolen from a drugstore.

Despite the medical examiner's determination that it was possible a boy as young as twelve could have committed the rape and murder, along with the suspect's inability to account for his whereabouts on the day Barbara was killed, the boy was never re-interviewed. Then Sheridan showed up one day in 2000 at the man's place of business, hoping to have some questions answered. "He made a big production in front of his employees, yelling, 'Hey, these guys think I killed a little girl!'" Sheridan recalled. The suspect offered to take a polygraph—then backed out.

After considerable back and forth, the suspect agreed to provide a DNA sample. In May 2002, following lengthy discussions between Sheridan and the FBI, as well as Detroit and state police, the suspect's attorney and several family members showed up at township headquarters to loudly decry the investigation. The suspect, who nervously stayed outside in the parking lot while all the commotion went on inside, had changed his mind about cooperating.

Sheridan is troubled by the suspect's equivocating. He issues a familiar law-enforcement refrain: "If someone has nothing to hide, you'd think that person would jump at the chance to prove himself innocent."

Most deviants have some sort of history involving molestation or child pornography. Working in this suspect's favor is the absence of an established sexual criminal past. "Maybe he's straightened out," Sheridan suggests, which criminal psychologists know is unlikely. "Or maybe he was never caught." Asked to assess the probability that the evasive businessman is the "mad slayer" of 1955 news reports, Sheridan says he's "eighty-percent sure." The evidence, all circumstantial, and the detective's hunches are together not enough to persuade Oakland County prosecutors to seek a court order to force the suspect to submit DNA samples or sit for a polygraph test.

Frank Gaca has always been stoic about his daughter's murder. No, he says, he's never had nightmares about Barbara. He saw his share of death as a sailor in the South Pacific during World War II. And he doesn't blame anybody or beat himself up over events. "I was upset, of course, but life went on," he said. "Heck, I had five other kids I had to take care of."

On this gray, snowy day, Gaca categorically appraises suspects, old and new. A scrapbook dedicated to the case lies open on the dining-room

Frank Gaca in 2005.
(Matthew Moore Collection)

table. The killer will probably never be found, he concludes. "It's been too long. Not unless someone comes forward and confesses." His wife died in 2004, believing the same. His children prefer that he not get false hopes up.

Many murders go unsolved. It doesn't help that certain evidence—including vaginal smears and Barbara's clothes—has been lost over the years. Sheridan admits the case is at a standstill. "Soon it'll just fade completely from everybody's memory." He pauses a few moments before adding, "Unfortunately."

When Barbara Gaca left home that final morning, she had with her items familiar to generations of Catholic schoolchildren: a white rosary, a pencil case, and a composition book. Detectives found them strewn about the crime scene. A page torn from the notebook included three neatly penciled lines written on her last day in school:

I love the angel
I see an angel
I have an angel

The words suggest more than a rote classroom exercise. The Gacas' Catholic faith told them that Barbara's life goes on—in some special harbor in the hereafter, where all God's children are safe from predators.

"When we think of Barbara today," said her brother, Robert, "we think of her as our guardian angel. I know there have been many times over the years when I could feel her hand on my shoulder."

The dedication of the Hazen S. Pingree monument on Memorial Day, 1904. (Author's Collection)

FIFTEEN
The People's Mayor

Shoemaker-turned-crusader Hazen S. Pingree was a populist who battled monopolies, championed the little guy, and became one of Detroit's greatest political figures.

After more than a century of watching the city he loved dissolve from a dynamic but orderly community "where life is worth living" into an urban moonscape with seemingly insurmountable problems, Hazen S. Pingree appears eager to jump down from his perch in Grand Circus Park, roll up his sleeves, and throw his considerable weight behind what's ailing modern Detroit.

It's possible that Pingree's name rings a bell, if only faintly, with today's generation. In the spring of 2000, after decades of neglect, the monument was sandblasted clean by the city as Grand Circus Park was spruced up for the opening of nearby Comerica Park. Probably not one in a thousand baseball fans walking past know anything of the old fellow with the Van Dyke beard seated somewhat uneasily in his concrete chair. That's a shame, because Pingree represents the kind of grassroots reformist zeal that has historically appealed to Detroiters, a zeal that many feel is essential to lifting the city out of its Third-World doldrums.

A couple dozen Detroit mayors have come and gone since the bombastic Burl Ives look-alike last occupied the office in 1897. While a handful of them—most notably Frank Murphy in the 1930s and Coleman A. Young in the 1970s—had tremendous effect on the city, no mayor before or since

Pingree has served the community better or had a greater influence on its course. Dust off the social reform programs long taken for granted in other big cities, and you'll find Mayor Pingree's fingerprints all over them. According to Pingree biographer and historian Melvin G. Holli, Pingree "established the first significant social reform administration in any large city of the time." His inventive crusading caused a panel of urban historians to select him as one of the country's ten greatest mayors for the book *The American Mayor.*

Pingree was a Yankee Protestant who came to Detroit after the Civil War to make his fortune manufacturing footwear. At the time, "boodle" was the time-honored grease of local and national political machines. Candidates concentrated on spoils, not issues. During the 1889 mayoral election, several leading citizens, hoping to break the Democratic stranglehold on the office, urged Pingree to run. "I'm too busy making shoes," was his response.

Pingree's friends prevailed, however, and after a victory at the polls he set about becoming Detroit's first truly notable mayor. To the delight of ordinary working-class folks, but to the chagrin of the conservative silk-stocking set that had originally supported him, Pingree proved to be a tireless reformer. During his four terms, the rotund Republican with the high-pitched voice successfully took on the utility and streetcar companies and other monopolies affecting the little guy. His battle with the private streetcar franchises was monumental, but in the end he—and the people—prevailed. In 1895, the first municipal streetcars appeared, their three-cent fare undercutting the private lines' standard nickel fare.

Pingree became a national figure during the severe countrywide depression of 1893–1894, which idled one-third of the local work force. At a meeting of the city council, the mayor suggested a plan allowing for starving families to grow vegetable gardens on vacant lots, both publicly and privately owned. A council member retorted: "Have the right people go to the homes of those who are destitute and if they have anything to sell, sell it, and don't add to the tax roll." At this, remembered a contemporary, "Mayor Pingree fairly blew up, as he always did when his sense of justice was outraged."

An avid horseman, Pingree sold his prize mount to raise money for his public vegetable gardens project during the depression of 1893–1894. (Burton Historical Collection)

Pingree, an avid horseman, sold his prize mount at auction for $387 (about one-third its real value) to raise money to buy seed and garden tools. Several citizens followed his lead, donating land and dollars to the cause. During the first year of the program, 945 families produced fourteen thousand dollars worth of vegetables on lots sprinkled around the city. Those numbers grew exponentially over the next several years. Grateful gardeners planted signs in their plots that read, "He who gives to others, gives to the Lord," and "The name of the man who originated this system will be handed down to prosperity."

The innovative public works program thrust "Potato Patch" Pingree into the national spotlight and became a model for Chicago, Minneapolis, Denver, Boston, and other cities. Pingree's selflessness endeared him to working-class Detroiters, many of whom crossed party lines to vote for him time and again.

Longtime city councilman John C. Lodge recalled an incident when Pingree was running for his third term against a seemingly formidable

Pingree's home on upper Woodward Avenue was located on the site where the Horace H. Rackham Educational Memorial Building now stands. (Burton Historical Collection)

opponent, businessman Marshall H. Godfrey. "On the Saturday before Election Day I found him at the corner of Fort and Woodward looking at a torchlight parade," Lodge remembered. "The marchers had torches made of small cans of kerosene, which they held aloft on a stick while marching. It looked like an impressive affair for our little city."

Pingree idly asked, "How many people are there in the parade?" Lodge said he didn't know; maybe a few thousand or so. Then Pingree asked: "How many are there on the sidewalk?"

"Probably four or five times that number," Lodge answered.

"Well," said Pingree, "just remember what I am saying to you. Marsh has the parade. I have the sidewalk." Pingree won handily.

Pingree's success is all the more remarkable because, before first taking office at age fifty, he had shown no political aspirations at all. Up until that time, his only related experience was as the president of the Michigan Club, a group of prominent Republicans whose roster included Detroit's social and business elite: James Vernor, Dexter Ferry, James F.

Joy, James McMillan, and Russell Alger. Their influence can be measured by the number of streets, parks, and buildings named after them.

But Pingree was quite content running one of the city's largest and most successful businesses, belonging to the right clubs, sitting on the right boards, and coming home every night to the elegant stone mansion he shared with family and servants on upper Woodward Avenue (on the site where the Horace H. Rackham Educational Memorial Building now stands).

"Pingree's taste for things French was fully indulged in his residence," Thomas W. Brunk wrote in *The Grand American Avenue*. "The central hall exhibited a tapestry that had reportedly belonged to Napoleon Bonaparte. The sitting room had French medallion-back chairs covered with expensive satin damask, heavy draperies, and marquetry furniture with marble tops. The drawing room was the most spectacular, with gilt Louis XV furniture covered with exquisite Gobelin tapestry, a large Aubusson carpet, crystal chandeliers, wall sconces, and an ornate marble mantel. The decorative effect was enhanced with Pingree's extensive art collection."

Nobody who knew Hazen Senter Pingree's background begrudged him his excesses. He was born August 30, 1840, into a poor Maine farming family of eight children. At fourteen he left home to work in a cotton factory. Six years later he began an apprenticeship as a leather cutter in a Massachusetts shoe factory.

In the summer of 1862, with the Civil War more than a year old, he volunteered for the First Massachusetts Heavy Artillery and almost immediately saw heavy action at the Second Battle of Bull Run. Two years later he was captured during the Battle of North Ana and sent to the notorious Confederate prison at Andersonville, Georgia. He spent five frightful months behind wire, doing his best to survive the rampant diseases, sadistic guards, and meager rations, and was finally able to escape during a prisoner exchange when he answered to the name of a fellow inmate who was too sick to respond.

It was while Pingree was in Andersonville that he first heard of the opportunities to be found in Detroit. He arrived in the city at war's end in 1865. Over the next quarter-century, he saw his fortunes rise with those of the growing community. He started by cutting leather in the shop of Henry P. Baldwin and soon entered into a partnership with Charles H. Smith to take over the business. From an eight-man operation grossing twenty thousand dollars in 1866, the firm of Pingree & Smith blossomed into a business with annual sales in the range of one million dollars. The firm's four-story shoe factory on Woodbridge at Griswold employed seven hundred people.

In 1872, Pingree married a Mount Clemens schoolteacher named Frances Gilbert, who was dead set against tobacco, alcohol, and foul language. Together the couple had two daughters and a son and "lived a quiet and well-ordered life," recalled a friend. Pingree moved his aging father from Maine to live with him.

When Pingree's elitist Republican friends handpicked him in the fall of 1889 to challenge Democratic incumbent John Pridgeon Jr., he was viewed as a man who was popular, energetic, resourceful—and, should he win, a compliant guardian of pro-business interests. That he also was an independent thinker with humanistic tendencies—the result of his experiences as an impoverished farm boy, half-dead prisoner of war, and bone-tired factory worker—seems never to have been considered possible sources of conflict by his upper-class supporters.

Pingree had almost no experience in civic affairs prior to entering the race. When challenged by reporters to state his qualifications, the neophyte insisted that he was an honest man and "no damn fool."

For all of the idealism he later displayed in office, Pingree also was a pragmatist. At the time of his first election, the majority of Detroit's two hundred thousand citizens were foreign-born. Assured of the support of native-born Republicans, he aggressively pursued ethnic voters. Looking to dispel rumors among Germans that he was a "dry" candidate, he launched his campaign in Baltimore Red's saloon. He drank "red-eye" whiskey with the Irish and courted Polish Catholic priests.

Election Day was typically rowdy, filled with fistfights and "floaters" voting early and often. When the sawdust settled on the floor of Baltimore Red's and other smoke-filled rooms throughout Detroit's sixteen wards, Pingree had won office by a margin as comfortable as the lifestyle he was about to leave behind. He responded to his unexpectedly high sup-

Pingree tosses a spadeful of dirt to launch construction of Grand Boulevard in August 1891. (Burton Historical Collection)

port among immigrant groups by placing several Germans and Poles in government jobs.

Pingree was sworn into office on January 14, 1890, and immediately went after the corrupt contractors responsible for the disgraceful condition of local roads. By the end of his first two-year term, the cedar-block main arteries had been replaced with asphalt, and Detroit was on its way to becoming one of the best-paved cities in the country.

Another victory was Grand Boulevard, a project stalled since 1879. Many ridiculed the creation of Grand Boulevard as being too far out in the countryside, but Pingree not only tirelessly championed the idea, one August day in 1891 he even got off his horse and ceremoniously tossed the first spadeful of dirt. The onetime farm boy then pulled off his suit jacket and took a turn behind the plow, showing that he hadn't strayed too far from his roots. Ultimately, the two-hundred-foot-wide landscaped boulevard wrapped around the entire city for a distance of twelve miles and featured some of Detroit's finest residences. Initially thought to represent the absolute outer limit of the city's expansion, by the early 1900s Detroit's explosive growth resulted in subdivisions built far beyond it.

Pingree also tackled the powerful school board during his first administration. "Why, actually members of this board have sold themselves out regularly to this and that and the other contractor," he charged. "It is frightful. . . . After they had been bought they frequently sold themselves again, and left the parties they first sold to."

Frequently tactless and bombastic, the new mayor rubbed many the wrong way. He often rushed into issues without gathering all the facts, allowing newspapers to have a field day reporting his mistakes and missteps. The press made up stories, some of them absurd. The *Detroit Journal* once accused him of poisoning his horses in the winter to save on feed. "It is cheaper to purchase new ones in the spring," the paper quoted hizzoner.

Over the years the embattled mayor gave as good as he got. When a bank dropped him from its board of directors because he was "antagonistic to corporate capital," Pingree responded, "This town needs somebody to tell the utilities crowd to kiss something else besides babies!"

On another occasion, after one of Pingree's corporate customers canceled a contract with his shoe company because the customer disagreed with Pingree's policies, the mayor had police surround the merchant's favorite whorehouse one day and declare it quarantined for smallpox. "Marching down the street with a coterie of newsmen and cronies," a newspaperman later wrote, "Pingree saw the troublemaker in a window. The mayor, feigning surprise, declared, 'I'll be damned.' There was a quick huddling of heads at the door of the house. Suddenly it was discovered that there was no smallpox in the house and the quarantine was lifted. The merchant flew out the back door and the shoe contract was quietly reinstated."

Constant battle with his critics wore on Pingree. Over time he gained weight, and his language grew coarser. Whenever nerves threatened to get the better of him, he responded in typically maverick fashion: he pulled out the dried codfish he carried in his coat and chewed on it as a tonic.

By his third term the "people's mayor" was indelibly identified with the working class. In the process he lost the support of the local aristocracy—

Pingree (*at left*) inside his office at City Hall. The four-term mayor was a hero to the working class. "It is your so-called respectable people who are the most dangerous," he declared. (Burton Historical Collection)

and his family pew in the tony Woodward Avenue Baptist Church. The social ostracism hurt. "It takes a lot of pluck to see your old associates pass you by without speaking and not get disheartened and want to give up the fight," he admitted. Nonetheless, in 1895 he ran for—and won—a fourth term. That year the crusading mayor racked up victories over the "utilities crowd" by establishing a cost-effective municipal lighting department and forcing the privately held gas company to drastically cut its rates.

Although Detroit's first "gas buggies" appeared on his watch, Pingree didn't live to see the auto industry's extraordinary impact on his horse-and-buggy town. Eager to practice his progressive policies on a larger scale, he ran for governor in 1896 and was elected while still serving as mayor. He held both jobs until the Michigan Supreme Court ruled that he had to decide between them. On March 22, 1897, he reluctantly said good-bye to City Hall.

Several months later, Governor Pingree gave a speech to the Nineteenth Century Club in New York, to which he spelled out his concerns for the average man and his welfare. So long as the citizenry depended on private companies to provide public services while those in government were open to bribes, citizens could expect poor service and high rates, he said. "I have been made painfully aware of the expenditure of large sums of money to elect corrupt officials. This money is contributed by men who stand high in the community, and who expect to be paid back a hundredfold from the public treasury. Their efforts to corrupt the people are resisted by the poor, the honest yeomanry.

"I have found it a necessity, and have continually practiced it, to pull the screens wide open in front of every man who was doing dirty work, call him by name, and show up his schemes. It is your so-called respectable people who are the most dangerous. Their cloak of eminent respectability hides them, and people hardly believe you when you show them up, especially when they are church members or carry long faces."

Pingree served two terms in Lansing, tackling the trusts, syndicates, and corporate giants with characteristic gusto. A populist and a progressive built along the lines of Theodore Roosevelt, the governor clearly was presidential material. But an untimely death from peritonitis while traveling abroad cut that dream short. Pingree died on June 19, 1901, in England, in the midst of Detroiters' preparations for the city's bicentennial. At his burial service in Detroit two and a half weeks later, twenty-five thousand citizens lined the funeral route.

Many of Pingree's aristocratic friends considered him a traitor to his class and shunned the memorial planned for Grand Circus Park. In keeping with his populist image, the seated bronze figure was funded largely through the pennies of schoolchildren and the nickels of ordinary citizens. It took longer than many wished, perhaps, but Detroiters finally dedicated the statue on Memorial Day, 1904.

Today, when the tumult from the nearby ballpark is great and the foot traffic is heavy, one can imagine how familiar it all must feel to the man perched restlessly on his concrete throne. More than a century after his passing, the idol of the people still owns the sidewalk, still has the roar of the crowd in his ears.

SIXTEEN

The Toughest Cop Who Ever Lived

Respected by some, despised by others, and feared by all, patrolman Henderson "Ben" Turpin was "The Law" to a generation of black Detroiters.

Depending on who is telling the story, Ben Turpin either was the most brutal and ignorant cop ever to work a beat in Detroit or an angel dropped to earth to protect law-abiding blacks. Many of those who grew up in the 1930s and '40s respectfully calling him "Mister Ben" later remembered him as "a son of a bitch" and "the sorriest excuse for a cop there ever was." He patrolled the Black Bottom neighborhood with head-splitting efficiency from 1927 to 1952, at various times punching out Coleman Young's father, gunning down a member of the Purple Gang, and straightening out a young Joe Louis. Turpin killed at least one person and maybe as many as twenty and at all times carried a brace of pearl-handled revolvers. Although he earned sixteen commendations in his quarter-century of service, he died in virtual anonymity. But if a life unremembered is the only true death, Ben Turpin still lives—an urban Paul Bunyan whose legend blankets the paved-over ghetto he last patrolled some sixty years ago.

"When you get to talking about Ben Turpin," warned Lieutenant Fred Williams, former head of public information for the Detroit Police Department, "you get to thinking the man was eight feet tall." Williams, who was born in 1930, grew up on the city's northeast side. He first saw

Turpin at a ballpark at Dequindre and Six Mile one Sunday afternoon in the early 1940s. As Williams remembers it, a woman was making her way through the crowded grandstand when she accidentally stepped on a large man's foot.

"You could at least apologize," the man said irritably. The woman cursed the man, who replied with a disparaging remark. Within seconds the two were wrestling in the aisle, prompting shouts of "Leave that woman alone!" Several men jumped to their feet to assist the embattled lady, when a cry of recognition stopped them short.

"Say!" someone yelled. "That's Ben Turpin!"

"Everyone sat right back down," Williams said. "Nobody there felt man enough to mess with him."

As always, Turpin's reputation had preceded him. Just as Judge Roy Bean was known as "the only law west of the Pecos" a century earlier in Texas, Ben Turpin represented to a generation of black Detroiters the most visible symbol of law enforcement east of Woodward Avenue, then the unofficial line of demarcation dividing the city into white and black spheres.

Turpin had a penchant for administering hands-on civics lessons with a nightstick, fist, or revolver. No one was immune from this kind of treatment, as Coleman Young, father of the future mayor, found out in the early morning hours of August 5, 1928. As recorded in a complaint to the police department, Young was making his way home from work down St. Aubin Avenue when he was arrested "without cause" by Patrolman Turpin, who "struck the said Coleman Young in the mouth with his fist and without provocation, and told the said Coleman Young that if he opened his mouth he would beat his brains out with his club."

Young added in his complaint that, "since the above attack, the said police officer has threatened the said Coleman Young and told him to keep off his beat." Turpin was reprimanded for this incident by white police officials, who privately considered the officer's swashbuckling, bullying ways the perfect deterrent to crime.

For all the controversy Turpin engendered, many of the black police officers who followed him into the ranks had a grudging respect for him. "He was effective at what he was doing," Williams said. "Those were

Patrolman Henderson "Ben" Turpin in 1927. (Author's Collection)

different times, and Ben Turpin was emblematic of policing the way it used to be.

"Today we'd all be fired if we tried operating like Ben Turpin did, but back then there was no hue and cry over constitutional rights, and there were no Miranda rights. Most cops were overbearing. What was valued was gruffness and roughness. There was no back-talking a cop or else you'd get slapped around and tossed in jail."

Williams, who joined the force in 1955, was for many years in charge of the department's archives, which are skimpy on the subject of black police officers. According to Williams, the first black officer, Joseph Stowers, was hired in May 1890. He was fired two months later, apparently because white officers had waged a successful letter-writing campaign accusing Stowers of "improper conduct toward white women."

It wasn't until 1914 that the city had its first black detective team. Daniel A. Smith and Warren G. Richardson, native Canadians, were paired to solve crimes in Detroit's burgeoning black community, which grew in population from 5,700 in 1910 to 41,000 in 1920. Despite the duo's success in nabbing pickpockets, robbers, murderers, and horse thieves, by 1920 there were only fifteen black officers on the three-thousand-member force. As Detroit's black population swelled past one hundred thousand during the 1920s, a mere thirty-two black officers were hired.

The 1920s was Detroit's most dynamic decade. A booming economy based on the automobile industry attracted hundreds of thousands of European immigrants as well as blacks and whites from the South. Included in this human wave was a twenty-seven-year-old former shoeshine boy from Kentucky named Henderson Turpin, who arrived in January 1925.

Turpin moved into a sixty-square-block neighborhood on the near east side of Detroit known as Black Bottom, where most of the city's black citizens were squeezed into dilapidated housing. The neighborhood's boundaries roughly were East Grand Boulevard on the north, Russell on the east, Jefferson on the south, and John R on the west. Pockets of Italians, Germans, and Greeks were sprinkled throughout, but, generally speaking, the only whites walking the sidewalks were landlords, insurance salesmen, and cops.

Despite the poverty and crime, residents of Black Bottom mostly were "law-abiding folks," insists Pearl Johnson, a former Detroit schoolteacher who grew up in a family of fourteen on Sherman Street. "I remember a happy time growing up," she said. "All the families looked out for one another. We didn't have our doors closed and windows locked like today. It wasn't necessary. You knew everyone on the block. Everybody sat on their front porch, so as you were going up the block, it'd be 'Good evening, Mrs. Patterson,' and then, 'Good evening, Mrs. Jones.'"

It was in this city within a city that Turpin, given badge number 2439 and assigned to the Third Precinct (Hunt Street) Station on Gratiot Avenue, cut a wide swath. Turpin, who had an eighth-grade education, had worked for eighteen months as a train porter at Union Station before being appointed a police officer on August 1, 1927. The new hire "didn't have to pass any kind of test to get on the force," said one contemporary. "He was hired for just one reason: to kick ass."

Turpin was a formidable looking lawman. He stood a shade under six feet tall and had a large shaved head that protruded like a howitzer shell from his stocky, 240-pound frame. He strapped two pearl-handled revolvers around his considerable waist and tucked a third pistol, a police service revolver, into his waistband. He tended to be tight-lipped but "kind of nervous," recalled Fred Ross, who grew up on Lafayette and St. Aubin streets and later served as president of the Jolly Old Timers, a social club of former Black Bottom residents.

In Ross's opinion, "Ben was a *real* policeman. He'd drive around in his sedan, and if he saw some guy hanging out on the street corner, he'd say, 'Don't be here when I come back.' He'd drive around the block, and if that guy was still there, he'd get out and smack him upside his head and move him physically."

Blacks had "a love-hate relationship" with Turpin, Mayor Coleman A. Young once told a reporter. Young, who lived on Russell Street in the early 1930s, thought Turpin was preferable to his white counterparts, particularly a six-foot-four flatfoot named Blondie Hayes who liked to tell blacks that his search warrant was his size-fifteen shoe. According to Young, Turpin "killed some twenty guys," but "he never shot a kid. Kids could run from him, but he knew all their parents and we knew he'd tell them."

"The mayor thinks Turpin was a great cop, but I know otherwise," countered Bill Black, longtime newsman on WJR radio. "He was nothing more than a bully who abused people, mostly black. He was a no-good bastard and the complete antithesis of what a good cop should be."

One afternoon in the middle 1930s, Black and his father were waiting to catch a streetcar on Hastings when Black's dad, an amateur boxer, dared to intervene in a scuffle between Turpin and a youth. "My father went chest-to-chest," Black recalled. "Turpin backed down. It's too bad. I would've loved to have seen Turpin try to stop one of my father's left hooks."

Fred Ross, however, defends Turpin. "On the other hand, he helped a lot of black folks out," he said. "When there were problems, they'd send Ben in. He was just mean enough in situations where white cops wouldn't go in."

At 11:30 p. m. on October 14, 1929, an off-duty Turpin strolled into a drugstore on St. Antoine to buy a newspaper. At the door he encountered a man whose face looked familiar.

"What the hell are you looking at?" the man asked.

"At you, ——," replied Turpin with customary surliness.

The man pulled out a pistol. Turpin pulled out his revolver and fired several shots. Louis P. Bryant, a Purple Gang bodyguard with a lengthy police record, fell dead on the sidewalk. Turpin was charged with first-degree murder, but a Recorder's Court jury deliberated just twenty minutes before acquitting him. The department gave Turpin a meritorious citation for "exceptional bravery" in killing a dangerous racketeer.

As Louis Bryant found out, Turpin was never off-duty or out of character. Pearl Johnson recalls going to the Catherine Theatre in the evening and finding Turpin there, holding court in the lobby. "He'd sit in a chair at the entrance doors and observe people as they came in," she said. "If the line in front of the candy counter needed to move, he'd say, 'Hey, fella, move up there.' And if someone had their hat on, he'd say, 'Hey, let's get that hat off.' He wasn't paid for it. He was just fulfilling his role as neighborhood guardian."

Turpin liked to hang out in a small restaurant across the street from the theatre. From there he kept his eye on a young group of toughs called the Catherine Street Gang. For a time one of its members was a teenager named Joe Barrow. Turpin "was tougher than anyone in that Catherine Street Gang," Barrow wrote in a ghosted autobiography some forty years after he had changed his name to Joe Louis and become the heavyweight champion of the world.

> *He used to keep me out of trouble. If he caught me out at night, he'd run me home or take me home himself. . . . He knew I was training to be a fighter and he didn't want anything happening to me. One time the gang tried to get me to hold somebody so they could rob him. I told them "no," but they kept trying to convince me. Ben Turpin was around that night. Thank God, he had some kind of policeman's instinct, and he*

Turpin and members of the baseball team he sponsored in the 1940s. (Author's Collection)

chased me away from the gang and took me home. I'll never forget the thankful look my mother had on her face when he pushed me through the door. Most of the gang wound up in jail.

"In his way, Ben had a heart of gold," Williams said. Unfortunately, Turpin's good intentions frequently were sabotaged by his temper. A case in point was the baseball team he formed in the late 1930s out of young men from Black Bottom. The dozen or so players wore uniforms sporting the initials T.A.C. for Turpin's Athletic Club. The team primarily competed on weekends against local church nines and occasional barnstorming professionals. One suspects that most close calls on the diamond went Turpin's way. He wore his pearl-handled revolvers while managing or squirreled them away in the catcher's equipment when playing. According to local legend, on one occasion Turpin took his team to Chicago, where it was demolished by a superior club. Turpin abandoned his players in a hotel without money or transportation home while he drove the team bus into the countryside in search of better talent.

An examination of Turpin's fragmentary departmental service file further fleshes out the man's irascible nature. On August 28, 1933, for example, Turpin was patrolling Eastern Market when, according to Turpin, "a man stepped up to me and with abusive words, accused me of nearly running over him a short time previous." This seems a reasonable accusation. By all accounts, a steering wheel was just another weapon in Turpin's hands.

The man "used such loud and abusive words towards me," Turpin explained, "that it was necessary to take him to the station, of which he refused to do until some force [was used], which caused a large crowd to gather."

Turpin drew crowds like a carnival barker—and was as subtle as one in his dealings with the public. In a complaint to the police commissioner dated June 17, 1935, a citizen named Ulysses G. Pearcy wrote of Turpin's "discourtesy" when Pearcy, obeying a traffic signal on Gratiot, inadvertently stopped his car in such a way as to prevent Turpin from crossing a side street.

"Dummy, if you were not so crazy you could pull up and let me pass," Turpin reportedly told Pearcy. When Pearcy took exception to this remark, Turpin responded, "I could jerk you out [of your car]. I'm an officer. I'm Turpin. Everybody knows Turpin."

"I was made to feel very humiliated," stated Pearcy, "and my wife being in delicate condition was made so nervous we feared for her. My five little children in the car with me were frightened and crying."

Turpin's nickname was inspired by the silent-film star, Ben Turpin. While Officer Turpin didn't have the comic actor's famous crossed eyes, he did unintentionally engage in the same kind of crude slapstick. On May 31, 1934, for example, officers were dispatched to Atwater and Chene streets to break up a ruckus caused when Turpin and a female friend were caught off-guard in his car. According to police reports, three passersby, "suspecting that a sexual intercourse was taking place, remarked, 'Give it to her, big boy.'" Turpin, trousers and revolver in hand, held the trio at gunpoint until "he was convinced that [they had learned] they could not get away with their smart remarks."

Even Turpin's legitimate arrests often involved dubious judgment and the questionable use of gunplay. Once he was escorting a woman to the Third Precinct lockup when the prisoner broke and ran. It being the end of a long day, Turpin was in no mood to give chase. Instead, he took aim with one of his revolvers and shot the heel off the woman's shoe, bringing her down.

On another occasion, Turpin spotted a moonshiner named Charles Jackson unloading two cans of hooch from his car. Turpin made the arrest.

"I'll carry the cans," suggested Jackson, "and put them in the back of the car for you. Then we can go to police headquarters."

Turpin was agreeable. Jackson bowed, got into the car, and then fled out the opposite door. Turpin immediately pursued him. After an extended chase, Turpin fired three shots, the last of which hit Jackson in the leg. While all this was taking place, a third person drove away with the car and the evidence.

So it went, as Turpin bounced erratically between buffoonery, bravery, and bullying. In 1939 he was made a detective, earning applause from his white superiors for cracking down on the city's black citizens.

But Turpin was far from being a white man's lackey. As Southern blacks and whites poured into the city during World War II to man the defense plants, racial relations became more and more strained. Turpin increasingly found himself protecting blacks who were being harassed by whites. On one occasion he ordered a paddy wagon from the Hunt Street Station to rescue several blacks trapped by a white mob at the Catherine Theatre.

On Sunday, June 20, 1943, Detroit exploded. A fistfight between white sailors and black teenagers on Belle Isle spilled over onto the bridge to the mainland. An apocryphal story spread through Black Bottom that a black woman and her baby had been thrown off the bridge, provoking attacks on whites by blacks. By Monday morning, a mob of some ten thousand whites roamed Woodward Avenue, overturning cars and dragging blacks off streetcars. Some Black Bottom residents retaliated by flushing out and beating up whites who wandered into the wrong neighborhood.

A car burns on Woodward during the 1943 race riot. (Walter P. Reuther Library)

"The 1943 riot was a *race* riot," emphasizes Fred Williams, whose recollections include whites stoning streetcars. "In 1967, the riot was just blacks and whites looting. In 1943, blacks and whites were at each other's throats."

Five thousand federal troops were sent in to restore order. By the end of the riot, thirty-four people had been killed. Twenty-five of those were blacks, seventeen of whom were killed by white policemen. Several had been shot in the back.

In the midst of this madness, Ben Turpin earned his legendary status among some of Black Bottom's residents. According to Pearl Johnson, "Blacks lost respect for black officers in general during the time of the riot. Black officers had to turn in their guns and were assigned to neighborhoods not affected by the riot." Turpin, however, went around to blacks' homes, convincing residents to stay inside and out of harm's way, said Johnson.

"The white cops were wholesale arresting blacks and carrying them off to the bathhouse on Belle Isle," recalled Fred Ross. "They killed some of them there. Turpin saved a lot of blacks, moving them out of trouble."

Turpin earned nothing for his actions except the enmity of certain white officers, who resented his interference. For his part, Turpin went back to manhandling people loitering on street corners and chasing down thugs. Sometime during this period, he took to wearing a homemade bulletproof vest, which fit awkwardly under his suit jacket. Though he'd always been suspicious of people, after the riots he became paranoid at times, once moving into the attic of the Hunt Street Station because of threats made on his life.

"There were a lot of people who disliked Ben, so it was probably necessary for him to wear the vest and carry all the weapons," Ross said. "He wasn't going to get left out, no way."

What finally brought down Detroit's most feared cop was not a bullet but diabetes. In June 1952, Turpin retired from the force at the age of fifty-four and was made an honorary special deputy sheriff by the Wayne County Prosecutor's Office, the first time such an honor had been bestowed.

Turpin spent the next ten years as a hotel detective, twice helping police make busts. He and his second wife, Margaret, lived in a small house on Jay Street, though his behavior became more erratic. He would answer the door brandishing a revolver and wearing his bulletproof vest.

Turpin lost both of his legs to diabetes. On August 8, 1962, he died in Harper Hospital of a stroke. His wife, blind and virtually penniless—Turpin's pension expired when he died—moved into the Brewster projects. Williams and other black officers took care of her until her death in the late 1970s. By then, thieves had already stolen Ben Turpin's pearl-handled revolvers from his widow, and the city had elected its first black mayor, Coleman A. Young, who gained office by promising to end police brutality in Detroit.

Bill Kennedy (*left*) hams it up with entertainer Jimmy Durante in 1967. (Author's Collection)

SEVENTEEN
Showtime with Bill Kennedy

For three decades, the flamboyant movie-show host and former B-movie actor was a welcome guest in Detroit living rooms.

How popular was Bill Kennedy? Consider this somber but illuminating anecdote. One autumn afternoon in 1963, the station switchboard at CKLW Channel 9 in Windsor lit up. Word was spreading that "Kennedy's been shot," and in the midst of the confusion some panicky and misinformed viewers on both sides of the Detroit River assumed it was the afternoon movie host, not the American president, who had been struck down.

Willard A. "Bill" Kennedy, whose engagingly lofty manner was more regal than presidential, was undeniably a local institution. As "Detroit's Hollywood connection" from the mid-1950s through the early '80s, the flamboyant, name-dropping showman offered viewers an entertaining blend of old films, celebrity interviews, Hollywood gossip, and movie trivia. At the peak of its popularity, Bill Kennedy's afternoon program regularly attracted one of every three people watching television in Metro Detroit. "Bill was unique," said Sonny Eliot, a good friend and frequent substitute host. "He had this acerbic sense of humor. And he knew more about how Hollywood operated, especially in the old days, than any other person I knew."

Prior to anchoring himself in the Detroit marketplace, Kennedy had spent fifteen years adrift in Hollywood, trying to establish himself as a star. He never made it, though one would never know by the way the former B-movie actor carried himself on the cheap paneled set he presided over, a clipboard in one hand, a cigarette in the other. "When he was doing his show," Eliot said, "he had this haughty, almost arrogant and larger-than-life personality, but he was so knowledgeable. And you always had the sense that it was all tongue-in-cheek, that Bill was just playing another role."

"From the moment he sashays onto the set (which looks like a room-addition den designed by Mr. Belvedere), his arrogance is apparent," an admiring critic once wrote. "As the theme music fades, the star announces, 'MY picture today is . . .' He makes it sound as if he'd written, produced and directed it. It's an engaging arrogance, though—the familiar arrogance of someone who truly loves motion pictures."

Detroit's longtime ticket to the movies was born in Cleveland Heights, Ohio, on June 27, 1908. His father owned three freighters used to ship coal up and down the Detroit River and around the Great Lakes. "I was so fascinated with movies, even when I was a kid," Kennedy remembered. "I loved watching Rudolph Valentino. John Gilbert was another great star, and I loved him, too. The first fan letter I ever wrote was to Fatty Arbuckle, and he sent me back a picture. I used to just love the silent movies when I was a kid. I always wished I could be an actor."

Kennedy attended Catholic schools and then spent two years at Assumption College before dropping out. As a young man he drove a milk truck and worked as a stockbroker, "neither of which was rewarding in any sense of the word," he said. In 1935 he broke into radio as a staff announcer for Cleveland station WTAM, then moved to Detroit's WWJ the following year. There he was the assistant to station manager and Tigers broadcaster Edwin "Ty" Tyson, a position that allowed him to indulge his lifelong interest in baseball. Kennedy had worked at Cleveland's Dunn Field as a youngster in the 1920s. Babe Ruth had been one of Kennedy's boyhood idols, and as a movie host he often kept a poster of the Bambino up on the set during baseball season. He also made sure to show the 1949 baseball movie *It Happens Every Spring* each year on opening day.

Kennedy was with WWJ for four years before landing a job as the Broadway-Hollywood news reporter for KHJ in Hollywood. One day, Hal Wallace of Warner Bros. heard Kennedy's voice on his car radio and invited him in for a screen test. Kennedy was given a scene from a play titled *The Second Man*. While sitting in a chair in the makeup room, Humphrey Bogart and Errol Flynn strolled in.

"They said to me, 'What's your name?'" recalled Kennedy. "After I told them Flynn turns to Bogie and says, 'You know, this guy looks like Jeffrey Lynn—with balls.'

"Then Bogie says to me, 'What scene are you doing?' I told him and he said, 'I did that show on Broadway.' I said, 'Well, that's great. I'm feeling pretty superstitious. Today's Friday the thirteenth and I'm going to do a test.' They said, 'Don't worry, you'll make it.'

"Later I thought: 'Wow, this is great. They sign me here at Warner Bros., I'm already a pal of Errol Flynn, I'm already a pal of Bogart.' After I got signed, whenever Bogart saw me he'd just say, 'Hi, kid.' Flynn was a little more friendly. I did a picture with him called *Northern Pursuit,* but he didn't remember seeing me in the makeup department at all, I'm sure."

Kennedy was the perfect leading man type: dark hair, tall, a strong jaw, a good physique, and a wonderfully masculine voice. However, his acting was suspect. He appeared in small roles in such movies as *Rhapsody in Blue, Escape in the Desert, Unchained,* and *Now, Voyager.* All told, he worked in about sixty films between 1940 and 1955, including a pair with Bette Davis. "I was one of her lovers in *Mrs. Skeffington,*" he said. "I got along very well with her, though as a person she was a miserable woman."

For all the romance attached to films, the actual process of moviemaking was not particularly glamorous, Kennedy conceded. "A lot of actors don't like it because there's too much sitting around between set-ups," he once said. "As far as I was concerned, I loved it. I loved meeting people on the set, like Ingrid Bergman and stars like that. She was terrific, just friendly as hell."

As Thierache the executioner, Kennedy burned Bergman at the stake in the 1948 film *Joan of Arc*. "Of course, I uttered one of the classic lines of all time in that movie," Kennedy recalled. "It was: 'We need some more fagots over here.' This was the big climactic scene of the whole movie. The director was Victor Fleming, a real martinet. He had directed *Gone With the Wind* and *The Wizard of Oz*. This guy was God. Anyway, I told

As Thierache the executioner, Kennedy burned Ingrid Bergman at the stake in *Joan of Arc*. (Ed Golick Collection)

him, 'Mr. Fleming, this "fagots" has a different meaning today than it had in the fifteenth century.' He said, 'Just go ahead and do the part or we'll get somebody else.' So I did it. I read the line, and when we had the preview in Pasadena the audience fell down laughing when they heard it. Only then did they cut it out of the movie."

As a movie host, Kennedy always demonstrated a special affinity for B Westerns and their stars, having appeared in many low-budget sagebrush sagas himself. During his career he was punched out by Gene Autry, rode with the Cisco Kid, got the drop on Johnny Mack Brown, and chased bad guys across the frozen North as a member of the Royal Canadian Mounted Police.

"In those days, when you tried to get a job in a western, you'd be asked three questions," he recalled. "Number one: 'Can you ride a horse?' You have to be able to do your own fast mounts. They made those movies so fast—six, seven days—they didn't tolerate any mistakes. You've got to make your mount and get the hell out of town, you know, with the posse following.

Kennedy (*second from left*) played a crooked real estate agent in the 1948 low-budget Western *Triggerman*, starring Johnny Mack Brown. (Author's Collection)

"Number two: 'Can you do your own fight scenes?' You had to do your own fight scenes because it saved them the cost of a stunt man.

"Then finally: 'Can you act?' That was third."

In *Silver City Bonanza,* Kennedy played the villainous Monk Monroe who knifed a blind man to steal his land but then had to contend with the victim's vengeful seeing-eye dog. "They paid me four hundred dollars for each dogfight scene," he said, "but only three hundred and fifty for my acting. That should have told me something."

Kennedy's parents never encouraged his acting career, considering it a precarious living, and Kennedy admitted that they were right. His original five-year contract with Warner Bros. called for three hundred dollars a week, a decent salary. Later it doubled. "The highest amount I ever made for one year was sixty-eight thousand dollars," he said. "That was pretty good in those days, but that was for only one year. After my contract with Warner's expired, I dropped way down. You could never make any plans because you never knew how much you were going to make as a freelance actor."

In between jobs, Kennedy sold aluminum siding door to door. "That was the most miserable job I ever had. A couple of other actors and myself would do that, but we'd always go to a town outside of Los Angeles so we wouldn't run into somebody that we knew. I managed to make a little money doing that, but it was a heart-breaking job. I didn't do very well at it and I didn't feel very good about it. There was so much misery involved. You know, you get rejection enough in show business, but when you're a door-to-door salesman you really get rejected: a door slam in the face or a dog chasing you over the fence."

Nearing forty, and desperate for a breakout role, Kennedy plunged eighty thousand dollars of his own savings into producing the 1945 movie *The People's Choice.* He convinced several friends to invest in it, as well. Kennedy played Abner Snell, a small-town radio announcer running for councilman who, in the end, wins the girl and the election. "*The People's Choice* is a corny film, but in a good way," said pop culture aficionado Ed Golick, who has been operating a web site dedicated to Detroit's television icons since 2002. "It's Bill's only leading role, and he really chews up the scenery. Most prints were struck in 16-millimeter, so that small towns with no movie theater could show the film in the school gymnasium, or at night on the side of a building. Sounds like a good idea, but the film bombed." Kennedy went bankrupt. *The People's Choice* remained a sore point for the rest of his life. It was the reason he had to continue working, he'd say.

Kennedy returned to Detroit in 1952, where he created an afternoon movie show called *Your Hollywood Host* on WWJ Channel 4. The show was canceled after a year when NBC brought in a whole lineup of network programs. Out of a job, Kennedy went back to Los Angeles, becoming the anchorman at KNXT. That job lasted two years until he was replaced by former war correspondent Clete Roberts, who became a fixture on Los Angeles TV.

While in California, Kennedy did a lot of voice-over work, including narrating the now famous opening of *The Adventures of Superman* TV series. "I did the narration standing on the stage with a microphone in

Rock Hudson (*left*) plugging *The Lawless Breed* in a January 1953 visit to the set of *Your Hollywood Host*, a short-lived program on WWJ Channel 4 that was the forerunner to Kennedy's afternoon movie shows on CKLW and WKBD. (Author's Collection)

front of me while producer Bob Maxwell was in the back, fiddling with the controls. The equipment in those days was not sophisticated at all. In terms of putting sound and picture together, you had to do it all the way through. There was no stopping. If you stopped, you couldn't pick it up, so it was back to the start again. I'd hear the squeak of the locomotive wheels, then the gun, and all of that had to be exactly synchronized with my lines: 'Faster than a speeding bullet! More powerful than a locomotive! Able to leap tall buildings in a single bound! Superman . . . strange visitor from another planet who came to Earth with powers and abilities far beyond those of mortal men! Superman . . . who can change the course of mighty rivers, bend steel in his bare hands, and who, disguised as Clark Kent, mild-mannered reporter for a great metropolitan newspaper, fights a never-ending battle for truth, justice, and the American way!'"

Kennedy and the producer worked from midnight until 4 a.m. to get it right. "I made a big mistake," said Kennedy, who also appeared in the opening episode. "I got a pretty big fee for doing the narration—I think it was three hundred and fifty bucks—but I should have insisted on screen credit. I had no idea the show would be as big as it became."

That Kennedy's last role in Hollywood was a bit part in the 1955 film *I Died a Thousand Times* seems entirely appropriate, given his checkered acting career. After shooting that role, he came back to Detroit for good. "I was smart enough to understand that once you reach a certain age, the chances of becoming a movie star are about a million to one," he said.

At the time, Abner Wolf, a grocery chain, was shopping around for someone to present a movie every Friday. Kennedy used the same formula he had earlier established with *Your Hollywood Host*—news items, guests, answering phone-in questions—and pitched the idea to CKLW. In 1956, *Bill Kennedy Showtime* debuted, and it was an immediate success.

"We had a lot of black and white, old-fashioned movies," he said. "I think we had a great selection. I don't know how many hundreds of pictures by Warner Bros. that we had signed up. A lot of RKO movies, too. I had *The Maltese Falcon, The Treasure of the Sierra Madre, Angels with Dirty Faces*. I had all the Jimmy Cagney movies with Bogie." This was an era when the availability of classic movies was limited. Film buffs could only dream of such innovations as VCRs, Blockbuster Video, NetFlix, DVDs, cable networks, and On-Demand. If the host happened to have had a bit part in the film, viewers were in for a treat. Kennedy would be identified throughout the film by a circle or arrow superimposed on the screen.

"I never considered myself as important as the movie I was showing," Kennedy insisted, "but having been in Hollywood, I knew movies. I knew how they were made and I knew stories about the actors who played in them. And I was honest. We showed a lot of great movies, but we also had a lot of turkeys, too. Whenever I had a lousy movie to show, that's when I had a lot of fun." The CKLW studios overlooked the Detroit River. Kennedy would inquire over the air if the crew on a passing freighter was watching the show, and often the ship's captain would blow the whistle to indicate yes. Once Kennedy read a long letter from a viewer that mocked his Hollywood career. When he was finished, he looked straight into the camera and said, "Better a has-been than a never-was."

One afternoon a bellhop called Kennedy from the Wardell Hotel on Woodward Avenue at Kirby. "Hey, Bill," he said, "you know Cary Grant's here?" Grant was in Detroit visiting actress Dyan Cannon. Kennedy got the room number and dialed the hotel switchboard. "Give me room 716," he asked.

"And who answers the phone but Cary Grant!" Kennedy recalled. "I said, 'Don't hang up the phone, Mr. Grant. I'm Bill Kennedy. Would you please turn on Channel 9? I'm talking to you from CKLW, Channel 9 in Windsor.' So he turns on Channel 9 and he sees me and we had a hell of a conversation. We talked about everything. It was a great moment."

Grant knew Kennedy from working with him in the 1943 war epic *Destination Tokyo*. "I was an officer on a submarine, and in this one scene with him I had to make this long speech," Kennedy said. "It was so long I couldn't handle it. They were on the verge of throwing me out and finding another actor. That's when Grant told them to rewrite the speech; it was too long. On the fourth take I finally got it right. That shows you the kind of person Cary Grant was. He didn't have to do that for me."

Above: Jeannette MacDonald visits Kennedy's show in 1959. At the time the actress was appearing in *Blythe Spirit* at the Cass Theatre. (Author's Collection)

Right: Visitors to the Windsor set of *Bill Kennedy Showtime* between 1956 and 1969 included Nat King Cole in 1958 (*top right*) and Liberace (*bottom right*) in 1960. (Author's Collection)

The movie host was in top form while schmoozing with the stream of celebrities who passed through the studio, their chats giving viewers an inside look at stardom and show business. Most were performing at local supper clubs and theaters, such as the Elmwood Casino, the Roostertail, or the Northland Theater. One afternoon Diana Ross and the Supremes crossed the river to perform their Motown hit "Come See About Me" in the studio. On another occasion Kennedy brought together Clayton Moore, television's Lone Ranger, and Brace Beemer, who had been the Masked Man on radio, for a chummy conversation that—as often was the case—was more fascinating than that day's movie. Jimmy Durante, Liberace, Jayne Mansfield, George Raft, Barbara Stanwyck, Jack Palance, Ray Charles, Ramon Navarro, Hedda Hopper, and Nat King Cole were just a few of the many stars who stopped by over the years. "Of course it was a great boost to the show to have someone like Debbie Reynolds or Clint Eastwood on," Kennedy said. "But they got great exposure, too. I remember when Jeannette MacDonald, the famous MGM star, was appearing in *Blythe Spirit* at the Cass Theater in Detroit. This was in 1959. The first three days at the Cass were dismal, until her regular appearances on my show took effect. Then she was a smash." The play, originally booked for a week, was extended to a full month.

Some guests Kennedy didn't care for, however. The annoyingly antic Jerry Lewis was one. Frank Sinatra Jr., whom Kennedy privately described as "a kid with no talent who had the attitude of someone who did," was another. When it came to old cowboy stars like Allan Lane, Kennedy was loyal to a fault. Robert Blake—who had played an Indian boy named Little Beaver in the *Red Ryder* western series of the '40s—once made the mistake of criticizing Lane on air. Kennedy took umbrage. When the show returned following a commercial break, viewers discovered that the afternoon's featured guest had left the studio.

According to Bob Cook, who worked as an engineer at CKLW from 1966 to 1969, the devil-may-care Kennedy was always a bit nervous before shows. In a lengthy, loving posting on a web site hosted by long-time Kennedy fan Jim Rees, Cook recalled: "He had a special foam mat that had about twenty different life-size women's breasts. It was given to him by one of his Hollywood friends. He always put it under the desk and he would play with it with his shoes off. One day we stole it for the fun of it and he went absolutely berserk. He refused to go on the set or do a show until it was returned. That joke backfired and brought out the only time he went 'off the deep end.' He had certain rituals while doing the show. He never used cue cards and all the shows were LIVE as we only had two video recorders and they were used to tape network feeds. This never bothered him.

"He had a fabulous memory. He knew every movie and every actor verbatim. It was amazing. We tried to stump him all the time but we never did. When he forgot he usually was able to remember by the following day. He never cheated. He could read over the lines to a one-minute commercial and do the commercial on a single pass. He was always at ease in front of a camera or while interviewing a person. He was able to make guests feel at home."

Despite Kennedy's gruff persona, Cook and others remember him as a thoughtful man and a gracious host. "When he traveled by air he always bought a life insurance policy for the studio crew and mailed it back to the station," Cook said. "He always did favors for the TV crew. He also held many birthday parties and paid for these out of his own pocket."

Kennedy was a heavy smoker, enjoyed his liquor, and, over the years, had become an expert pool player. The latter, he said, was the result of killing time in Hollywood while waiting for the phone to ring. He had three of his own children and two stepchildren from two marriages. His second marriage, in 1971, was to Suzanne "Suzy" Wiggins King, whose great-grandfather, the flamboyant "Pop" Wiggins, had founded the famous Temple Theater in Detroit.

As one of Detroit's most recognizable figures, Kennedy enjoyed playing the role of a bon vivant. He lived in a stately house at the corner of Beaupre and Hillcrest in Grosse Pointe Farms and drove around in his 1962 Rolls Royce and a '57 Thunderbird (the latter of which was a gift from the Ford family), flaunting his celebrity but never his money. Unlike some of his ruder contemporaries, he had time for everybody. And he exuded the sense that he was reveling in the adulation and approval that had eluded him in Hollywood.

Detroit mayor Jerry Cavanagh (*right*) was a guest on the first show of *Bill Kennedy at the Movies*, which debuted in the Southfield studios of WKBD on September 9, 1969, and ran for fourteen years. (Author's Collection)

In 1969, the contract of the highest-paid employee at CKLW was not renewed. The Canadian government had passed a "local content" law that required stations to meet Canadian programming quotas. "It was a lot of jealousy, basically," Kennedy said. "Why should an American make all that money?" Kennedy shopped around, playing a couple of Detroit stations off each other, before signing a deal with WKBD Channel 50. The renamed *Bill Kennedy at the Movies* debuted on September 9, 1969, from the station's Southfield studios. It lasted fourteen years and frequently outdrew the soap operas on the other channels.

Part of the charm of Kennedy's show was that, even though technology and viewers' expectations were rapidly changing, it was always mid-century on his set. "In this day and age, when even network news shows use squeeze zooms and special effects until the viewer is seasick, it's refreshing to hear Bill Kennedy request a shot of the picture 'on the easel,'" wrote Mary Ann Watson, a telecommunications instructor at Michigan State University. "The production values of *At the Movies* never transcend the level of TV Directing 101. Camera operators sneeze and

Kennedy blesses them. He can't remember what's coming up next, so he asks." To Watson, who thought Kennedy "a Detroit classic," the best parts of the show were the phone-in segments:

> *He makes you feel there really is such a thing as a DUMB question . . . and the disembodied voices don't let him down. One caller wants to know if Cheryl Ladd and David Ladd are related in any way other than their former marriage. With a furrowed brow Kennedy rolls his eyes and says, "They had relations when they were married." The wisecrack is wasted on the confused caller.*
>
> *Sometimes children call. Sometimes regulars. Sometimes nervous first-timers. And Kennedy abuses them all. He doesn't hesitate to tell his viewers to "Speak up—project!" in the way an imposing teacher intimidates a bashful pupil. He bristles when he's challenged and lightly dismisses questions he can't answer right off the bat. If he can supply information that's related—but not asked for—he'll press the caller with a one-uppity "Did you know that?" No one has ever accused Bill Kennedy of resorting to tact when a caller is using up too much time. "This is a question and answer period," he testily reminds someone about to embark on a personal-experience story of their own.*

Watson's "An Ode to . . . Bill Kennedy?" appeared in the December 1982 issue of *Monthly Detroit,* the same month the seventy-four-year-old movie host completed a move from Grosse Pointe to the balmy climes of Palm Beach. Kennedy, at that point semi-retired, agreed to do the Sunday show from a Florida studio while Sonny Eliot hosted the weekday movies. The new arrangement lasted just one unhappy year. "I didn't like the set-up," Kennedy later explained. "Say I'd be showing a Bette Davis movie and, as usual, I'd have her pictures up on the easel. I had to send the pictures to Detroit to be photographed, along with a tape of the show, and they were getting them all mixed up. It just wasn't coordinated." Worse, station management tried to change Kennedy's theme song, "Just in Time" from the 1956 musical *Bells Are Ringing.* "I thought, 'Jesus, you don't change Bob Hope's theme song just because he's in Germany.' You'd never change 'Thanks for the Memories,' but they tried to change mine."

Kennedy's last show was taped poolside of his Palm Beach villa on Sunday, December 14, 1983. He showed *The Sons of Katie Elder,* starring John Wayne and Dean Martin. "It wasn't one of the Duke's better movies," Kennedy said. "I would've preferred to do *Red River* or *She Wore a Yellow Ribbon.* But I got a 15 rating for that final show. It felt very good going out that way." At the end of the show Kennedy said "Sayonara" and melodramatically tossed his champagne glass into the pool. "And do you know that for several months after that, I kept on having the same dream?" he said later. "I'd be going to work to do the show, but something was always keeping me from getting to the studio. My car would stall out or I'd get in an accident or I'd be in the hospital. Sometimes I'd get to the studio but they wouldn't let me in."

A local station in Florida approached him to host a show similar to the one he'd had in Detroit. "But in the way of paying, they think sunshine is money," he said. "The attitude is, as long as you're living down here, you shouldn't expect to be paid much. I think they wanted to pay me one hundred dollars a day to do it. Which is better than a kick in the ass, but it's not the kind of money I want to work for." Instead he concentrated on enjoying daily swims in the pool and visits from the grandchildren.

Kennedy rarely returned to Detroit. His "fabulous files," the voluminous files containing hundreds of thousands of clippings and movie stills, were donated to the Detroit Institute of Arts in 1987. In 1990, he participated in a pair of Bill Kennedy specials to help celebrate WKBD's twenty-fifth anniversary. Later, he was awarded an honorary Emmy by the Detroit chapter of the National Academy of Television Arts and Sciences. He remained fondly remembered by countless Detroiters, who had enjoyed having him as a guest in their living rooms throughout decades of remarkable technological and social change. When Kennedy was laid up in a Palm Beach hospital with a broken hip, loyal fans flooded his room with 2,500 cards and letters. Rose Kennedy, patriarch of the famous political family, was in the hospital at the same time. "She only got ten letters, and she was wondering, 'Who the hell is this guy,'" Kennedy recalled with a laugh. "Nobody on the staff had ever heard of me."

Despite the inevitable mellowing that accompanied his advancing years, status remained immensely important to "the other Kennedy."

He never forgot his days of working as a lowly paid booth announcer, a sack of sandwiches at his feet, repeatedly saying, "We'll be right back . . . ," when he returned to Detroit after failing to make it in Hollywood. In 1992, when a writer in a Detroit magazine mistakenly referred to him living in the considerably less affluent city of West Palm Beach, Kennedy blew a gasket. "I was broke in Detroit many times—the last time in 1952—so I *want* people to know that I live in a Palm Beach villa worth two million dollars," he complained in a letter to the writer.

> *Through some marvelous real estate deals that my wife Suzy conducted—she has a tremendous instinct for deals—we have enhanced our financial position ten times over what we had in 1983. Also, we have been accepted socially in Palm Beach, mostly because of my wife, who was a socialite back in Grosse Pointe Shores. Of course, I can be amiable at times, too.*
>
> *I guess only a failure would want his success to be known. Because I want it to be known! I have heard it said that living well is the best revenge. Not for me—I want it known to a lot of bastards in Detroit and Hollywood that Bill Kennedy made it big in Palm Beach. Many others with piles of money have failed to crack society down here.*

To Kennedy's credit, social climbing took a backseat to meeting the needs of his fans. He continued to answer the scores of letters he received each month, often writing pages of longhand in response to a single question. The many years of smoking gradually caught up with him, as in his eighties he battled throat cancer and emphysema. Word of his illness caused another flood of letters—and tears. "Some made me cry when they told me how much my shows meant to them, and that they still miss me after all these years," he told *Free Press* columnist Bob Talbert.

Kennedy was irascible to the end. During his final month of hospitalization, when he was too weak to talk or summon a nurse, he relied on a police whistle someone had given him. "When he didn't think the nurse was getting there fast enough after he buzzed for one, he'd blow the whistle until they came—waking everybody up in the middle of the night," Suzy said. "He wasn't going to give up his whistle."

Kennedy died at home on the morning of January 28, 1997. He was eighty-eight years old. He was cremated and his ashes were given to a family member. While Kennedy's hauteur often was brought up in the appreciative remarks that followed, longtime friends who knew "the real Bill" defended him. "That was not it at all," insisted Sonny Eliot. "He always said the arrogance just covered up his own insecurity."

In Kennedy's latter years, a cult of Asian film buffs sprang up around a 1945 serial he starred in called *The Royal Mounted Rides Again*. The thought of his character, a Canadian Mountie, palavering with cowpokes in Taiwanese had held a certain absurd appeal for the old hambone. "Now that," he said, "is show business."

EIGHTEEN

A Week in Hell

During one week in the summer of 1936, a scorching heat wave turned Detroit into a virtual furnace and claimed at least 364 lives.

The heat was on, and so was Susie. For the ninth time that day, a broiling hot Sunday, the headline actress of the Jo Mendi Theatre at the Detroit Zoo gave a crowd of admirers a gracefully vigorous show, roller skating, pedaling a bicycle, pushing a scooter, walking a tightwire, and performing other tricks with her fellow chimpanzees.

She was adorable, she was beloved, and by the following morning she was dead. The six-year-old chimpanzee had succumbed to heat exhaustion after an entire day of nearly nonstop performing. "With her checkered skirt and blouse awry, she was carried from the caged arena," reported the *Detroit News,* "a limp and hairy heroine of public demand."

Mary Lou, another chimpanzee, also collapsed, but she recovered. Zoo director John Millen admitted afterward that it "really was too hot for Susie and the others to go on, especially for nine performances." But all of the chimps "were good troupers, and they were willing when they saw the great crowd that had gathered Sunday to see them perform." Millen insisted that the zoo was "going to hunt up another educated chimp to fill her place for the rest of the season. In other words, the show will go on as usual, the way Susie would want it to. She was a trouper."

For man and for beast, it was the week from hell, those seven scorching days in Depression-era Detroit when the populace was subjected to a roasting of unprecedented intensity. On July 12, 1936, the same day Susie was stricken, the heat killed sixty people across the city, pushing the toll to 122 after five straight days of hundred-degree temperatures. The majority of victims died inside their un-air-conditioned homes or shortly after being admitted to the hospital with an overtaxed heart or aching head. Most were elderly people, though infants and adults in the prime of life also were struck down. On this Sunday the victims included Betty Lou Crawford, a fourteen-month-old girl who passed away from heat prostration at Children's Hospital, and twenty-three-year-old Patricia Mezzole, who died in St. Mary's Hospital from a heat-induced heart attack. Thirty-four-year-old Walter Balko was found slumped in his car outside his home on Greeley Avenue. "He was badly sunburned and died of internal hemorrhage," reported the *Free Press.*

But that was only the beginning of the dying. Over the next two torrid days, until the run of triple-digit readings finally snapped, the body count exploded, with residents at one point passing away at the rate of one man, woman, or child every ten minutes. Hospital corridors were filled to overflowing, hospital corridors were crammed with victims and shrieking relatives, and even the mad were driven insane, as some psychiatric patients—convinced that they were in the grip of a cold spell—fought with attendants to remain bundled in blankets. Medical examiners conducting the never-ending stream of autopsies ran out of white sheets to cover the bodies. "A great city," declared the *Detroit Times,* "is dying of the heat."

Detroit has endured other notable heat waves. In 1953, for example, residents sweltered and pavement buckled as temperatures hit 90°F for eleven consecutive days. That sticky stretch was surpassed by a dozen straight days of 90°F-plus heat in 1964. The entire summer of 1998 remains the warmest on record, with daytime highs and nighttime lows averaging out to an uncomfortable 74.5°F.

However, the great heat wave of 1936 came at a time when air-conditioning in cars, homes, businesses, and municipal buildings was virtually unknown. Cooling centers and better-informed public health measures were decades in the future. Prior to 1936, the city had never experienced

Detroiters do their best to cool off at Waterworks Park on July 10, 1936, in the midst of a record heat wave. (Walter P. Reuther Library)

two consecutive days of triple-digit heat, at least not in the sixty-three years that the U.S. Weather Bureau had been keeping records. In fact, since 1873 there had only been seven 100°F days ever recorded in Detroit—a total that in 1936 was equaled in one murderous week.

Of all the calamities Detroiters endured during the Great Depression—bank failures, factory closures, labor strife, political upheaval, the lawlessness of Prohibition—the killer heat wave of July 8–14, 1936, is the one least talked about. Its particulars are imprecisely remembered, if at all. To the citizens who lived through it, it was just one more extreme weather event that came, wreaked its havoc, and then left—a portion of one summer to be lumped in with all the other periods of unbearably hot and stuffy weather one encounters in a lifetime of summers. "We really didn't care about records," a retired roofing contractor said in 1986, reflecting on the fiftieth anniversary of the disaster. "Those are good days to forget and I mean that."

During the 1930s, the Southwest suffered drought conditions immortalized by the searing images of dust bowl farm families who appeared in *Life* magazine and in the travails of the fictional Joad clan in John Steinbeck's classic novel *The Grapes of Wrath,* which was made into a film of the same title. The human, economic, and environmental devastation wrought by the extreme weather seemed of a piece with all the other miseries that afflicted the country during the Depression.

However, in 1936 much of the country, including Detroit, appeared to be on the rebound. That year's July 4th weekend featured pleasant and clear weather, with an unprecedented number of people crossing the Ambassador Bridge into Canada. In those pre-Weather Channel days, most people were blissfully unaware that a mass of blast-furnace heat, steadily building in the Southwest and aided by an enormous high-pressure system off the West Coast, was headed their way. On July 6 the temperature reached a record-breaking 121 degrees in North Dakota, a harbinger of what was to soon hit Detroit.

The temperature was already in the low 80s°F when most Detroiters started work on the morning of Wednesday, July 8. By midafternoon the thermometer had officially hit 104.4°F, just shy of the all-time single-day mark of 104.6°F, set on July 24, 1934. The soaring temperature caught many by surprise, with men and women collapsing at work, at home, and on the street. One man was overcome by the heat while driving on Davison and crashed his car into the back of a truck.

Theodore Raulink was working on a farm at Ann Arbor Trail and Telegraph when he pitched over and died. George Boyle dropped dead inside the laundry he worked at on McGraw Avenue. Peter Kasmonos, a house painter, was rushed by taxi to Receiving Hospital, but by the time he was admitted it was too late. These three men, all in their forties, were the earliest known fatalities. By midnight there were at least five others.

On the following day, the thermometer topped out at 102°F, forcing many offices and factories to close by afternoon. A dozen more deaths were attributed to the heat. Harried weather bureau clerks answered every phone call by shouting "102 degrees" into the mouthpiece before hanging up. The federal forecaster said no relief was in sight. In fact, only the presence of some clouds, which deflected the sun's rays, kept Detroit from experiencing its highest-ever reading on Thursday. The entire midsection of the country, from Oklahoma to the Upper Midwest, was baking in record heat. Many communities set marks that, three-quarters of a century later, have yet to be broken, including the highest temperature ever recorded in Michigan: 112°F in Mio.

Hordes of people crowded playgrounds and city parks, looking for some relief in shade or any cool breezes to be found; others splashed in the warm waters of local lakes. The official temperature of the water in Lake St. Clair, at Mount Clemens, was a bathlike 80°F. Some people with plenty of time on their hands packed a lunch and bought an all-day pass on one of the Detroit-Windsor ferries, sailing back and forth on the Detroit River for hours. Health officials issued tips to the populace: don't overeat, and avoid fatty foods; don't overexert yourself or wear heavy or dark clothing; drink plenty of fluids, but be careful to drink ice-cold water slowly; and put a pinch of salt in each glass of water. Above all, they warned, don't worry how hot it is—an upset nervous system makes a person even more susceptible to sunstroke.

Friday, July 10, was the third straight day of triple-digit temperatures. Nineteen Detroiters died that day. Wrestling promoter Nick Londes canceled that evening's match between Vincent Lopez and Chief Little Wolf at Brodhead Naval Armory. "It's asking too much of fans to go inside this hot weather," he said. With people staying home, switchboard operators were kept unusually busy, handling about 1.25 million telephone calls, roughly thirty thousand more than normal. "People are phoning to break engagements because of the heat, to postpone dinner parties, to order goods instead of shopping for them," explained a phone company official.

Those who dared to drive were far more likely to have an accident in the extreme heat than during milder weather, the city's traffic director warned. "Don't drive if you are sleepy, don't drink too much beer, and keep your eyes on the street and not on the girls." The last was a sound bit of advice. The asphalt was softening, and the pavement in some places buckled; a four-foot mound at McNichols and Livernois frustrated motorists in all directions. The public works commissioner did his best to sound reassuring about any possible road hazards, saying the department wasn't looking for "any serious trouble until thermometers hit 220."

Detroit was nearly halfway there. The weekend was consistently, monotonously, and unmercifully hot: the thermometer officially registered 101°F on Friday, Saturday, and Sunday. The average person could do little more than take the punishment. One editorial referenced the recent Joe Louis–Max Schmeling bout. On June 19, Detroit's own "Brown Bomber" had been unpityingly pummeled by the German heavyweight while absorbing the first loss of his professional career. Citizens, "like Joe Louis from the fourth round on, must stay in there and take it," said the *Detroit News*. (Curiously, Louis's stepfather, Pat Brooks, the man who had raised him, died of a stroke on the second day of the heat wave; however, his death was not attributed to the weather.)

Meat sales plummeted while sales of lemons—used for lemonade, iced tea, and mixed drinks—skyrocketed. Seven freight cars' worth of lemons, about 700,000 overall, were quickly sold one day at the produce terminal. The price of lemons doubled, reaching a dime each; watermelons, the second most favorite summer fruit, sold for fifty cents apiece.

Cheating the heat required ingenuity. Some families who evidently didn't care about their electric bills turned their entire kitchens into improvised iceboxes. First, a family sealed all the windows and doors with paper. Next, they propped open the door of their refrigerator and placed a fan inside. Finally, they spread out a mattress and pillows on the kitchen floor, producing a "guaranteed" night of rest, said one practitioner. Other enterprising types placed a fifty-pound cake of ice in a bucket next to the bed and positioned a fan, strategically tilted, to blow over it.

Of course, for any of this to work, one first had to have a fan. At Ray Jewelry on Griswold, customers could purchase a $7.95 model on credit: 45 cents down, 50 cents a week. Shelves there and elsewhere were quickly emptied of the precious appliances while storeowners, anxious to replenish their stocks, desperately called wholesalers around the country. A man who was caught stealing a fan from Kinsel's drugstore insisted that he be allowed to bring it to his jail cell—a request the judge denied. The thief was right to worry about possible liquefaction. One day, with the mercury stuck above 100°F, the central heating plant accidentally turned on the radiators inside the top-floor lockup at police headquarters for several hours. The *Detroit News* reported the Albert Kahn–designed building actually had a cooling system installed when it was built, "but it never has worked. The only result ever attained by putting on the cooling system has been to blow soot out of the apertures and onto the faces of everyone in the building." Elsewhere, inmates at the Wayne County jail did time in relative comfort. "Guards and turnkeys at the correctly termed 'cooler' say the 261 prisoners are more comfortable than they are," the *Detroit Times* reported. "It seems the thick walls keep the heat out as well as the prisoners in."

"I lived in an apartment house on Cass then, so I know heat," said Helen (Malone) Dodd of Highland. She was seven years old in 1936. All the heat waves of her childhood blend into one composite memory of four walls acting as a kind of multistory brick oven, baking the renters within. "All the windows were thrown open, but that didn't do much good," she recalled. "We lived at the front of the building, overlooking Cass. I'd stay up into the wee hours of the morning, it was so hot, and I'd look out the bedroom window, just watching people. I saw lots of things that way, probably some things that a little girl shouldn't have."

Sometimes, on unbearably hot nights, the Malones gathered up blankets and pillows and headed for Cass Park, a block away, where a frazzled family could put down a blanket and pick up a breeze. Dodd assumes they did so in 1936. "We'd sleep out in the open. In a way it was kind of fun," she said. If friends and neighbors shared the same grassy venue, socializing among the adults and horseplay among the kids sometimes derailed the quest for serious shut-eye. Conversely, snoozing in the dark among a park full of strangers produced no nightmares, she says. "In those days there weren't any problems of people bothering you. Detroit was a different place back then."

Belle Isle was the nocturnal refuge of choice for a small army of sleep-deprived Detroiters carrying cots, hammocks, and blankets, but any grassy space would do, including one's own lawn. Sleeping outdoors, an innocuous activity, did lead to one unusual weather casualty. Earl Brown decided to bed down one night in the vacant lot next to his house

In the days before air conditioning, Detroiters often tried to beat the heat by sleeping outdoors. Belle Isle was a favorite communal sleepover. (Walter P. Reuther Library)

on Nevada; a short while later, the fifty-year-old man was run over by a car when his son pulled into the darkened space to park.

With so many people trying to find respite in the water, the number of drownings climbed. Two people drowned on Belle Isle while the water was crowded with waders. The body of a little boy who had disappeared while swimming with friends was recovered near the Grosse Pointe Farms municipal pier, not far from where his shoes had been found at the water's edge. The body of another missing Detroit youngster was recovered from Quarry Lake near Trenton. There were scores of drownings around the state. One victim was an off-duty Hamtramck fireman who, overcome by the heat, toppled off a boat while fishing at Marysville. Another man, swimming with his sister and a female friend in the Paw Paw River, was forced into a gut-wrenching decision. Unable to save both floundering women, he rescued his sister.

Despite such distressing news items, swimmers were not to be denied. "The fact that the Belle Isle beach closed at 9 o'clock meant nothing to heat-weary citizens," observed one reporter. "They merely scaled a 12-foot spiked fence and the river was theirs."

Maintaining decorum was a struggle in the heat. Bathing suits and sunsuits were fine for young children, and skinny-dipping (at least among boys) was tolerated in isolated lakes and streams, but adults dressed modestly in public. String bikinis were unheard of, and it was considered scandalous for a man to appear shirtless away from the beach. Inside the clammy municipal buildings, attorneys, judges, bailiffs, and court employees were required to keep robes, coats, and ties on. Only defendants were allowed to appear in shirtsleeves.

Store employees also remained professionally dressed. For women this meant a sausagelike confinement of girdles, slips, and stockings, though Hudson's and Crowley's at least offered workers and customers air-conditioning to ease the suffering. Few other stores did. The owner of the Elbel Music Company, declaring that it was "time to be sensible about men's clothing for summer," made front-page news by allowing employees at his Ann Arbor shop to wear short pants. This was quite a jolt in an era when men were expected to always wear shirts and slacks, no matter what the weather—and few adult males at that time wore shorts on any occasion. "I was fearful of the reaction of the public," Robert Elbel, Jr., told reporters, "but it has been received as a grand idea. If the hot weather continues I predict other stores in Ann Arbor and other places will fall in line."

A few knobby-kneed music store clerks aside, such a revolution was not forthcoming. Customs of dress remained firmly—and discomfortingly—in place. Detroit police not only continued to wear leather puttees and dark uniforms, but an inspection scheduled months in advance went ahead as planned. Patrolmen stood at attention in ten-pound wool overcoats and other winter gear while superiors determined whether an officer's clothing was good enough to last another year on the beat. A scheduled police courtesy course was jeopardized when "a lot of patrolmen said they didn't give a —— whether it was courteous or not, they wouldn't turn out for school in the current weather," reported the *Detroit Times.* A stern warning from the department's commissioner ended the revolt.

Main thoroughfares leading to Belle Isle and riverside parks were jammed with thousands of cars, causing waterfront communities to divert police officers to traffic duty, but most other streets were eerily empty. People chose to ride out the heat in basements, parks, saloons—anywhere away from pavement, though some Detroiters playfully fried eggs on curbs and sidewalks. Vapor lock became a big problem for motorists as the heat caused engines to stall.

Air-conditioned theaters, all sporting "It's cool inside" signage, were packed. Some movie houses stayed open all night, allowing folks to grab a few winks in the dark. The Eastown on Harper opened its lobby to perspiring housewives looking for someplace other than their kitchen to finish their ironing. Manager Joe LaRose said the lobby could accommodate as many as thirty ironing boards, maybe more. "And why not?" he said. "It's nice and cool for them to iron in the theater and it doesn't hurt me a bit. All they have to do is buy a ticket to get in." The women didn't even have to lug an ironing board with them; they were provided for free by a furniture company on Van Dyke. "I don't blame them," said the store's manager. "I'd like to stay there the rest of the day myself."

With people drinking more water, taking more baths, and sprinkling lawns (and themselves), the water department reported record usage. At its peak, the city was pumping 417 million gallons daily, enough to fill a ditch ten feet deep, a hundred feet wide, and ten miles long. Judging by local beer consumption during this same period, many would have loved to see such an imaginary trough filled with ice-cold Goebel's or Stroh's. It was estimated that thirsty Detroiters were drinking two million eight-ounce glasses of beer each day. A bartender drawing drinks inside an air-conditioned saloon on Kercheval collapsed, more likely from overwork than the heat.

Sandlot baseball games, always a big draw, were sparsely attended. The defending world champion Detroit Tigers were in the midst of a three-week road trip during the great heat wave of 1936, but catcher-manager Mickey Cochrane's boys didn't escape the wilting temperatures. The East Coast also was smothered by record readings. The concrete-and-steel ballparks that Charlie Gehringer, Goose Goslin, and company visited—

including Washington's Griffith Field, Philadelphia's Shibe Park, and New York's Yankee Stadium—held the heat like oversized skillets. All games were played in the afternoon, the hottest part of the day. Doubleheaders went on as scheduled.

Players, broiling in their wool uniforms, wore wet cabbage leaves under their caps to prevent sunstroke. Conditions were even more brutal for umpires, who were forced to wear the traditional dark suit and knotted tie no matter how hot and muggy it got. Trainers put oatmeal in the water bucket so that nobody would gulp too much and get cramps. After games, players quaffed generous amounts of cold beer to help replenish the dozen or more pounds they had lost running around the parched grass and dust-choked infield; at night they wrapped themselves in wet sheets and tossed and turned in their hotel beds.

The rising temperatures coincided with a modest winning streak by the underperforming Tigers. In New York, Tigers coach Ralph Perkins explained to a local columnist that Detroit was a hot-weather team. Why, speedball pitcher Schoolboy Rowe had just beaten the first-place Yankees. "He needs hot weather," Perkins said. "We have it now. He will be devastating, colossal, stupendous, from now until the first snowfall." The same held true for shortstop (and future city councilman) Billy Rogell, who was battling a slump. "He is the greatest hot-weather player in the world. In a record heat wave they would have to pick that fellow to play shortstop in the All-Star game—for both sides!" To the disappointment of their fans, the Tigers blew hot and cold all summer, ultimately finishing a distant second to the Yankees.

As the days wore on, the oppressive heat building up inside homes, apartments, and institutions reached intolerable levels. One double tragedy saw a seventy-four-year-old woman die inside her home on Magnolia Street; the following day her forty-two-year-old daughter passed away in the same house. Twenty-three people died on Saturday, July 11. On Sunday, the full scope of the catastrophe became evident. Eloise Hospital, which on a typical day recorded two deaths, reported that eighty-six patients had died since Wednesday. The superintendent explained that nearly all were elderly and already suffering physical disorders. "Usually

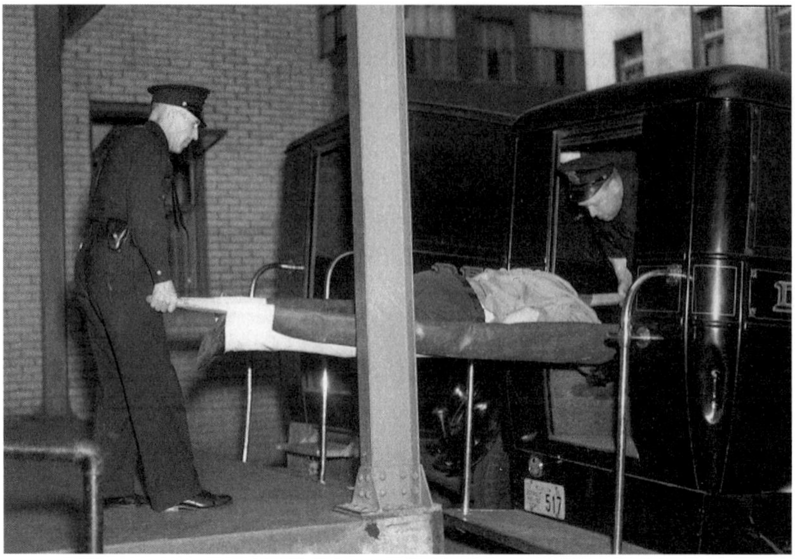

A heat victim is carried into Receiving Hospital on July 12, 1936. (Walter P. Reuther Library)

there is a letup, a breathing spell, when we have such hot weather, but now we have had no breathing spell for five days."

At Receiving Hospital, a steady stream of perspiring policemen and ambulance drivers brought the stricken in on stretchers. The *Detroit News* described the scene: "The admitting room and corridors of the hospital were filled with patients and weeping relatives, all screaming for attention. Doctors and nurses worked at [a] feverish pace, administering relief to prostration victims who were placed in ward rooms, on temporary cots in the corridors and even on benches." Victims, their chests heaving, mouths twitching, and faces beet red, were cooled down with wet cloths and given saline injections. The lucky ones gradually regained their sanity and were sent home after a day or two; the unlucky ones wound up at the Wayne County morgue.

At the morgue, mounting bodies threatened to overwhelm employees and overflow the building. For the first time in memory, the morgue was filled to its 280-crib capacity. Scores of other bodies lay on wheeled stretchers in the dark hallways, awaiting a final official verdict on cause of death. Medical examiners hurried to release bodies to undertakers, performing fifty autopsies on Sunday alone—five times the daily average. Meanwhile, phones rang incessantly, and attendants dealt with a mob of relatives anxious to identify and claim the bodies of loved ones. Never before, said Dr. W. D. Ryan, chief medical examiner since 1918, "has there been anything like this for such a protracted period." To speed the processing of victims, city treasurer Albert E. Cobo loaned the morgue several clerks from his office.

Monday's high was 100°F. The forecast called for "Continued warm, no immediate relief in sight." In each of the daily newspapers, long lists of the dead started on page one and jumped to inside pages. That was a different era in terms of thinking about animal welfare, so it's difficult to estimate how many overstressed horses and neglected pets were also dying in the heat, but to judge by anecdotal news items, the toll was considerable. At the Detroit Zoo, where Susie the chimp was literally worked to death, keepers marveled that animals from Arctic or moderate climates appeared less stressed by the heat than those from tropical regions.

Tuesday, July 14, brought more of the same draining, death-dealing heat. By midnight, another 144 Detroiters were gone, the second-highest twenty-four-hour toll in the city's history. Only the influenza pandemic of 1919 had claimed more victims on a single day. At 2:15 in the afternoon, the temperature hit an official 104.3°F. Once again, the city was on the cusp of setting a new all-time single-day high.

And then, seemingly with a snap of Mother Nature's fingers, the heat wave broke. Starting around three o'clock, the mercury began a steady slide. The temperature fell into the 90s . . . the 80s . . . and then the 70s, as a storm front moved in. Cool, blessed rain fell, symbolically dowsing Detroit's week in hell. By early the following morning, the weather bureau reported an official temperature of 62°F, an overnight free fall of forty-two degrees from Tuesday afternoon's high. Butchers "sold a record amount of steaks and chops," reported the *Detroit Times*. "Suddenly as the temperature dropped, the city discovered it was hungry. Thousands of housewives hastened home from parks to feed the family its first real meal in seven sweltering days."

The human cost was almost unprecedented in the city's long history; only cholera and influenza epidemics had ever been so lethal to the general public. Over the course of a week, during which the daily highs had averaged a sizzling 101.9°F, at least 364 Detroiters had died. (Across the river, twenty-two people died in thinly populated Windsor and surrounding Essex County.) Elsewhere around the state, an additional 206 people—many of them farmhands toiling in fields—had perished. Several million dollars' worth of crops had been ruined by the extreme heat. Nationally, some five thousand deaths were blamed on the heat, with Michigan's toll of 570 victims surpassed only by Ohio's.

Belle Isle, which had been packed with thousands of overnight campers, was practically deserted on the evening the killer heat wave passed. The few people who had planned to spend the night brought along extra blankets. The forecast called for cool temperatures, and they wanted to stay warm.

WILD WEATHER

Metro Detroit is no stranger to outlandish weather. Here's just a small sampling of the region's many extreme weather events.

Fluky Flakes

Detroiters should have suspected that Mother Nature was up to something in the spring of 1923: Easter that year fell on April Fool's Day. Six weeks later, on the afternoon of May 9, temperatures plunged some thirty degrees and a half-foot of snow fell on the city. By the following evening, the white stuff had melted, but it remains the latest significant spring snowstorm in local history. However, some random flakes were recorded on May 31, 1910, officially making that date the latest that any trace of snow has been known to fall on Detroit.

Bummer of a Summer

One of the strangest weather-related phenomena in history occurred in 1816, "the year without a summer." Throughout areas of Canada and the Northeast, snow fell in June, ponds iced over in July, and the gloomy cold killed crops and led many starving farmers to fear that some kind of Biblical apocalypse was at hand. England and Europe suffered famine and food riots, a bleakness that inspired British novelist Mary Shelley to write *Frankenstein*. It wasn't until almost a century later, in 1913, that scientists surmised that a series of volcanic eruptions in the Far East had spewed so much ash into the atmosphere that it blocked out the sun around much of the northern hemisphere. Southeastern Michigan was sparsely populated in 1816, hence the paucity of contemporary accounts, but modern meteorologists assume that the area experienced some of the same abnormalities of climate. Ironically, the catastrophe helped spur the region's development, as many afflicted New Englanders headed west. Rochester Hills, for example, was settled in 1817 by James Graham of New York.

The Devil's Wind

The deadliest Great Lakes storm in recorded history hit without warning on November 8–9, 1913, as snow squalls smacked heavy lake traffic on the still ice-free waters. Sustained winds of sixty miles per hour roared across the eastern part of lower Michigan, from Detroit up through Port Huron, whipping up thirty-five-foot waves that treated large freighters as if they were bathtub toys. Dozens of ships sank on Lake Huron, including eight freighters. Canadian beaches were littered with frozen corpses afterward, but the majority of the 256 sailors lost in the storm were never found.

The C-c-c-old Facts

Our ancestors could recite some teeth-chattering figures from more than a century ago. The coldest winter ever recorded in Detroit was the three-month period from December 1903 through February 1904, when the temperature averaged a mere 18.7°F. The coldest day on record in Detroit is December 22, 1872, when Christmas shoppers braved temperatures that dropped to -24°F.

Twisted Killer

The last single tornado to kill more than a hundred people in the U.S. occurred on the evening of June 8, 1953, when a funnel cloud with winds of up to 318 miles per hour punched a half-mile-wide path through the northern Flint community of Beecher. The Flint-Beecher twister was rated an F5, the most powerful ranking on the Fujita scale. It killed 116 people, injured 844 more, and destroyed hundreds of homes. Many of the victims were children who had been put to sleep for the night; thirty-seven of the dead were under the age of ten. A survivor recalled walking dazedly around in the aftermath and seeing an elderly neighbor "still in her bed but her house was gone and the bed was in the middle of the street." The same system spawned several smaller tornados in southeastern Michigan that day, resulting in nine additional deaths.

NINETEEN
Knuckles

As one of the ringleaders of the Chicago "Black Sox" who threw the 1919 World Series, Eddie Cicotte brought everlasting shame upon himself and the family he loved.

In the summer of 1923, a baseball team from Bastrop, Louisiana, was tearing up sandlots and cow pastures in every direction. The semipro nine featured a round little pitcher named Moore, who dazzled batters with a virtually untouchable assortment of junk pitches, and an outfielder named Johnson, whose slugging and fielding prowess never failed to astonish. "The team has been cleaning up in Morehouse Parish," marveled a local newspaper reporter, "and has walloped almost every club it has met in north Louisiana and south Arkansas."

Before too long, the identities of the team's stars were revealed. "Johnson" actually was "Shoeless Joe" Jackson, an illiterate country boy generally considered the finest natural hitter the game has ever seen. "Moore" was Eddie Cicotte, a lifelong Detroiter widely admired as one of the "brainiest" pitchers around. A few years earlier, they had been members of one of the greatest major-league teams ever assembled, enjoying careers that would have put both in the Hall of Fame. Now both were pariahs, banished from organized baseball after confessing to their roles in throwing the 1919 World Series.

The sad, sordid tale of the Chicago "Black Sox" scandal is embedded in American culture, its cast of characters—soulless, double-crossing gamblers; scheming, gullible ballplayers; penurious, vindictive owners—represented in such films as *Eight Men Out, Field of Dreams,* and *The Godfather,* and novels like *The Natural* (also made into a movie) and *The Great Gatsby.* "Say it ain't so, Joe," a boy reportedly pleaded to Jackson when news of the players' betrayal shook the country. While there has always been some room for doubt about the complicity of Shoeless Joe in the fix that "play[ed] with the faith of fifty million people," as F. Scott Fitzgerald wrote, there has never been any question of Cicotte's role as a ringleader. In fact, Cicotte was the first of the eight Black Sox players eventually tossed out of baseball to admit his wrongdoing. Without the guilt-racked pitcher's confession, it's very possible that the scandal would have remained a noisy but unconfirmed rumor instead of becoming the blackest episode in the long history of the national pastime.

Cicotte paid for his latent honesty for the rest of his days. "I don't know anyone who ever went through life without making a mistake," he said in a rare interview a few years before his death. "Everybody who has ever lived has committed sins of their own. I've tried to make up for it by living as clean a life as I could. I'm proud of the way I've lived and I think my family is, too."

Family was so important to Cicotte that on a train ride in the summer of 1919 it caused the thirty-five-year-old pitching ace to seriously consider selling out his employer, his teammates, and the public. As the Chicago White Sox headed to New York on a road trip, "Somebody made a crack about getting money, if we got into the Series, to throw the Series . . . and said they would go ahead and go through with it if they got this money," Cicotte later explained. In New York, he got in touch with a pair of low-level gamblers, Billy Maharg and Bill Burns, tipping them off that "something good was coming up."

First baseman Chick Gandil, an ex-boxer with established underworld ties, brought Joseph "Sport" Sullivan, a Boston bookmaker banned in Detroit's ballpark and elsewhere, into the conspiracy. Ultimately, Shoeless Joe Jackson, pitcher Claude "Lefty" Williams, shortstop Charles "Swede" Risberg, outfielder Oscar "Happy" Felsch, and infielder Fred McMullin were swept up in the scheme. Third baseman Buck Weaver

Eddie Cicotte broke into the major leagues with his hometown Detroit Tigers, but the pitcher made his reputation—both good and bad—as a member of the Chicago White Sox. (Library of Congress)

knew of their plans but said nothing, a decision that caused him to be lumped in with the guilty.

The White Sox won the American League pennant in 1919, which put them in a best-of-nine-games play-off against the Cincinnati Reds in the World Series. The National League champs were big underdogs, but Cicotte and Gandil let it be known that their cabal would roll over for $100,000. New York gangster Arnold Rothstein was to funnel the money through his lieutenant, ex-prizefighter Abe Attell.

Cicotte pitched the opener in Cincinnati. He hit the first batter he faced, a sign that the fix was in. Chicago lost, 9–1. They dropped two of the next three contests, with Cicotte committing two key errors in a 2–0 loss in Game 4. However, gamblers stalled when the players demanded their payouts. Exactly who got paid and how much they received is open to debate, but it appears that as little as $25,000 of the bribe money was actually distributed. Down four games to two and facing elimination, the double-crossed conspirators decided to play to win. Cicotte pitched masterfully to win Game 7, 4–1, but the Reds won the next day to take the Series. Gamblers supposedly had gotten to Lefty Williams, threatening to kill him and his wife if he didn't lose his third start of the Series.

Cicotte, who once claimed, "There is no good substitute for brains in our profession," was the only conspirator with the foresight to demand his share up front. The day before the Series began, he found the money under his pillow. "There was $10,000," he said. "I counted it. It was my price."

Edgar Victor Cicotte (pronounced SEE-kot) was born June 19, 1884, in Springwells, a township later absorbed into Detroit. He was the youngest of seven children. His father, who descended from one of the city's old-line French families, was a laborer who died when Eddie was ten years old. Looking to help his mother make ends meet, the youngster dropped out of school to work in a box factory. In his free time he played sandlot ball and went to Bennett Park (the future site of Tiger Stadium) whenever he could to watch the Tigers play.

The stocky right-handed pitcher broke into organized ball in the Upper Peninsula. There he compiled an overall 38–4 record with teams in Calumet and Sault St. Marie. The location also allowed him to satisfy his love of the outdoors, especially fishing and hunting. The Tigers invited him to a tryout in 1905, after which they optioned him to Augusta, Georgia. On May 16 in Augusta, Cicotte married Rose Freer, a French-Canadian girl from Detroit. The Augusta Tourists' lineup included a native Georgian, Ty Cobb. One day Cicotte traded blows with Cobb after the skinny eighteen-year-old, nonchalantly eating a box of popcorn in the outfield, ruined Cicotte's bid for a shutout by muffing a fly ball.

Cicotte and Cobb came up to Detroit in the last weeks of the 1905 season. On September 5, Cicotte notched the first of his 209 big-league wins, beating the White Sox in front of friends and family at Bennett Park. While Cobb eventually spent twenty-two summers with the Tigers, Cicotte bounced around the minors for the next three years, experimenting with his knuckleball. He re-emerged in 1908 with the Boston Red Sox. During his five years in Boston, Cicotte was an underachieving pitcher who frequently clashed with management. "He was suspended

Eddie Cicotte (*middle row, second from left*) and Ty Cobb (*top row, third from right*) were teammates on the Augusta Tourists in 1905. (National Baseball Library)

without pay so much of the time that it was like having no job," observed one sportswriter.

In July 1912, Cicotte was sold to the White Sox. He initially refused to report, saying he would retire and tend to the little neighborhood café he ran in the off-season. Sportswriters knowingly said he would reconsider when he weighed the difference in earnings. They were right. Thanks to a superior supporting cast and his growing mastery of an arsenal of trick pitches, most of which were perfectly legal at the time, "Knuckles" Cicotte hit his stride in Chicago. In 1917 he developed the "shine ball," which helped him to a breakout season. "He'd have some transparent paraffin on his trousers or somewhere, or some talcum powder, and every chance he'd get he'd rub the ball there," catcher Bob O'Farrell told author Lawrence Ritter in *The Glory of Their Times*. "That would make the ball slide off his fingers and put a real break on it when it came up to the plate. Acted something like a spitter." Cicotte won a league-high twenty-eight games, including a no-hitter, and posted a 1.53 earned-run average, best in the majors. In the 1917 World Series against the New York Giants, Cicotte's flutterballs accounted for a 2–1 victory in the opener. The Sox went on to win the Series in six games. Cicotte returned to Detroit a world champion—an underpaid world champion, he complained.

Cicotte was an easygoing sort, popular with players and reporters. When the Red Sox went on to the win the 1912 World Series after he was dealt at midseason, his former teammates thought enough of Cicotte to present him with an expensive gift. The following year he accompanied the White Sox and New York Giants on an epic six-month barnstorming tour of Asia, the Middle East, and Europe, returning to the States on the *Lusitania,* the liner doomed to be sunk by a German U-boat in 1915. The globe-trotting was a remarkable experience, especially in an era of limited travel, and was just one more opportunity afforded him because of his major-league status. "The first rule I would tell any young pitcher is to live a normal, healthy life," he told *Base Ball Magazine* in 1918. "I am not a prohibitionist. In fact, I enjoy a glass of beer as well as the next man." But it was essential for a professional ballplayer to keep regular hours, avoid dissipation, and "learn to use your head at all times."

Following a sub-par 1918 season in which he led the league with nineteen losses, Cicotte signed a $5,000 contract for 1919. Baseball lore has it that Chicago owner Charles Comiskey agreed to give the pitcher a $10,000 bonus if he won thirty games, then ordered him benched in the season's final weeks so he wouldn't have to pay it. This supposedly was Cicotte's impetus for agreeing to rig that year's World Series.

The facts don't bear this out. The contract Cicotte signed makes no mention of a bonus. Furthermore, it was Cicotte who asked to go home to Detroit after his twenty-ninth win. For the second time in three years, he topped all American League hurlers in wins and innings pitched. Cicotte wanted to rest his overworked arm for postseason play but instead wound up starting two more games in late September, including the pennant-clincher, though he did not receive credit for the victory. If Cicotte really did narrowly miss out on the alleged $10,000 bonus, it didn't matter, for he soon found that exact amount under his pillow.

What impelled Cicotte and others to throw the World Series? In a word, greed—though in their minds it was a justifiable kind of greed. Cicotte, like many players, believed himself to be chronically underpaid. For many years he lived on Central Avenue, near Vernor. In 1919, the large brick house, which still stands, was bursting with family members. In addition to being the sole support of his pregnant wife and their two young daughters, Rose and Virginia, Cicotte had taken in his wife's parents, his brother and wife and their young daughter, and Rose's sister and husband. He owned a garage, co-managed with his brother, and had taken out a $4,000 mortgage on a farm in Livonia Township, near present-day Seven Mile and Merriman roads. Cicotte later related that he had used the tainted money to pay off the mortgage and install new floors in the farmhouse and barn. He also bought livestock and feed.

In the aftermath of the 1919 World Series, there was widespread talk that gamblers had gotten to the Sox, but no proof had been found. Meanwhile, Comiskey doubled Cicotte's salary to $10,000, making him one of the game's highest-paid pitchers. Cicotte responded with another fine season. On Sunday, September 26, 1920, he beat the Tigers at Comiskey Park for his twenty-first win. A poor hitter, he even contributed a pair of singles to the 8–1 victory. It was the last major-league game he ever played. The following day, a Philadelphia newspaper published an interview with Billy Maharg, who verified the rumors of a fix. He named Cicotte as the man who had cooked up the plot.

Cicotte went to Comiskey's office and confessed. "Yeah, we were crooked," he said, sobbing.

"Don't tell me," Comiskey said. "Tell it to the grand jury."

Cicotte, Shoeless Joe Jackson, and Lefty Williams quickly signed confessions, all without consulting a lawyer. They described the plot and named the co-conspirators. Cicotte used the opportunity to unburden his troubled soul. "I needed the money," he said. "I had the wife and kids. The wife and kids don't know about this. I don't know what they'll think." Cicotte said he experienced pangs of guilt during the opening game of the Series and afterward played to win. "I wanted to win," he told the grand jury. "I could have given [the money] back with interest, if they only let me win the game that day."

The late Gene Carney, considered by many to be the greatest authority on the scandal and its participants, once gave writer Todd Schulz his take on what motivated Cicotte to come clean. "He had the keenest conscience. This really bothered him. He was a Catholic and he talked to his priest and other friends about it. If he doesn't go to the grand jury this really could have been slipped under the rug. There was no real evidence that anything had happened. But when a player confesses he took money, that ended the cover-up."

None of the gamblers implicated in the fix were ever found guilty of a crime. Neither, for that matter, were the Black Sox, who stood trial in the summer of 1921 on charges of defrauding the public. During the trial, the confessions of Cicotte and others mysteriously disappeared. The jury deliberated just a short while before declaring all of the defendants not guilty. Cicotte was so happy, he jumped up and grabbed the jury foreman. That evening, players and jurors celebrated together at a local restaurant.

The acquitted players, who had been suspended since the last week of the 1920 season, assumed they would be able to resume their careers. But they hadn't reckoned on Judge Kenesaw Mountain Landis, the theatrically thunderous federal jurist hired by owners in late 1920 to clean up the game. Baseball's first commissioner declared the players banished for life. Anyone in organized ball who had anything to do with them also would be tossed out of the game.

Over the next few years, members of the Black Sox played "outlaw" ball around the country, typically for semipro and town teams and often under assumed names. Cicotte found the experience less than satisfying. On one occasion, he was signed to pitch the deciding game in a championship series between the Illinois towns of Colchester and Macomb. Cicotte easily blanked Macomb, leading a disgruntled fan to point to Cicotte's red, white, and blue socks and say, "You've got a lot of guts to wear those colors." On another occasion, Swede Risberg assembled a barnstorming squad called The Ex-Major League Stars. Just before the tour started in Minnesota, Risberg refused Cicotte's demand for full pay up front. Cicotte lost two teeth in the fistfight that followed.

In 1927, Cicotte's name popped up again in connection with a wide-ranging gambling investigation conducted by American League president

Ban Johnson. According to credible testimony from former players, in 1917 Cicotte contributed to a cash pool given the Detroit ball club for laying down in a crucial series with Chicago. Cicotte refused to travel to Chicago to testify. In a statement released by his attorney, the pitcher said he "doesn't even remember" the games in question.

Cicotte's selective memory extended to conversations with his son, born shortly after the 1919 World Series. They talked a lot of baseball, recalled Eddie Jr., who played briefly in the minor leagues, but they never talked about the scandal that had defamed the family name. "He was a wonderful man," Eddie Jr., once reminisced. "He was a family man. I grew up by his side. When I was a little kid he'd say, 'C'mon Eddie, we're going fishing today.' We hunted together and fished together all the time."

Cicotte worked briefly as a Michigan game warden before landing a job at Ford. His employment history at the auto company is filled with holes. During World War I he worked in the off-season as a stock manager in the Rouge boatyard. He evidently returned to the plant in 1924, working as a mechanic and also possibly for Harry Bennett's security department. Some accounts placed him at the infamous "Battle of the Overpass" on May 26, 1937, when Bennett's security force—filled with ex-athletes, former convicts, and small-time hoods—beat up Walter Reuther and several other members of the fledgling United Auto Workers outside the Rouge. Cicotte's exact participation in this seminal event in labor history is unclear. A plausible explanation is that his familiar face was spotted at shift change, when the melee occurred. In any event, he was not one of the many participants required to testify in the federal hearings that followed.

Cicotte retired from Ford in 1944. He followed baseball on radio and TV but never attended a game. The feisty Billy Rogell, a shortstop with the Tigers in the 1930s and later a city councilman, was a regular visitor. "One of the nicest guys God put on this earth," was Rogell's recollection of Cicotte.

Rogell had grown up poor and streetwise in Chicago, cheering on Shoeless Joe from the outfield bleachers. "The Black Sox? Hell, I was still a kid then," he said. "Well, sure, it bothered me, 'cause those guys were my idols." Over the years Rogell tried repeatedly to take Cicotte to the ballpark. "I'd invite him, but he'd never go. I guess he wasn't allowed to." As adults enjoying each other's company, the subject of the 1919 World Series never came up, Rogell said. "Was he sorry about what he did? Well, what the hell, I never asked him. Listen, he was my friend. I liked the guy. We never talked about it. I didn't look at him as an old Black Sock. I liked the guy, that's all."

In 1957, Cicotte had the satisfaction of seeing Al Cicotte, the grandson of his brother Alva, break in with the Yankees. The journeyman pitcher played for six teams during his five big-league seasons, including a brief stint with the Tigers. There were stories, vigorously denied by family members, that he deliberately mispronounced his surname in order to distance himself from his infamous relative.

Rose died in 1958, leaving Cicotte a widower after fifty-three years of marriage. He kept busy by raising strawberries on his little farm and selling them from a roadside stand. He still drove a tractor and helped clear his neighbors' driveways. In 1965, now a mellow octogenarian, he told a visitor that he'd become calloused to being called a crooked ballplayer. "I admit I did wrong," he said, "but I've paid for it for the past forty-five years." He continued to keep a low profile, though his children had to contend with rude remarks throughout their entire lives. "A lot of people try to get in dirty digs, even now," Eddie Jr., then sixty-eight years old and himself a Ford retiree, complained in 1988. "I try to let it go over my head. I was at the VFW or Legion here once and some wise guy said something. I felt like popping him. But I'm getting too old to do that—and he was probably as old as I was."

Cicotte was treated for cancer and a heart ailment. He died at Henry Ford Hospital on May 5, 1969, at the age of eighty-four. Few were on hand for the burial at Parkview Cemetery in Livonia. The flat bronze marker over his grave—not unlike a pitcher's slab—gives no indication of his major-league career or a hint of the turmoil and shame left behind. Simply listed are his name and the dates of his birth and death. Above it all is a single word: Father.

TWENTY

Cold Cases from a Hot Decade

Detroit saw its share of spectacular murders during the Jazz Age, including several unsolved cases that grabbed national headlines and remain part of the city's lore.

It was, in every sense of the phrase, murder most foul. The odor emanating from the unclaimed steamer trunk at the American Railway Express warehouse in New York grew stronger with each passing day. Finally, freight office employees could take it no longer. They opened the cheap trunk—and gagged at what they found. Inside was the decomposing corpse of a young woman, her heart, lungs, and other internal organs missing. Police determined that the victim had been murdered in Detroit and then shipped to New York.

It was July 23, 1920. The Twenties, a decade renowned for its decadence, was off to a roaring start. It wasn't the last time during this period that Detroit seized national headlines for a murder that titillated the public and perplexed detectives. Exactly ten years later, in the predawn hours of July 23, 1930, the city's most popular and influential radio commentator, Jerry Buckley, was gunned down inside the lobby of the La Salle Hotel on Woodward. The assailants fired nearly a dozen bullets into the crusading "Voice of the People," including six to the back of the head.

Although unrelated, the two murders serve as bookends to an era that saw a soaring number of homicides in Detroit. Many were gang-related, the distressingly routine by-products of turf battles over liquor trafficking during Prohibition. Some were so singular in their motive or execution, they immediately became part of the city's lore. What follows are several sensational homicides from Jazz Age Detroit. Because there is no statute of limitations on murder, these cases officially remain open to this day—which is not to say that investigators at the time didn't usually have a good idea of who was responsible. Most homicides "are not deep mysteries or even aggravating riddles to detectives," veteran Detroit crime reporter Charles Givens wrote in the 1948 book *Detroit Murders*. "In nine out of ten unsolved cases they are virtually certain who the murderer was. Proof is another thing. Ask questions of detectives who handled these so-called mysteries and in the majority of cases you get the same answer: 'We know who the murderer was but there were no eyewitnesses and he had sense enough to keep it simple.' A shrug of the shoulders . . . the simple art of murder."

The LeRoy Trunk Murder Mystery

Throngs of morbid New Yorkers flocked to the rail express warehouse on East 44th Street on July 23, 1920, as word spread of the monstrous discovery of a mutilated woman's body crammed into a trunk. The unclad body "had been laid open, as if with a surgeon's knife, from throat to pelvis, and all internal organs removed," reported the *New York Times*. Was a new Jack the Ripper on the loose? Policemen kept the rubberneckers at bay as the body was removed to the morgue and investigators started their grim work.

The trunk was addressed to James Douglass in care of the American Express Co. Paperwork showed that it had been shipped by A. A. Taiturn of 105 Harper, Detroit, on June 10 and moved into storage on June 17. Detectives discovered that the sender's name was supposed to be Tatum. Clerks had misread the scribbled handwriting as "Taiturn," which explained why they had been unable to locate the trunk for a deliveryman who told police he had been hired by a certain "E. Le Roy" to claim it for the fictitious Douglass. Police theorized that the man who had paid the deliveryman for his unsuccessful pickup had been the killer.

Allan Tatum, the purported sender, surrendered to police in Birmingham, Alabama. Tatum, a Linotype operator, had recently returned to the South after spending several months in Detroit. He had nothing to hide. In fact, he was so scared of Le Roy—a man he had never met—that he opted to remain jailed for protection.

The woman in the trunk was soon identified as Katherine Lou Jackson, a petite divorcée who had been the common-law wife of Eugene Le Roy. The couple had met the previous year while staying at the Interurban Hotel; both were newcomers to the city. By the spring of 1920 they lived in a third-floor room at the apartment building on Harper.

Le Roy was known to be short-fused. According to Tatum, Jackson had told Tatum that Le Roy had once chased her out onto the street with a knife, threatening to kill her. Jackson and Tatum had known each other in Birmingham, and, after the knife incident, Jackson requested that Tatum come to Detroit to comfort her. Whether they also were lovers is unknown. Le Roy, who at the time was enjoying his own affair with an actress, obviously thought they were.

Police surmised that Le Roy had killed Jackson out of jealousy, possibly using chloroform to knock her out. No bloody clothes or blankets were ever found, leading investigators to speculate that the killer had burned them in the basement incinerator. Le Roy used Tatum's name as a sick joke and a false lead when shipping her remains out of town. He had apparently intended to pick up the trunk and destroy its contents, a plan that backfired because of a simple misreading of the shipping label.

Le Roy was faintly recalled by acquaintances as having been employed in the auto industry, either as an engineer or mechanic, though that may have been a ruse. He was variously described as "ferret-faced," a man of medium build, dark complexion, and "shiny black hair," who wore "sporty clothes" and was "frequently in the company of women." He was said to use perfume "lavishly." New York police quickly implicated him in two hotel murders, including that of a seventeen-year-old woman. The perpetrator reportedly used several aliases, including P. P. Poulvrer, O. J. Woods, and O. J. Fernandez.

Whatever the fugitive's real identity, he had a much larger and considerably less-documented world to move around in than today. There were no national crime databases, DNA registries, computers, or even Social Security numbers to assist the authorities in 1920. It was still possible for a wanted man to reinvent himself or simply vanish. So it was with Eugene Le Roy. For several years following Jackson's murder, sightings of Le Roy occasionally inspired headlines and lifted detectives' hopes. Men resembling Le Roy were spotted in Mexico, arrested in Cheboygan, and detained in Uruguay. Each time, however, what seemed to be a promising break in the case came to nothing.

The last flurry of activity occurred in Chicago. In February 1925, a carnival worker named Frank J. Le Roy was arrested, principally because of his name and a unique scar that matched the one the suspect was thought to have on his left leg. However, police soon determined that the man had been in a Cleveland jail at the time of the Jackson murder. That November, a waiter matching Le Roy's description was picked up in the same city. He, too, was soon set free.

With that, an already cold trail slipped into deep freeze. No trace of Eugene Le Roy was ever found. Neither was a second trunk that the killer was known to have shipped from Detroit on the same day as the first—this one presumably containing the missing heart, lungs, and viscera of Katherine Lou Jackson.

The Milaflores Massacre

The Thompson submachine gun, an assault weapon originally designed to sweep German trenches in World War I, was one of the iconic symbols of the Roaring '20s, but it wasn't until March 28, 1927, that the "Tommy gun" made its murderous debut in Detroit. About 4:45 that morning, residents of the Milaflores Apartments at 106 East Alexandrine were blasted out of their sleep by chattering bursts of automatic gunfire. Those arriving on the scene encountered a grisly sight. In the hallway outside apartment 308, the shredded bodies of three men—Joe Bloom, George Cohen, and Frank Wright—lay in slick pools of blood. The fusillade of .45-caliber slugs had produced a macabre Swiss-cheeselike effect, tearing away chunks of wood, plaster, and flesh. Bloom and Cohen were nearly cut in half, while Wright, riddled by at least fourteen bullets, managed

Through the mid-1920s a Thompson machine gun could be purchased from hardware stores, though its use by criminals like Fred "Killer" Burke—a key suspect in Detroit's first Tommy gun murders—soon caused their sales to be limited to law enforcement agencies. (Author's Collection)

to linger a short while in the hospital before dying. "The machine gun worked," Wright said. "That's all I remember."

Even in the Wild West atmosphere of Prohibition Era Detroit, the city's first Tommy gun murders stood out as a sickening new low in violence. The police quickly identified the victims as second-drawer hoods and assumed the massacre was tied to yet another underworld beef. But who were the executioners?

Signs pointed to a loosely organized, up-and-coming band of thugs known to be involved in bootlegging, extortion, and kidnappings. The press had started referring to them as the Purple Gang, though the exact origins of the name are fuzzy. Items found in a police search of apartment 308 suggested that the place had been used as a hangout by several individuals associated with the gang, including Abe Axler and Eddie Fletcher, a pair of sociopath career criminals from New York who had set up shop in Detroit.

Detectives theorized that the chain of events began with the shotgun murder of Johnny Reid, a liquor agent for the Purples, on Christmas night 1926. Wright, an all-purpose punk from Chicago, was suspected of having been hired by local Italian mobsters to kill Reid. After Wright killed another known associate of the Purples a few weeks later, allies of both victims responded by kidnapping one of Wright's friends, gambling hall operator Meyer "Fish" Bloomfield. A phone call lured Wright to the third-floor apartment at the Milaflores, where Bloomfield's release would presumably be arranged. Bloom and Cohen came along. The three walked into an ambush, with the assassins emerging from behind the fire door at the end of the hall, blasting away. Reporters later counted at least 110 bullet holes.

The day following the murders, police pulled over a car on Woodward Avenue and found weapons inside. Taken into custody were Axler and Fred "Killer" Burke. With his dead eyes, flat expression, and cropped mustache, Burke was a particularly menacing figure. It took a special "feel" to handle a powerful weapon like the Thompson, and Burke was reputed to have a jeweler's touch with the trigger. Police speculated that, aside from taking on the job of killing Wright for professional reasons, Burke would have had a personal motive, as he and Reid were close friends who had once belonged to a St. Louis gang known as Egan's Rats.

Other Purples and their associates were interviewed. Nobody knew anything. The seized weapons proved not to have been used in the killings. At a habeas corpus hearing two days later, investigators could offer no substantial evidence to warrant the further detention of Axler and Burke. The judge had no choice but to order their release. Like so many other investigations involving gangland killings, this one quickly dried up. The murders did, however, result in a state ban on the sale of Tommy guns to private citizens through hardware stores and other retail outlets. Henceforth, only law enforcement agencies and the military could legally buy them. ("It's the safest gun to shoot in city streets," declared one advertisement.)

Nobody ever stood trial for the Milaflores Massacre, a crime whose brutality established the Purple Gang as the lords of Detroit's underworld. Four years later, another sensational triple homicide—this time of rival gangsters at the Collingwood Manor Apartments—resulted in the murder convictions and imprisonment of several key Purples, effectively breaking the gang's back.

Axler and Fletcher, principal suspects in the Milaflores Massacre, managed to stay out of prison, only to be found shot to death inside a parked car in Pontiac in 1933. Burke, who had a falling-out with the Purples before going to work for Al Capone's outfit in Chicago, was by then serving his own life sentence for killing a policeman in St. Joseph, Michigan. A raid on Burke's residence uncovered a small arsenal, including a pair of Thompsons that ballistics tests tied to the ultimate gangland rubout of the era: the St. Valentine's Day Massacre in 1929.

Dr. Loomis and the Other Woman

The evening of February 22, 1927, was wet and cold. Despite the rain, Dr. Frank O. Loomis later told police, he decided to take a walk. When he returned to his home on the 1300 block of Marlowe about forty-five minutes later, he found his wife, Grace, dead on the floor of the sunroom. Her face had been battered, and there were deep cuts on her arms and fingers. A window had been smashed. The hundred dollars Loomis said he had given his wife to buy clothes for their two young children, who were sound asleep at the time of the murder, was missing.

Loomis was known as an upstanding citizen, a doting family man whose medical practice included many charity cases. There was no apparent motive for him to kill his wife, a nurse he had married in 1914. But detectives didn't buy his story. They found a scorched wooden stake and a pair of pearl buttons in the basement furnace, indicating to them that Loomis had burned the murder weapon and his bloodied shirt before notifying authorities. Moreover, two people walking on Marlowe reported hearing a shrill scream around 9:05 p.m. It was at about that time that a telephone operator handled a call from an unknown woman who let out a long shriek before a man's voice came on the line. "Never mind," he said, then hung up. Loomis contended that he had been blocks away on his walk at that particular time.

Loomis was arrested and put on trial. Every day hundreds of people tried to squeeze into the small courtroom where prosecutor Robert Toms and Louis Colombo, the latter one of the city's top defense attorneys, heatedly clashed. Colombo contended that a Peeping Tom had watched Loomis hand his wife the hundred dollars, then waited until the doctor left before breaking into the house and fatally beating Grace, taking the money and the murder weapon with him as he fled. It was a simple, straightforward, and plausible scenario. But then there was Gertrude Newell.

Detectives and reporters knew quite a bit about Gertrude, even if the jurors weren't allowed to. Described as an "auburn-haired charmer," the slender, flighty divorcée had been spotted while being squired to speakeasies by Loomis several times prior to Grace's murder. After the murder, police apparently had planted listening devices in Gertrude's Wabash Avenue apartment, though whatever they may have learned was inadmissible. The prosecutor "brought her name in, rather timidly, some thought, and Loomis admitted that he had had a cocktail with her once, and dinner with her and her parents another time," wrote crime reporter Charles Givens; however, "she was declared a hostile witness and therefore could only be called to the stand on rebuttal."

Loomis had a reputation for being hot-tempered, but during cross-examination the thirty-six-year-old suspect was cool, methodical, and unbending in his testimony. Meanwhile, Colombo parried the prosecution's expert witnesses with those of his own. After a three-week trial, the jury took just thirty-five minutes to arrive at a verdict: the doctor was found not guilty.

For the next year, Loomis was hounded by the press and shadowed by police, forcing him to constantly change his office and residence. As he renewed his oft-contentious relationship with Gertrude, his practice fell into disarray, and his debts piled up. "He was just so wrapped up in her," said a friend, "he couldn't think of anything else."

On the evening of May 18, 1928, the two quarreled. "I know a hell of a lot more about you than you know about me," neighbors heard Gertrude yell. The next morning, Loomis was found dead inside a dentist's office adjoining his own, head down on a desk. He had inhaled illuminating gas. A half-empty whiskey bottle and an opened Bible were nearby. The doctor's friends speculated that he had been an innocent man unable to live down the stigma of the trial.

Loomis left three suicide notes. One was to a friend, which read in part: "G. drives me crazy. . . . My God! How I love her! Perhaps we will meet again when both of us may be more reasonable." Another was written to a local newspaper and began: "I am not guilty of murder. My conscience is clear." Detectives strained to parse Loomis's words. Even in death he continued to insist that he had not committed murder, which technically was true if he had killed Grace in a fit of rage. In the eyes of the law, such an unpremeditated act is considered manslaughter.

The last note was addressed to the police: "A newspaper article will be published in twenty-four to forty-eight hours explaining this action on my part. Please be patient until then." If Loomis had indeed written and mailed a clarification of events—possibly even a confession—it never arrived. Meanwhile, Gertrude suffered a nervous breakdown and repeatedly attempted suicide. She soon left town. Where she went and what happened to her afterward is unknown.

Slaughter of the Evangelist Family

As a faith healer and self-styled prophet, Benny Evangelist was immersed in the dark world of voodoo. This association may have cost him and his family dearly. On the morning of July 3, 1929, a neighborhood realtor let himself into the Evangelists' home at 3587 St. Aubin, near Mack and discovered Evangelist sitting upright in a trancelike state at a desk, his arms crossed on his chest. "Evangelist's plight was devastatingly apparent," *Free Press* reporter Royce Howes later wrote. "His head lay on the floor beside him." In the upstairs bedrooms, the decapitated mystic's wife, Santina, and four children—Eugenia, 4, Margaret, 5, Angelina, 7, and 18-month-old Mario—lay in "a gory shambles." All had been hacked to death, evidently with a machete. At the time it was the worst mass murder in Detroit's history.

The funeral of the six members of the Evangelist family, slaughtered one July day in 1929. The mother and youngest child were buried in a single coffin. (Larry Calcaterra Collection)

Evangelist, an Italian immigrant born Benedetto Evangelista in 1896 and a carpenter by trade, had founded a cult called the Great Union Federation of America. Worship services took place in the basement of his family's home. The *Free Press* described Evangelist's religious sanctum: "Eight or ten wax figures, each hideous and grotesque to the extreme, and each presumably representing one of the 'celestial planets,' were suspended on the altar in a circle by wires from the ceiling. Among them was a huge eye, electrically lighted from the inside, which Evangelist referred to in his bible as 'the sun.'" The walls and ceiling were lined with light green cloth. A large sign in the basement window, visible to passersby, bore the words "Great Celestial Planet Exhibition."

Police, unaccustomed to handling such a wholesale domestic slaughter, made a hash of the case. Hundreds of policemen, reporters, and gawkers tramped through the crime scene, destroying whatever clues the killer may have left behind. Detectives even forgot to take Evangelist's fingerprints prior to burial, resulting in the need to have his body secretly exhumed one night for the task and then reburied. Frustrating investigative efforts was the notoriously tight-lipped and clannish Italian immigrant community. Not a single one of Evangelist's "disciples" could be located, and despite the fact that hundreds of people had come to him for cures, only a handful even admitted to knowing the man.

In the end, nobody ever was charged, though police pursued several promising angles. One involved a semi-secret band of criminals known as the Black Hand, which Evangelist and distant members of his family seem to have been involved with in some fashion. Police uncovered several notes, including one dated six months before the murders that warned Evangelist: "This is your last chance." It was signed "The Vendetta" and was accompanied by the crude drawing of a hatchet. Other minor circumstantial evidence kept the Black Hand angle an open avenue of inquiry, but the various strands could never be woven into a satisfactory hypothesis.

Detectives also explored the possibility that Umberto Tecchio, the last man to see Evangelist alive, was the killer. Tecchio stopped by Evangelist's home on the evening before the murders to make the final payment on a house that Evangelist had sold him. A friend who accompanied Tecchio stated that there was nothing unusual about the transaction and that he and Tecchio—who three months earlier had knifed his brother-in-law to death in an argument over an unpaid debt—went out drinking the rest of the evening before going home to their boardinghouse to sleep. However, years later a paperboy told police that he had seen a scowling Tecchio on Evangelist's front porch early the following morning, about the time police estimated the murders had taken place. Tecchio died in 1934, and a key witness was deported to Italy, thwarting investigators.

The most intriguing supposal could serve as the story line of a low-budget "slasher" video. Evangelist had previously lived in York, Pennsylvania, where he had known a railroad worker named Aurelius Angelino. Both were natives of Naples, Italy, and shared a fascination with the occult. In 1919, two years before Evangelist moved to Detroit, Angelino attempted to kill his entire family with an axe, managing to hack two of his children to death before being stopped. Angelino was sent to an insane asylum, where he escaped twice and was recaptured each time. In 1923, he broke out a third time—and was never seen again. Had Angelino somehow made his way to Detroit, where his old friend had set up his eerie basement shrine? As Howes wrote, the massacre of the Evangelist family "is much more suggestive of the fanatic run amok than it is of the neighborhood bad man."

"Evangelist, no doubt, was insane," said the parish priest who oversaw the family's interment at Mount Olivet Cemetery. "I do not believe Evangelist was sincere in practicing the creed he had established. Rather, I believe he founded the mysterious cult with all of its weird props and practices with the sole idea of making money." What Evangelist ultimately made were headlines—and a mystery that endures to this day.

Silencing the People's Mouthpiece

During the 1920s, Detroit recorded 1,284 homicides and had one of the highest murder rates in the country. The killing didn't stop once the calendar flipped to 1930. Until a growing economic depression and the repeal of Prohibition saw murders drop and property crimes rise, the new decade was simply a continuation of the old. In the first two weeks of July 1930, at least eleven gangland figures were killed in various shootouts. Mayor Charles Bowles was viewed as inept, aloof, and in the pocket of criminals, leading frustrated citizens to successfully petition for a special recall election.

Bowles's most powerful critic was WCHB radio host Jerry Buckley, who since 1928 had nightly used the power of the airwaves to attack corruption and espouse humanitarian causes. Buckley, age thirty-nine, came from an old Corktown neighborhood family and was revered for his populist stances. Curiously, the "voice of the common man" did not originally support the recall, calling it undemocratic; however, he changed his mind just before the election.

Detroiters voted overwhelmingly on July 22, 1930, to oust Bowles. After spending the night covering election returns at City Hall, Buckley returned to the La Salle Hotel, where WCHB had its studios and the

Popular radio commentator Jerry Buckley was slain in the early hours of July 23, 1930. (Author's Collection)

The bullet-riddled chair inside the lobby of the La Salle Hotel where Jerry Buckley met his end. (Author's Collection)

commentator kept a suite. A phone call from an unidentified woman brought him down to the lobby, where he took a chair and waited. At 1:45 a.m., three men strode in, drew revolvers, and fired a flurry of shots at point-blank range. After the gunmen fled into the night, a stunned hotel employee used the newspaper Buckley had been reading to cover his shattered skull.

The assassination sickened citizens already fed up with lawlessness, helping to make Buckley's funeral one of the largest Detroit had ever seen. But grief turned into disbelief when the press published unflattering revelations about the martyred crusader. The most damning was that Buckley had extorted money from racketeers in exchange for "going easy" on them. Sometimes he played both ends against the middle, shaking down opposing parties. Suddenly his about-face on the recall suggested something other than a sincere change of heart. Beyond the allegations of blackmail was Buckley's reputation for womanizing and enjoying the high life. Any of these activities could have made him a target.

A grand jury was convened. After months of investigation, it returned indictments against three men, all linked to eastside gangster Pete Licavoli. Ted Pizzino had been a tenant at the La Salle; police found him in bed shortly after the murder, still partially clothed. His roommate, Angelo Livecchi (whose wife lived in New York), was nabbed in New York just as he and his wife were hastily arranging a trip to Italy. "Scarface Joe" Bommarito also was arrested. All three were charged with first-degree murder.

"The court battle raged on for weeks and public interest was sustained to a proper pitch throughout," wrote *Free Press* police reporter Charles T. Haun. "Theory after theory for Buckley's murder revolved around the jury's collective heads. Buckley was killed because of his action against those interested in keeping Mayor Bowles in office . . . killed because of a double cross . . . killed because of a woman. You could take your choice." No matter what the scenario, argued prosecutors, the bottom line was that the defendants had been the hitmen.

A key witness, Frank Tara, was brought in under heavy police guard. Tara testified that he had been standing outside the hotel's Adelaide Street entrance when he heard gunshots in the lobby. Moments later, two men he identified after the fact as Pizzino and Livecchi rushed past him and jumped into a waiting getaway car. But after newspapers published his photograph, Tara refused to take the stand again. "It's my death sentence," he exclaimed. The terrified witness was held in contempt, and his testimony was stricken, dealing a major blow to the prosecution.

After six weeks, the case finally went to the jury. Loud arguing was heard behind closed doors. Thirty-five hours later, jurors emerged with a verdict: not guilty.

Many questions about Buckley's murder and Buckley himself have gone unanswered. Today some armchair criminologists name a different set of Licavoli gunmen—John Mirabella, Joe English, and Russell Syracuse, all of whom fled to Youngstown, Ohio—as the likely killers, though the exact motive behind such a high-profile slaying remains open to conjecture.

Detroit has chalked up more than twenty-five thousand homicides in the eighty-plus years since Jerry Buckley was gunned down in the lobby of the La Salle. After all this time his murder is still "on the books," a classic cold case that serves as a chilling reminder of what human beings are capable of doing to each other, no matter what the era.

Johnny Miler was Joe Louis's first ring opponent. (Author's Collection)

TWENTY-ONE
The Man Who Licked Joe Louis

In his very first amateur bout, Detroit's Brown Bomber took it on the chin against a fighting footnote named Johnny Miler.

Joe Louis is fondly remembered as one of Detroit's favorite sons, and rightfully so. Arguably the greatest prizefighter of all time, he packed drama and dignity into a career that included some of the most memorable moments in ring history: the knockouts of Primo Carnera and Max Schmeling on the eve of World War II . . . his remarkable comeback against Billy Conn in 1941 . . . his final fight against an up-and-coming Rocky Marciano in 1951. The bout Louis counted as his most memorable, however, was the one he wished he could forget: a three-round shellacking at the hands of a fellow Detroit amateur boxer named Johnny Miler in his very first fight.

The shy teenager who stepped into the ring that long-ago winter day bore little resemblance to the champion he one day became. Dissatisfied with the idea of spending his life working at some dead-end job, Joe Louis Barrow decided to try his luck at the profession so many young men in Detroit turned to during the Depression: boxing. His friends at the eastside Brewster Center gym, where he often hung out, saw that he had raw talent, most notably a jackhammer right hand.

Joe was still something of a mama's boy. He'd been a quiet, oversize twelve-year-old when his family came to Detroit from rural Alabama in 1926. He had grown even larger in the four years since, when he entered the Bronson Trade School, an all-boys vocational school, at age sixteen. Not long after Joe began learning how to build pieces of furniture at Bronson, his mother came up with another use for his hands: playing the violin. It seems incredible in retrospect, but Lillie Barrow had convinced herself that her budding heavyweight had the makings of a musician—this despite the fact that Joe's only acquaintance with an instrument had been fooling around with a mouth harp when he was a little boy. Somehow she scraped together the change needed for weekly lessons and instrument rental.

Joe felt awkward with the violin placed in his big mitts, and the sound he coaxed from the instrument stood hair on end. He took a great deal of teasing as he lumbered, shamefaced, to and from his lessons at a small music school at Woodward and Warren avenues. Once some wise guy called violin-toting Joe a sissy; fed up, Joe crashed the instrument over his tormenter's head.

One day inside Bronson's gym, Joe tugged on a pair of boxing gloves and started fooling around with a fellow student. He floored his opponent with a single left-handed punch. The swift execution caught the attention of promising amateur fighter Thurston McKinney. "Man," McKinney said in awe, "throw that violin away."

From then on, the story goes, Joe used the fifty cents his mother gave him for each music lesson to pay for boxing instruction at Brewster. To further deceive Mrs. Barrow, a God-fearing woman who abhorred violence of any type, Joe ultimately dropped his surname and boxed as Joe Louis.

Joe was intoxicated by the saunalike air of the gym and by the *whap-whap-whap* of the speed bag. He enjoyed doing his roadwork on Belle Isle, gulping in the early morning air and relishing the solitude as he rumbled along the pathways of the scenic park. He loved the rough camaraderie and singleness of purpose that characterized workouts. Having grown infatuated with the idea of developing into a professional fighter, he dropped out of trade school to concentrate on training.

Joe, who quickly grew tired of being used as a sparring partner for fellow Brewster boxers, was itching to test himself. By late 1931, the growing youngster had passed 154 pounds—then the ceiling for middleweights—and moved into the light-heavyweight class.

Brodhead Naval Armory, site of Joe Louis's first fight. (Author's Collection)

An opponent was found. The Christ Church Athletic Club, one of the city's premier centers for boxing instruction, was managed by Billy Stewart, whose stable of amateur champions included his twin sons. One day Louis discovered that he'd been scheduled to meet another of Stewart's prize pupils, Johnny Miler, in a three-rounder at the Brodhead Naval Armory on Jefferson Avenue.

The rest of the Brewster crew had heard of Miler. They knew he was one tough customer. "Are you afraid?" Louis was asked. "No," he replied. But he should have been.

Miler, born Johnny Miletich in Hocking, Iowa, in 1910, had dropped out of tenth grade to follow his father into the coal mines. At the age of twenty he moved to Detroit and got a short-lived job on the assembly line. Laid off and with nothing better to occupy his time, the strapping six-foot-one, 175-pounder started to rattle the speed bag under Stewart's instruction.

Miler—as he was known after a ring announcer mangled his Croatian surname—quickly acquired a reputation around local gyms as a hard-nosed craftsman. At the time he was to face Louis, he already has as many as twenty amateur bouts under his belt. "He was no knock-out artist," Stanley Evans, another promising fighter of the time, later said of Miler. "He was tough, but he was cagey—a bee on a horse's rump. He wasn't about to stand in there and punch it out; his tactic was to bite and scram."

Louis was seventeen years old, four years younger than his savvy opponent, when the match took place one day in the winter of 1931–1932. Curiously, the exact date of Louis's debut has never been fixed. Even the circumstances of this historic match remain cloudy. Was it a sanctioned affair in the preliminary round of that year's Golden Gloves tournament, the annual amateur competition that attracted thousands of hopefuls from across the city? Or was it a warmup match for Miler, who had his eyes set on the upcoming 1932 Olympic trials in San Francisco? No newspaper accounts of the fight have ever been found, and memories regarding the particulars seem always to have been fuzzy. The only thing everyone agrees on is that, in his very first organized fight, Joe Louis Barrow fought Johnny Miler.

"Fought" is a generous term. "Survived" would be more precise. According to Freddie Guinyard, one of several friends of Joe Louis in attendance that night, the novice confidently thought his size and powerful right hand would slow Miler down. But that strategy quickly flew out the armory window.

The bell sounded, and Louis, moving cautiously, fired a left jab and then landed a right to Miler's jaw. Joe stepped back to watch Miler fall. But instead of toppling over, Miler was all over his opponent, finally depositing Louis on the seat of his pants. As Louis later recalled, his head was "going around like a top" when the bell ending the round ended. His handlers revived him with splashes of water. "They must have poured half of Lake St. Clair on me," he said.

At the beginning of the second round, a right hand "landed on the only unbruised spot on my chin," said Louis, who was punched to the canvas six more times. Angels were singing in his head, he confessed. At the bell, his handler "picked up the pieces that used to be me and dropped them on the stool in my corner."

The wobbly legged novice gamely answered the bell for the third and final round. He managed to stay on his feet until the end, although he later attributed that small victory to Miler's arm being weary after landing so many punches.

As far as is known, Louis and Miler never crossed paths again. Miler collected a twenty-five-dollar merchandise check for his victory over Louis. A short while later Miler captured the local Golden Gloves championship in the light-heavyweight class. He then went on to become the first Detroit boxer to represent the city in the Olympics, losing a controversial decision to Ireland's James J. Murphy at the 1932 Games in Los Angeles.

After the Olympics, Miler served as a sparring partner for Max Schmeling, the German fighter who had just lost the heavyweight title to Jack Sharkey. Miler then broke into the professional ranks with a $250 payday against Leon Jasinski in Grand Rapids. In early 1933, Miler pummeled "Flash" Riser in front of three thousand fans at Olympia Stadium to become Michigan's new heavyweight champion.

Meanwhile, it had taken time for Louis's battered body and ego to recover. He was "all skinned up" after the Miler mauling, remembered one of his friends. All he had gotten for his beating was a seven-dollar merchandise check, or exactly one dollar for each time he had been floored. Louis dejectedly handed over the check to his mother and stepfather, receiving a stern lecture in exchange. Surely there were better and easier ways to make a living, he was told. Not long afterward, Louis woke early one morning to join a long line of similarly hungry and dispirited men looking for work outside the gates of Briggs Manufacturing.

Briggs was known as "the slaughterhouse." Louis was assigned one of the traditional "Negro jobs": pushing truck bodies to the paint sprayer on the assembly line. It was hot, grueling work, he remembered. "The tape would come off the body-covers and land on the floor, sticky side up. The tape would gum onto the dolly wheels, and you'd get a real workout pushing those truck bodies. I would leave the factory around 5 o'clock, go home for dinner, and then go over to the gym."

Joe's confidence was restored a few months later when, in his first fight since getting mauled by Miler, he knocked out a promising young boxer named Otis Thomas. He kayoed his next thirteen opponents en

Joe Louis (*second from right*) and the Detroit contingent of Golden Gloves champions in 1934. (Author's Collection)

route to entering the 1933 Golden Gloves tournament, where he emerged as the light-heavyweight champion. The following year he repeated his win, then turned pro with a first-round knockout of Jack Kracken in Chicago. This time he received fifty-nine dollars in cash for his efforts. He was on his way.

By comparison, Miler's professional career, which included an unsuccessful title shot at "Slapsie" Maxie Rosenbloom, was undistinguished. As Louis made headlines climbing up the heavyweight ranks in the 1930s, Miler bounced around smoky gyms throughout the United States, England, and Australia, picking up one puny paycheck after another. He once fought an exhibition against heavyweight titleholder Max Baer, who stopped in Des Moines en route to making a movie in Hollywood. Baer "smashed and clowned his way to a one-sided victory," the Associated Press reported. "After permitting the serious Miler to slap harmless punches to the face and body for most of the first round, the . . . champion suddenly cut loose with a terrific right that sent the Iowan reeling against the ropes. A kindly bell ending the round undoubtedly saved the badly outweighed Miler from a knockout." Baer received $25,000 for barely breaking a sweat—more than Miler made during his entire career.

By the spring of 1937, Miler had all but lost interest in the fight game. Not long after losing a bout at Olympia, he announced his retirement. One week later, Louis knocked out James Braddock in Chicago to become the new heavyweight champion of the world.

Louis went on to hold the title for the next dozen years, an unprecedented achievement. Among his string of successful title defenses were stirring victories over Schmeling and Billy Conn, ring classics that established him as a sporting and cultural icon.

Miler moved back to Iowa, where he became a policeman. He died in 1976, a footnote content to spend his final years on a farm tending his petunia garden.

Meanwhile, the man whom columnist Jimmy Cannon had immortalized as "a credit to his race—the human race," continued to inspire songs, books, films, paintings, and sculptures long after his own career ended with a loss to Rocky Marciano during an ill-advised comeback bid. In Detroit, a hockey arena was named after him, and a giant replica of his fist was installed at the corner of Woodward and Jefferson avenues. Since 1986, *Sports Illustrated*—which donated the controversial two-ton sculpture known as "The Fist"—has annually presented the Joe Louis Award to a member of the local sports community.

Even after Louis died in 1981, the honors kept coming. In 1993, the U.S. Postal Service released a first-class stamp recognizing the fabled "Brown Bomber." It was issued before self-adhesive stamps became the norm, giving millions of ordinary Americans the opportunity to do what Johnny Miler did in such convincing fashion one long-ago winter day: lick Joe Louis.

Tom Tyler starred in the 1941 serial *Adventures of Captain Marvel*. (Author's Collection)

TWENTY-TWO

The Adventures of Tom Tyler

Vincent Markowski left Hamtramck for Hollywood one day in 1923. He returned three decades later, his good looks and career ruined by a rare and crippling disease.

If life actually were like a Saturday matinée serial, the further adventures of Vincent Markowski would have had a more upbeat, action-packed ending. However, this was Hamtramck, not Hollywood, and Markowski—better known to the world as Tom Tyler—had come to his sister's large frame house on Moenart Street to suffer a slow, tedious death. At not quite fifty years old, the celluloid action hero and Western movie actor was afflicted by a rare and frightening disease that had already cost him his looks, his marriage, and his livelihood.

As the eponymous hero of the *Adventures of Captain Marvel*—widely regarded as one of the finest serials ever produced—Tyler had played a character dubbed "The World's Mightiest Mortal." The irony probably was not lost on Tyler's sister, Katherine Slepski, who at the end was helping bathe and dress him. "He was a little grumpy, a little demanding," remembered Ray Slepski, who gave up his bedroom to his ailing uncle. "But who could blame him? Here he'd been this big, strong, handsome guy, a champion weightlifter, and now his features are distorted, his hands are like claws, he's helpless. It really was pathetic to see him in that condition. It was hard to believe that just a few years earlier he'd been a matinée star."

Film buffs generally consider the dozen chapters of the Captain Marvel saga the apex of Tyler's screen career, a thirty-year stretch that spanned the period from silent films through the early years of television. All told, Tyler appeared in seven serials and more than 150 movies, including minor roles in such classics as *Gone With The Wind* and *Stagecoach*. He associated with some of the greatest names of Hollywood's golden age, both on and off the set, and had a fling with one of the era's legendary actresses. He was a versatile, hardworking, and well-liked professional who thought no role was beneath him. As his illness advanced and his film career dried up, he took dozens of bit parts on such popular television shows as *The Lone Ranger, The Roy Rogers Show,* and *Sky King*. His last role was in a never-aired TV pilot directed by the infamous B-movie director Ed Wood.

Despite his long career, Tyler is easily overlooked today as just one more obscure laborer in the dream factory of American cinema. This is unfortunate, according to film historian Don Miller, who believes that Tyler could have had a much higher screen profile than he did: "The feeling persists that with creative and intensive guidance, the attributes of Tom Tyler, buried as they were under an avalanche of neglect and carelessness, could have been transformed into a screen image approaching the highest plateaus."

Vincent Markowski was born August 9, 1903, near Port Henry, New York. Despite the Polish-sounding surname, the family actually was Lithuanian. Vincent's immigrant father and older brother, both named Frank, worked in the nearby iron ore mines. In September 1918, Frank Markowski Sr. moved the entire family to Detroit and got an assembly line job at Ford. The Markowskis lived in a two-family flat on Mitchell.

Vincent, one of five siblings, briefly attended local Catholic schools, but like many teenagers of the era he dropped out to enter the workforce. Factory jobs were plentiful in industrial Detroit, and he soon found one. During this period he became interested in weightlifting and spent much of his free time chiseling his already sturdy six-foot-two-inch frame. One weekend he was competing in a bodybuilding contest at the local Martha Washington Theater when a talent agent suggested that he try

Tom Tyler (*née* Vincent Markowski) in an early publicity still. (Author's Collection)

his luck in Hollywood. Brawny good lucks were always in demand in the nascent film industry. With his younger sister, Molly, lending him some money, Vincent and a neighborhood friend, Emil Karkoski, set off for California in the summer of 1923.

The two pals worked their way across the country until Karkoski changed his mind in Denver. While his friend turned back, Vincent continued west, eventually arriving in Hollywood, where he found a cheap apartment and began making the rounds of studios, scrounging for work. His first part was as an extra in a 1924 movie called *Three Weeks.* After that he appeared in such minor roles as an Indian in *Leatherstocking* and a chariot driver in *Ben-Hur.* These early roles owed more to his muscular torso than anything else, as much of the time he appeared on-screen bare-chested. According to biographer Mike Chapman, during this period he usually was credited as Bill Burns.

Between acting gigs, he worked day labor jobs, took modeling assignments—sometimes posing in the nude for sculptors and painters—and continued to hone his impressive physique through weightlifting and acrobatics. He developed into one of the top lifters in the country in the 1920s. While competing as a member of the Los Angeles Athletic Club, he was the national amateur heavyweight champion in 1928. He weighed two hundred pounds, had a forty-five-inch chest (unexpanded) and a thirty-two-inch waist, and was the first American to lift more than three hundred pounds in the clean-and-jerk, a lift that put a premium on brute strength. He qualified for the 1928 Olympics, but the U.S. decided against sending a squad of lifters to Amsterdam. His disappointment wasn't as keen as it might have been, because by then he was an established silent-movie star.

His break came when Joseph P. Kennedy—the father of future president John F. Kennedy—decided that cheap Westerns were the easiest way to make money for his FBO studio, the forerunner of RKO Pictures. He wasn't the only movie mogul to seize upon the genre as an attractive option to the more expensive feature-length productions. According to film historian David Robinson, the formulaic hourlong B Western was the "perfect vehicle for the producer working on a shoestring budget who could not afford a sound stage or construct lavish sets." All a studio had to do was "hire a few actors, rent a half dozen horses and travel a few miles outside Los Angeles, where nature provided the kind of spectacular scenery that could give an extra boost to even the most shaky productions."

Few people understand the genre better than Bobby Copeland of Knoxville, Tennessee, who has a collection of some fifteen hundred Westerns and has written or contributed to dozens of books about the subject. The film buff fondly recalls a childhood spent inside dark neighborhood theatres, cheering on the guys in the white hats and hissing those wearing black. "I think the real appeal was that the hero always had good, strong values," he said. "He didn't drink, swear, or carouse. If he hit a guy, he'd pick him up afterwards. Instead of killing the villain, he'd shoot the hat off his head. For kids who didn't really have a role model—and that includes me—these figures were like your father, preacher, and Sunday school teacher, all rolled into one. You'd come out of the theatre feeling like your soul had just been cleansed."

FBO held a casting call in 1925 and was impressed by the young man from Hamtramck. The muscular city slicker was asked if he could ride a horse. "I said 'yes' and didn't even gulp," he recalled later. "I knew if there was a way to stick on, I'd find it. I contacted a friend who was an expert horseman and it wasn't long before I was riding very well." An FBO executive flipped through a phone book and came upon the name Tyler. Coupled with Tom—borrowed from Tom Mix, the most popular Western star of the time—Vincent Markowski became Tom Tyler.

At barely twenty-two years old, Tyler was the lead in a series of quickie Westerns. His first FBO effort, *Galloping Gallagher,* did well in theaters. Publicity photos for the picture showed the new star in a bathing suit, hoisting a huge piece of wood above his head. The accompanying caption read: "This is Tom Tyler, the strongest man in Hollywood, who carries trunks of trees on his head and doesn't think anything of it." By the following year movie exhibitors considered him one of the country's top box-office draws. He was "a likeable hero with a low-key personality on screen," wrote one critic.

Tyler rarely made it back to Hamtramck, though family members visited him on several occasions. His brother Frank came out to California and decided to stay. Frank found a studio job as a gaffer and best boy, spending most of his career with Columbia Pictures. Tiring after a time of being asked why his and Tom's names were different, he changed his last name to Tyler, too.

By 1930, Tom Tyler had worked in more than forty movies, most of them low-budget Westerns. All were silent films. His transition to "talkies" was rocky, screenwriter Oliver Drake recalled in his autobiography: "When sound came in, things were tough for me in the picture business, but my friend Tom Tyler was having it much tougher. He had a slight Lithuanian accent and it seemed no one wanted him for a talkie. He had to move out of his house in Beverly Hills, sold his car, and was slowly going down the drain." Drake put Tyler in touch with a voice coach, who "liked Tom very much and continued coaching him over the next few months, long after Tom's money ran out."

With his tremendous work ethic, Tyler soon rebounded, appearing in fifteen movies in the 1931–1933 period. He also worked in five different serials for Universal Studios, stepping out of his established cowboy persona to play lead roles as a pilot, an African big-game hunter, and a Canadian Mountie. Most actors looked down on serials, but to Tyler the low-status work represented a regular paycheck for the few weeks it took to shoot one.

Back home, nobody cared whether he appeared in a feature or a two-reeler, a silent film or a talkie. He was "Hamtramck boyhood's greatest movie hero"—or so he was described when attending a New Year's Eve party for forty boys at St. Ann's Community House in 1931. "His prowess and horsemanship won for him a place in the hearts of millions of kids throughout the country," reported a local newspaper, "but no group of youngsters accorded his pictures a greater reception than those in his own hometown.

"His appearance at the party was held as a surprise for the boys, ranging from eight to fifteen years in age. When he entered the dining room, they immediately recognized him and sent up a tremendous cheer for him. Tom Tyler had dinner with them and then addressed the assemblage. In his talk, he referred to them as pals and, in Popeye fashion, advised them to drink their milk. They complied with a toast of milk to him."

A lobby card from the 1935 western *Trigger Tom*. Its star was described as "Hamtramck boyhood's greatest movie hero" when he came home for a visit in 1931. (Author's Collection)

Three years later, Tyler again came home for the Christmas holidays, making personal appearances at midnight shows at the Martha Washington Theater. "If I had known I was going to stay two weeks," he told the *Hamtramck Citizen*, "I would have brought my wonder horse, 'Lightning,' with me."

On screen, a cowboy's chief love interest was supposed to be his horse. In the real world, Tyler never lacked for female companionship. His sister Katherine remembered that when he was growing up in Hamtramck, girls who passed by on the sidewalk would always glance back. In California, he had his choice of starlets. At one point in the mid-1930s, he had an affair with Marlene Dietrich, the glamorous German-born actress who, in one biographer's words, "oozed sex." Actress Marion Schilling, who worked with Tyler, considered him "a handsome, big mass of muscle" and a conscientious actor who she would have liked to know better. He was "very quiet" on set, and she thought she knew why: "He was in the midst of a torrid love affair with Marlene Dietrich and during the day was probably in 'recovery.'"

On September 8, 1937, following a five-month romance, Tyler married actress Jeanne Martel in a small ceremony in Los Angeles. The violet-eyed brunette, described as a Joan Crawford look-alike, had lived in Detroit for a time when she was a girl. She was several years younger than Tyler, who told the press that he was "mainly interested in Jeanne as the grand wife she is and not the great star she might some day become." He called her "Punky."

In the mid-1930s, Tyler was making upward of five hundred dollars a week, a good income at a time when most Americans earned between twenty and forty dollars a week and a new car cost just a few hundred dollars. He bought an adobe Spanish-style house and proudly sent his family pictures of him posing in front of it. He was a homebody, enjoying gourmet cooking in the kitchen and cabinetmaking in his basement workshop. He also took flying lessons. However, his film career stalled as he bounced around the smaller studios. The breakthrough roles went to others, like Gary Cooper in 1937's *The Plainsman* and John Wayne in *Stagecoach* two years later. "The problem with actors who started with poverty-row studios is that they could never really get away from them," Copeland says. In order to keep the cash coming in between roles, Tyler toured for several months as the headliner of the Wallace Brothers Circus, showing off his strongman abilities to Depression Era audiences eager to see a familiar film figure in person.

With a new wave of younger stars to compete against, including a slew of singing cowboys like Gene Autry and Roy Rogers, Tyler's leading-man days in Westerns were over. He had to be content with second and third billing in Westerns and bit roles in larger budget films in which he often didn't receive screen credit. He's easy enough to spot, though. He's the deputy handcuffing Casy (John Carradine) in *The Grapes of Wrath,* for example, and the boxing referee in Abbott and Costello's *Buck Privates.* He pops up for a few seconds midway through *Gone With The Wind,* playing the courtly Confederate officer on horseback who tells Scarlett O'Hara

(Vivien Leigh) that it's time for her to move on during the evacuation of Atlanta. "Sorry, ma'am, we've got to march," he says. Brief as Tyler's appearance is, it was one of only fifty speaking roles in the three-and-a-half-hour movie, which had a cast of more than twenty-five hundred.

In *Stagecoach,* director John Ford gave Tyler a small but meaty role. This time he was cast as a homicidal heavy, Luke Plummer. Near the end of the movie Plummer is shot and killed by the Ringo Kid, played by John Wayne. It's no ordinary death, wrote Don Miller, with "Tyler ambling into the saloon after the gunfight, smiling benignly at the gathered tipplers, then keeling over." Ten years later, Tyler appeared in another Ford-Wayne collaboration. In *She Wore a Yellow Ribbon,* he played a wounded corporal operated on by a surgeon inside a moving, dimly lit wagon. "It's a tiny role, but I think it's one of the best performances he ever gave," Copeland said.

During the intervening decade, Wayne had escaped from the wasteland of B Westerns to become a big-screen star while Tyler had not. What was the difference?

"One of the things that hurt him a lot was his voice," said Ray Slepski, Tyler's nephew and godson. "He didn't have a good voice. It was kind of gravelly. You'd hear him talk, it just didn't hit you right." Tyler tended to overly enunciate his lines—an ongoing effort, some thought, to cover up his accent.

"He really wasn't cut out for major studio work," Copeland said. "He had a monotone voice—never went up or down—and he was pretty wooden in love scenes. Actually, despite his impressive physique, he really wasn't that good of a physical actor. He could look awkward in fight scenes. He didn't have major movie-star potential, however that's defined. You know it when you see it. Tom Tyler didn't have it—but his star still shone pretty brightly for a while."

Luck, as always, also played a big part. In 1931, Tyler auditioned for the title role in a new Tarzan film being produced by MGM. Although his physique made him seemingly perfect for the part of the jungle hero and the studio publicly acknowledged that he was the leading candidate, ultimately Olympic gold medalist swimmer Johnny Weissmuller was cast in the role. The film's director explained that Tyler was "not muscular

Captain Marvel fends off knife-wielding assailants in Siam in a chapter from the popular serial. (Author's Collection)

enough." The wooden Weissmuller became an instant worldwide star and grew rich off the Tarzan franchise, while Tyler was left to imagine what he might have been able to accomplish in a loincloth instead of a Stetson.

Tyler was thirty-seven years old when his sinking career was rejuvenated by a Republic Studios serial based on the cartoon character Captain Marvel. The red-clad super hero had debuted in Whiz Comics in early 1940 in response to the runaway success of Superman. As the story went, Captain Marvel really was Billy Batson, boy reporter. Upon saying the magic word, "Shazam!" Batson would be struck by a bolt of lightning and transformed into the superhero.

In the *Adventures of Captain Marvel,* Tyler warded off machine gun bursts with his hands, hoisted giant trees, hurled a twenty-ton engine, and fought off knife-wielding adversaries in remote Siam. Republic breathlessly hyped the action: "See the amazing feats of Captain Marvel. He flies like a bird! Bullets bounce off his body! He is the most awe-inspiring character ever seen on a screen! A one-man blitzkrieg!" As the big screen's first flying hero, Tyler had to endure hours strung up in a harness and rigging while being filmed in front of a process screen, recalled stuntman Davie Sharpe. The "pain must have been almost unbearable," he said. "Yet, he never let out a peep. What a pro!"

Casting Tyler as "the mighty muscleman" was considered "sheer genius" by one critic: "Visually suitable, he did such a great job and is so well remembered by fans for this very role that it is difficult to imagine any other actor in his place." Observed another: "Although primarily identified with Westerns, he was not so much a cowboy but simply a *hero* type."

Filming the twelve chapters of the *Adventures of Captain Marvel* took exactly thirty-nine days over the winter of 1940–1941. "At a large studio you would have a trailer as a dressing room and a catering service for your meals," Frank Coghlan, Jr., who played Billy Batson, told Tyler biographer Mike Chapman. "At Republic, you dressed where you could, had a box lunch and fought off the ants." For his work as Captain Marvel, Tyler was paid $250 a week. A few months later, Republic signed him to a two-year contract: $7,800 for the first year, $10,400 for the second.

During this period Tyler worked in several films in Republic's long-running "Three Mesquiteers" series of B Westerns. Each movie featured a trio of cowboys in a modern-day setting. While the actors (who at various times included John Wayne and Bob Steele) were interchangeable, the characters' popularity remained intact until the series finally ran its course in 1943. At the end Tyler was playing a character named Stoney Brooke and the trio was battling Nazis.

In 1943, Tyler was signed by Columbia to portray the title character in *The Phantom,* another serial based on a comic-strip hero. Although he was by that time forty years old, the trim actor wore his skintight purple costume as the masked "Ghost Who Walks" well. The action this time took place in the wilds of Bengali and involved hidden treasure and the Lost City of Zoloz. The role required Tyler to wrestle a stuntman in a gorilla suit and share screen time with canine sensation Ace the Wonder

Dog, a German shepherd known as "Devil" in the serial. It was formulaic fare, but youngsters ate it up and critics were impressed. William C. Cline later wrote that Tyler bore "an almost uncanny" resemblance to his character. Noting the actor's stilted speech and movements, Cline suggested that Tyler was "the Gary Cooper of B films."

Unlike millions of American males, Tyler did not serve in uniform in World War II. For one thing, he was too old. For another, by the middle 1940s he was starting to experience signs of the illness that eventually drove him out of movies and killed him. His joint pain and swelling was initially diagnosed as rheumatoid arthritis; however, the true nature of his ailments, which didn't manifest until years later when his skin began tightening and his features grew deformed, were not yet apparent.

The superhero was suffering from an uncommon autoimmune disease called scleroderma. A few thousand new cases are diagnosed every year in the United States. Most of the afflicted are between the ages of thirty and fifty. Three-quarters of the victims are women. Its cause remains unknown. Slepski said nobody else in the family, before or since, ever exhibited symptoms of the disease. Its severity can vary widely, but there is no cure.

In addition to thickening of the skin, the disease also can wreak havoc with the victim's internal organs. According to literature from the Scleroderma Foundation in Byfield, Massachusetts, "The same process going on in the skin can enmesh the lungs in strands of scar tissue so dense that the victim struggles for air. Scar tissue in the esophagus makes swallowing painful and troublesome. In the digestive tract it inhibits the absorption of nutrients. Joints all over the body might throb with pain. Kidney involvement is particularly treacherous. It leads to high blood pressure and kidney failure."

Tyler's young wife could not live with his condition. "They got divorced," Slepski said. "The story we always heard was that she ran off with some other guy." Republic also dumped him, deciding not to renew his two-hundred-dollar weekly contract. For the rest of the 1940s and into the '50s, Tyler determinedly tried to cobble together a living with a series of bit parts in film and TV while also fighting off the advances of his insidious disease. "Out of all the people I worked with, Tom loved his work the

Tyler, pictured with Ace the Wonder Dog, was the title character in *The Phantom*. (Author's Collection)

most," Clayton Moore, television's Lone Ranger, once said. "Through all the ups and downs, and there were plenty of both for all actors, he never complained and was always upbeat. He just loved the work."

In addition to minor roles in such movies as *They Were Expendable* and *Samson and Delilah,* Tyler appeared in several TV shows, including *Cowboy G-Men* and *Dick Tracy.* Longtime Detroit movie host and former bit actor Bill Kennedy worked with Tyler on a couple episodes of *The Gene Autry Show.* "We all knew that Tom was terminal and that Gene had hired him as a tribute," Kennedy said in a 1997 interview. "We loved Gene for this gesture. Tom gave a superlative performance in both segments. We spent a week with Tom and I got to talk to him about his fascinating career. He knew Doug Fairbanks, Valentino, John Gilbert, Tom Mix, William S. Hart, Chaplin. John Ford liked him, as well as many other famous directors of that time."

Tyler's last role was as Deputy Ed in *Crossroad Avenger: The Adventures of the Tucson Kid,* a television pilot directed by Ed Wood. Wood, zealous and inept, later gained posthumous fame as "the worst director of all time," thanks to Johnny Depp's portrayal of him in Tim Burton's 1994 Oscar-winning biopic. Wood's amateurish production was never picked up by a studio, which was just as well, considering Tyler's health. While Wood went on to produce another unsold TV pilot, *Dr. Acula,* with another terminally ill actor, Bela Lugosi, Tyler left Hollywood for Hamtramck.

He arrived at his sister Katherine's house one November day in 1952, virtually penniless. Ray Slepski was then a young teenager. He surrendered his bedroom—which was directly across from the only bathroom in the house—and moved into another one down the hall. "The bathroom had one of those steam cabinets, and he liked to use it," Slepski explained. "It seemed to help his hands and his skin a little."

Ironically, just as Tyler was slipping into obscurity, many of his cowboy films were airing on television, introducing him to a new generation of viewers. Unfortunately, he had not secured any rights to his work, which meant that he received no royalties. Like many actors, he had displayed little business sense. He and a partner once opened a realty office on North Vine in Hollywood and somehow managed not to make any money during Southern California's real estate boom. "One time some guy wanted him to invest eleven hundred dollars in distributing a new lemon-lime soft drink, but he said no," Slepski recalls. "The soft drink was 7 Up."

Tyler spent most days in a chair in the sunroom, overlooking a grassy lot. In nice weather he sometimes sat on the front porch and patiently answered neighbors' questions about Hollywood and its stars. He shuffled instead of walked, and his gnarled hands had a hard time gripping his favorite summer food, corn on the cob. His lips retracted, and his teeth and eyes bulged. His skin was taut, discolored, and leatherlike. "He was not pleasant to look at," Slepski said. "It really took a toll on my mother. She was a saintly woman. She never complained and neither did my dad. In those days, family took care of family. There never was any question that we would take care of Uncle Tom."

On the morning of Saturday, May 3, 1954, Tyler, who was having difficulty breathing, was taken by ambulance to St. Francis Hospital in Hamtramck. "He'd been looking a little better, so it actually was a shock when he died that night," Slepski said. The official cause of death was a heart attack brought on by hardening of the arteries, which had been caused by scleroderma. It took a while for the hospital to realize who the deceased patient was.

"Word got out that, hey, this was a movie actor," Slepski said. "He was laid out at Wysocki Funeral Home on McNichols, a couple blocks from our house. It was a small funeral parlor, and I remember it being so crowded. People were coming from all over the country. Guys with cowboy hats, old actors, kids who saw him on TV, just a ton of people." A police escort was needed for the sixty-five-car procession from the funeral home to Mount Olivet Cemetery, where Tyler was buried in the Markowski family plot. A stone marker bears an image of him in a cowboy hat.

Today Tom Tyler remains eternally young and invincible, thanks to the reissuing of several of his cowboy films and superhero serials on DVD. "It's been, what, how many years since he died?" Slepski said. "People still call, they just want to talk about him. Some guy from Ohio's going up north next week and he wants to stop by and say hello. It's incredible, really, and I don't mind. It's good that he's remembered."

Robert Blake in the 1960 movie *The Purple Gang*. (Author's Collection)

TWENTY-THREE
Purple Reign

The lawless years of Prohibition in Detroit were dominated by a ruthless band of toughs known as the Purple Gang.

They're all gone now, the once feared members of Detroit's infamous Purple Gang. During the *rat-a-tat-tat* years of Prohibition, the storied Jewish mobsters strode through town with breezy confidence and sneering lips, dispensing threats, bullets, and twenty-dollar tips at will. Rival thugs feared them, law enforcement respected them, the Jewish community they preyed on loathed them, and those on the outside—reporters, show girls, and Grosse Pointe swells—were fascinated by them.

"The Purple Gang was a hard lot of guts, so tough they made Capone's playmates look like a kindergarten class," jazz musician Milton "Mezz" Mezzrow recalled in his memoirs. "Detroit's snooty set used to feel it was really living to talk to them hoodlums without getting their own brains blown out." Mezzrow was no different, frequently bragging about how he smoked opium and drank rotgut with the Purples.

In the case of the Purple Gang, those in the vicious center of events faithfully kept the unseemly particulars to themselves all the way to the grave. Paul Kavieff, a local crime buff who tried harder than most to get them to talk, sidled up to them at such favorite haunts as Max Silk's Left Field Deli, across the street from Tiger Stadium. One Purple who occasionally dropped in to see his old friend Max was Harry Keywell, who spent thirty-two years behind bars for his part in shooting three unarmed

This police lineup in 1928 includes Purple Gangsters Harry Keywell (*second from right, rear*) and Ziggy Selbin (*fourth from right, rear*). (Author's Collection)

men to death in 1931. As they all sat at the diner on one occasion, an acquaintance of Kavieff's tried his best to reconcile the age spots, thinning hair, and crepe-paper skin with the old Purple's murderous reputation. He thought the frail octogenarian looked like an accountant.

"What did you expect?" responded Kavieff. "You think these guys all wear black shirts and white ties and carry violin cases?"

Thanks to such popular depictions of criminal life in *The Godfather* or *Guys and Dolls,* there's an almost irresistible tendency to romance gangsters—especially from a safe distance. The dark truth is that the men who made the headlines during Detroit's most lawless years were more along the lines of the sociopath Joe Pesci portrayed in the movie *GoodFellas.*

There was, for instance, Ziggy Selbin. While never an important Purple, he was representative of most members of the gang: young, Jewish, and wildly unprincipled. Selbin was born in Detroit in 1910, the son of a deli owner who also dabbled in petty crime. By the time he was a teenager, Selbin had committed several contract murders and was doing considerable freelance work. Once Selbin got into an argument with a drinking companion who refused to surrender a ring that Selbin admired. He solved the stalemate by cutting off the man's finger.

Despite his dirty work for the gang, the hard-to-control Selbin had become a public embarrassment. One day in 1929, a gunman walked up to Selbin on a downtown street and emptied his pistol into him. It was just one of the five hundred or so murders the Purples are thought to have committed during their heyday.

"These guys were just cowboys," said Kavieff. "And that's why they didn't last long."

The Purple Gang was the true power of Detroit's underworld for only a short while, from the mid-1920s through the early '30s. They were, however, a force to be reckoned with. Generally preferring muscles to brainpower, they bullied their way into a variety of activities, including kidnapping, extortion, and labor racketeering. The Purples also controlled an extensive bootlegging empire, providing clients such as Al Capone with a steady supply of liquor from Canada. Above all, they were unblinking killers for hire who participated in scores of hits, including that quintessential gangland slaying, the St. Valentine's Day Massacre in 1929.

After Harry Keywell and other Purples were sent to prison three years later for their roles in the infamous Collingwood Massacre in Detroit (a triple murder in 1931, described in an earlier chapter), individual Purples continued to operate through the 1940s, although internecine warfare and the Italian mob combined to make them little more than a footnote in crime annals once Prohibition was repealed. By then, however, their reputation had been secured for all time.

To understand the Purple Gang, one has to understand the environment that spawned them. Unlike many of today's urban gangs, they were not products of crushing poverty, broken homes, or widespread economic despair. Most were raised in middle-class households in the east side neighborhood around Hastings Street. Their parents were religiously conservative Jewish immigrants who owned delicatessens and scrap yards or worked brutal hours at Dodge Main and Briggs Manufacturing.

At the core of the group were three sets of brothers: Abe, Joey, Ray, and Izzy Bernstein; Harry and Philip Keywell; and Harry, Sam, and Lou Fleisher. Except for the much older Abe Bernstein, who was born in Russia in 1893, the boys grew up within several years of one another. Most of them attended Bishop Ungraded, a trade school on Winder Street. The playground was the site of daily card and crap games, where the impressionable youths picked up a few tricks and ran errands for older hoods. In the years following the First World War, these restless adolescents graduated from stealing fruit at Eastern Market to shaking down neighborhood merchants.

Exactly how this loosely organized band of budding gangsters acquired its name is open to conjecture. One theory is that a shopkeeper forced to pay them for "protection" described them as being "purple—like raw meat." Other versions suggest that they were named after an early leader, Sam "Sammy Purple" Cohen, or by an imaginative member of the press. Whatever the origin, one thing about the Purples is clear: they may have outgrown petty thievery and moved on to respectable professions if not for the advent of that great social experiment known as Prohibition.

Far from solving the universal problem of drunkenness, Prohibition was responsible for the birth of modern organized crime. Nowhere was this more apparent than in Detroit, which was, during the 1920s, an industrial boomtown of 1.5 million hard-drinking citizens. "Soused and serene" is how one national publication described the city during its fifteen-year (1918–1933) "dry" period. A local newspaper estimated that some twenty-five thousand blind pigs were operating in the city, including one run by Max Silk, a school chum of Ray Bernstein.

Born in Canton, Ohio, in 1907, Silk moved to Detroit as a teenager. His family, like so many ordinary but opportunistic citizens of the day, became minor players in the booze business. The Silk family set Max up in a deli that was really a front for a bootlegging operation. While Silk always maintained that he never did jobs for the Purples, he admitted that they "knew each other." He also worked the same territory and followed a similar pattern of crime, including a bread-and-butter activity of the Purples: hijacking someone else's liquor shipment.

Detroit police raid a still. By 1928 the illegal booze trade was worth an estimated $400 million and employed 50,000 people, making it the city's second-largest industry behind auto manufacturing. (Walter P. Reuther Library)

Under the guidance of mentors Charlie Lighter and Henry Shorr (the latter of whom was the father of Mickey Shorr of radio and electronics-store fame), who ran the Oakland Sugar House on Oakland Avenue, gang members eventually made and shipped their own brand of booze. But they still found it more convenient to simply steal what other operators had taken the time and risk to haul across the Detroit River from Canada.

Few were better at stealing hooch than Harry Fleisher, the soft-spoken son of a scrap yard dealer. Born in 1903, he was admired as a man who "did his own work." A favorite tactic of his was breaking down the door of a garage suspected of housing a still and promising a vagrant five dollars to transfer the booze to his truck. After the loading was finished, so was the loader: passersby would eventually discover the bullet-riddled body in the alley. Like most Purples, Fleisher was arrested scores of times for everything from murder and kidnapping to assault and drug possession.

In 1928, Silk was arrested for robbing a "hell of a load of booze" at gunpoint. Whether he was working for himself or the Purples, he wound up spending a dozen years in Jackson and Marquette prisons. There he walked the exercise yard with Purples like Irving Milberg, Philip Keywell, and Morris Rader. The latter two were sentenced to life in prison for killing a fourteen-year-old boy who happened to peek into a garage that the gang was using as a distillery.

Strictly speaking, card-carrying members of the Purple Gang never really existed. Certainly none of them ever referred to themselves as Purples. "Purple Gang?" Izzy Bernstein complained from his jail cell in 1929. "Aw, ferget it. This Purple Gang stuff makes me sick. The Purple Gang, the Purple Gang! All the time the Purple Gang! Who got up that name? Everybody's a Purple. It's the bunk!" More than anything, the name was a media device, an attempt to impose order, logic, and organization on a wide range of illegal activities perpetrated by individuals who often resisted all manner of order, logic, and organization. However, in May 1929, Joey Bernstein represented the Purples at an Atlantic City meeting of several crime groups, including gangsters such as New York's Dutch Schultz and Lucky Luciano. The attempt to carve out individual territory represented the first step toward organizing the American underworld, an irony not lost on Paul Kavieff. The Purples were never structured like the Mafia families, he explained. "Certain groups might get together to pull a heist, but they did their own thing most of the time, which was the problem in the end. It was hard keeping these guys in line for any length of time."

The Purples first made headlines in the fall of 1925, when a group of cleaning wholesalers, looking to fix the price of cleaning suits in the city, hired them for one thousand dollars a week to "convince" independent shops to join the association. Abe Bernstein, the acknowledged brains behind the muscle, orchestrated a long series of bombings, kidnappings, and murders. The level of violence in the four-year "cleaners and dyers war" appalled the wholesalers, who at one point tried to back out of their agreement with the association. The group had a collective change of heart after the association's leader, Sam Polakoff, was found shot to death inside his car on Dexter Boulevard.

Vice turned Detroit into a frontier town. In 1926, the bloodiest year of the Roaring '20s, the city recorded 326 homicides. Most were gang-related and went unsolved. In a two-year span, 1927–1928, the police killed 70 people and wounded 134 more. On the other side of the ledger, eight policemen were shot to death, and another were 25 wounded.

According to one study, by 1928 the smuggling, manufacturing, and distribution of illegal booze was worth an estimated $400 million and employed 50,000 people, making it the city's second-largest industry behind auto manufacturing. With so much money on the street, the city was rotten with corruption and vice. To handle the explosion of crime, the police department doubled in size, but the effect was to put more cops on the various underworld payrolls. One-third of the officers in the class of 1926, for example, were either dismissed or indicted for corruption by 1932. They joined an ever-growing list of public officials, including mayors and police chiefs, who were booted out of office or tossed in jail during the era.

The opportunities presented by Prohibition attracted countless out-of-town hoodlums with major crime bosses or their representatives coming from St. Louis, Chicago, and other cities for a look-see at the country's main port of entry for booze. At a 1927 meeting inside the Book-Cadillac Hotel with Abe Bernstein and other local gang leaders, Al Capone was told in no uncertain terms to "stay the hell out of Detroit." Even so, Capone liked the Purples' style enough to hire them to transport his favorite Canadian whiskey to Chicago.

Abe Axler and Eddie Fletcher—two "Yorkies," as the Purples called transplants from New York—arrived in Detroit about 1926. They were inseparable pals. Fletcher, a onetime boxer, was a particularly natty dresser, typically sporting spats, a diamond stickpin, a brightly colored silk suit, and a wide-brimmed hat. Like Axler, who had spent time in Sing Sing, he could just as well have worn a hood and carried a scythe, for both are thought to have personally dispatched scores of men for both personal and professional reasons. In early 1927, the pair was widely suspected of pulling off the first Tommy gun murders in Detroit, gunning down three rival gangsters inside the Milaflores Apartments at 106 East Alexandrine. And they assisted in numerous freelance hits for payoffs that usually numbered several thousand dollars. Axler and Fletcher may have had a peripheral but important role in the most famous gangland slaying of them all. On February 14, 1929, seven members of Bugs Moran's gang were slaughtered inside a Chicago garage while waiting for a load of hijacked whiskey. Only one member of the hit team has ever been positively identified: Fred "Killer" Burke, a St. Louis transplant who did occasional work with the Purples, including the triple murder at the Milaflores. Axler and Fletcher are thought to have acted as lookouts for the St. Valentine's Day Massacre, which eliminated Capone's chief underworld rival.

The term "underworld" could be applied only loosely to the high-profile Purples as they were regularly seen about town—stirring coffee at Segal's Drug Store on 12th Street, shooting pool at Nick's on Cass Avenue, fanning the breeze with Tiger stars from their box seats at Navin Field, or taking steam at the Oakland Schvitz. The Cream of Michigan Restaurant on Grand River had so many known gangsters sitting around its tables, sipping barley soup, and idly building igloos out of sugar cubes that the press dubbed the café the "Crime of Michigan."

At night gang members squired teenage show girls around the city's countless speakeasies. They might spend the evening at Ruby Jones's Montmarte cabaret, where the diminutive singer would croon "Big Bad Bill (Is Sweet William Now)," or at Morey's on Michigan Avenue, where a rendition of "My Yiddish Mama" was always good for a five-dollar tip from Ray Bernstein. However, all-night orgies at Oakland County roadhouses or downtown opium dens were also part of the lifestyle for some Purples. Harry Millman, in particular, was known for his almost inhuman consumption of booze, cocaine, heroin, and women.

Being in the Purples' wake sometimes meant crossing paths with a bullet. Mary Lou Neiger grew up in the upper flat of a house at 1963 West Euclid. The flat's owner, a Jewish man she called "Mr. L," was a bondsman for the Purples. "Warm, motherly Mrs. L" had brothers and a cousin in the gang. "I was only four or so," said Neiger, "but I can remember sitting on a gangster's lap in the kitchen. He let me play with his gun." One day, little Mary Lou wandered farther than she was allowed. "I was leaning against a telephone pole when this long, black touring car drove slowly by," she recalled. "When it drove past about the third shop from the corner, they started shooting. I could hear gunfire and glass breaking." After Mr. L's bodyguard was found murdered, his body unceremoniously deposited in their trash can, Mary Lou's father decided to move the family to a safe location in Palmer Park.

For years, such Wild West shootouts drew close scrutiny only when innocent citizens happened to get caught in the cross fire. This attitude was beginning to change by "Bloody July" of 1930, when a dozen gangsters were gunned down on city streets. That month, citizens finally fed up with years of lawlessness recalled Mayor Charles Bowles in a special election. A few hours after the polls closed, popular radio commentator Jerry Buckley was shot to death in the lobby of the La Salle Hotel. Police rounded up the usual suspects, including several Purples. But no one was ever indicted for Buckley's murder, which insiders attributed to the broadcaster's double cross of certain criminals friendly to Bowles.

The uproar should have persuaded Bernstein and company to lay low. Instead, on September 17, 1931, they pulled off a triple murder that effectively broke the gang's back. That day, Ray Bernstein, Harry Keywell, Harry Fleisher, and Irving Milberg invited three members of a group of bootleggers called the Third Avenue Navy to an apartment in the Collingwood Manor at the corner of 12th and Collingwood. The meeting was set up by a bookie named Solly Levine, a friend of Bernstein's who innocently assumed that the talk was to be of the upcoming American Legion convention, which promised a windfall in liquor sales.

Instead, midway through the meeting a car in the alley started backfiring—a signal for the Purples to draw guns and pump sixteen shots into their unarmed guests, who had incurred Bernstein's wrath by encroaching on his territory. As Levine and the Purples were fleeing toward the getaway car, a gun fell to the floor. His companions asked Levine to pick it up. Levine did, then realized that he had sealed his fate by putting his fingerprints on one of the murder weapons.

Protected by a personal bodyguard of twelve policemen, the bookie agreed to testify against Bernstein, Keywell, and Milberg. All received life sentences. Harry Fleisher, who had disappeared after the shootings, showed up one year later (by which time he had been implicated in

Ray Bernstein, Irving Milberg, and Harry Keywell are sent to prison following their convictions in the Collingwood Massacre. (Author's Collection)

the Lindbergh baby kidnapping). Levine had long since fled. Without testimony, authorities had no choice but to let Fleisher go.

Repeal was right around the corner, and so was the end of the Purples' short reign. With their primary sources of revenue gone and their leaders behind bars, individual Purples fell victim to the eastside Italian mobs and to one another.

Jackie Sherman, a ham-and-egg boxer in the early 1930s, remembered what happened to his manager, Eddie Fletcher. "Sure, I knew Eddie and Abe Axler were killers," said the former welterweight. "But they were all right by me. He never had me lay down in a fight. He'd tell the tough guys around the gym, 'Leave the kid alone. He's a good kid.'"

One November night in 1933, Fletcher and Axler left a bar in Pontiac. A constable later found them inside their car on a gravel road near Telegraph and Quarton. Each had been shot several times in the face. "Eddie

A crowd quickly gathers outside Boesky's Restaurant on 12th Street on November 25, 1937, as word spreads that Harry Millman has been gunned down. (Walter P. Reuther Library)

The body of gangster Harry Millman is loaded into the county coroner's hearse. (Walter P. Reuther Library)

and Abe were in the backseat," said Sherman. "They were holding each other's hands when the bullets hit them."

Henry Shorr, who was thought to be ready to testify against some remaining Purples, disappeared one day in 1935. No one was ever indicted, although Harry Fleisher had his car reupholstered two days after Shorr was reported missing.

Harry Millman met his end on Thanksgiving eve 1937, at Boesky's Restaurant on 12th Street. (The owners were parents of future Wall Street trader Ivan Boesky.) Two men emptied their pistols into the burly brawler, whose post-Prohibition career had consisted largely of shaking down whorehouses controlled by Italian gangs. "The wops got him," Millman's girlfriend said, crying.

Detroit's Mafia, led by Joe Moceri, Joe "Scarface" Bommarito, "Papa John" Prizola, "Black Bill" Tocco, and Joe Zerilli, quickly filled the vac-

Purple Gangsters Harry Fleisher (*left*) and Myron "Mike" Selik (*right*) were called to testify in the Hooper murder investigation in 1945. (Author's Collection)

uum left by the Purples' demise. The gang's name, however, continued to surface in the news during the war years. During that time the warden of Jackson Prison was accused of giving Ray Bernstein and his incarcerated lieutenants special treatment. Among the charges listed were: bookies allowed to operate within prison walls, Purples occasionally given liberty to travel to Briggs Stadium to watch the Tigers play, and prostitutes smuggled into the infirmary.

The most sensational post-Prohibition Purple development was the unsolved murder of state Senator Warren G. Hooper one cold January night in 1945. Hooper, who had admitted to taking bribes, was killed before he had a chance to reveal who was behind the payoffs. The triggermen were thought to include two old Purples, Harry Keywell and

Ray Bernstein, who used their privileged position to leave prison for the short while it took to shoot Hooper in his car on a lonely Jackson County road.

The Purples' reputation worked its way into postwar pop culture, with Elvis Presley including them in his 1957 hit, "Jailhouse Rock" ("the whole rhythm section was the Purple Gang") and Hollywood releasing a movie version of the mob's story in 1960 titled *The Purple Gang*. Robert Blake starred as "Honeyboy" Willard in his first feature film.

Few Purples finished their lives in prison. Ray Bernstein died shortly after his release in 1964, proclaiming to the parole board that "crime does not pay." Others, like Keywell and Harry Fleisher, moved to places such as Florida and Las Vegas and faded quietly away. Since then, occasional historical exhibits featuring the Purples have come under attack from the local Jewish community. "As far as most older Jews are concerned, the Purple Gang never existed," said Steve Rosman of Southfield, who once organized an exhibit on Detroit's Jewish community of the 1920s and '30s that included the infamous mobsters. "They're considered an embarrassment. But I think that, deep down, many of these same people remain fascinated with the image."

The Detroit Stars inside Mack Park in 1919. Tenny Blount (*center, wearing sweater*) was the club's manager. (Author's Collection)

TWENTY-FOUR
Black Diamonds

During the apartheid era of professional baseball, black stars like Turkey Stearnes and Ray Dandridge were forced to play in a league of their own.

Turkey Stearnes was the greatest baseball player that Detroit never saw.

Several generations ago, inside the emerald confines of old Mack Park on the city's near east side, Norman "Turkey" Stearnes regularly thrilled crowds with feats of batting and fielding brilliance that, had he been born a white man, would have won the wiry centerfielder fame, money, and a starring role with the Detroit Tigers or any other major league club. Instead, Stearnes's style and accomplishments merely made him the most conspicuous member of the Detroit Stars, a charter entry in the Negro National League in 1920, and the city's first and foremost black professional baseball team.

"He was one of the darlings of the crowd," a fan remembered years later. "Some chick would cry out, 'Hit that ball, Turkey Breast! Hit it, baby!' When Turkey swung and missed, it would set up a Pentecostal wind in Mack Park."

More often than not, though, Turkey would connect. Parlaying powerful shoulders with one of the oddest batting stances ever—chest puffed out, the toe of his right foot pointed skyward—Turkey Stearnes swatted a truckload of home runs. In 1923, his first season with the Stars, he hit thirty-five home runs. He walloped more than fifty the following season, after which point he hit so many home runs that he "just quit counting," he said. He hit them far, too. One round-tripper carried 470 feet out of Mack Park, while another blast in St. Louis soared an estimated 500 feet.

Stearnes compiled a lifetime batting average of .350 in Negro League play and led the league in home runs several times. In 1930, while across town the Tigers were floundering in fifth place, Stearnes almost single-handedly propelled the Detroit Stars into a play-off with the St. Louis Stars for the Negro National League pennant. Although Detroit lost in nine games, Stearnes put on a one-man show, cracking out five base hits in the second game alone. The excitement and level of play at crowded Mack Park approached that of the white major leagues' own World Series, but in *The Sporting News,* long the self-proclaimed "bible of baseball," there was not a single mention of the heroics of Turkey Stearnes and his black contemporaries. It was almost as though black baseball didn't exist—which, in a very real sense, it didn't.

Invisible men. That is how one historian described them, this legion of black athletes, many blessed with extraordinary talent, who toiled in obscurity in baseball's gulag during the first half of the twentieth century, their deeds and faces absent from the sports pages and bubble gum cards of white America. For these men, denied a chance at the major leagues and all that it represented in terms of achievement, recognition, and security, the notion of the national pastime in a segregated society proved a myth; their anonymity in the professional sports world was a cruel joke. "I'd go out on the street," lamented Ray Dandridge, a superb third baseman who broke in with the Detroit Stars in 1933, "and the kids didn't know a thing about our Negro baseball."

Ray Dandridge and Turkey Stearnes—both of whom were belatedly enshrined at the National Baseball Hall of Fame—were only two of the many black diamonds who sparkled during the heyday of black baseball, a period measured roughly from the formation of the Negro National League in 1920 to 1947, when Jackie Robinson finally shattered the major leagues' color barrier as a member of the Brooklyn Dodgers. Robinson's immediate and spectacular success that year led to opportunities for similarly gifted black athletes. Within a decade the Negro League folded like a house of cards, robbed of its finest talent by the same league it had hoped for so long to integrate. It was a bitter and ironic ending to a game that had, in the black community, evolved into a cultural institution of the highest order.

On February 13, 1920, a group of black men met in a Kansas City YMCA and put up five hundred dollars each toward the formation of the Negro National League. Prior to that, all-black teams had existed in Detroit and elsewhere on an independent, semiprofessional basis, barnstorming through the countryside and playing games whenever an opponent and ball field could be found. The new league, though, represented the first successful attempt to organize black teams along the lines of the white major leagues.

Andrew "Rube" Foster, the league's chief organizer and president (and today known as "the father of Negro baseball"), correctly foresaw a burgeoning interest in his league in the country's emerging Northern ghettos: New York's Harlem, Chicago's South Side, and Detroit's Black Bottom, among others. Franchises came and went, owing to their generally tenuous financial backing, but before the Negro National League temporarily folded during the Great Depression, its teams were playing before weekend crowds of several thousands, with some of its star players drawing a salary of upward of four hundred dollars a month.

The Detroit Stars, a charter member of Foster's league, existed for several years as a nearly unbeatable semi-pro team prior to 1920. John "Tenny" Blount, a Paradise Valley sports promoter and numbers racketeer, headed the Stars' operation, renting Mack Park, near Southeastern High School, for league games and exhibitions.

The 1920s were the zenith of black baseball in Detroit. The Stars, who usually played exciting and winning baseball, were supported by a black community that had grown from just 5,700 in 1910 to more than 41,000 a decade later. Henry Ford's assembly lines provided work for the sudden influx of blacks from the Deep South, and the Stars afforded black workers and their families one of the few recreational activities available to them in a segregated city.

John Glover, a photographer whose own family migrated to Detroit from Alabama in 1919, remembered Mack Park in the '20s: "At that

Catcher Leon "Pepper" Daniels played for the Stars during the 1920s. (Larry Lester Collection)

time, Mack Park was considered way out of town. We used to take the Mack streetcar down, and if you were the least athletically inclined you could hop off the car before the conductor came through and collected fares. I don't know how many the park officially held—maybe three or four thousand. But it was always filled when I was there. You even had a few whites in the stands."

Glover has his own special recollection of Turkey Stearnes, who one afternoon spied Glover and two friends trying to sneak into the park through a hole in the centerfield fence. "Turkey was playing centerfield," said Glover. "He called time and stopped the game to personally escort us out the same hole in the fence, all the while saying some uncomplimentary things about me."

Lawrence Carter, an occasional columnist for *The Detroit News,* years later remembered some of the excitement surrounding the only black professional athletes in Detroit. "On Sundays," he wrote, "Mack Park would be jam-packed to watch the Stars play the Kansas City Monarchs with their peerless pitcher Bullet Rogan, the Pittsburgh Homestead Grays with the legendary home run hitter Oscar Charleston, or maybe the Cuban All-Stars. . . . Across Gratiot at St. Antoine near Beacon was 'Brosher the Biscuit King' . . . a fervent booster of the Detroit Stars. When they won, Brosher, a stompin'-down good piano player, would celebrate with music and eats. It was a great time."

Thanks to a booming economy, Detroit in the Twenties was able to support two baseball teams: one black, one white. And while blacks were allowed into Navin Field to cheer for the Tigers, few dared dream of one day playing for them. Even Detroit Mayor Coleman Young, who as a youth growing up in Black Bottom thrilled to the Tigers' radio broadcasts, once admitted as much. "We were more likely to dream about playing for the Homestead Grays," Young said.

That it took eighty-four years after slavery was abolished in the United States before the major leagues issued its own Emancipation Proclamation is unsurprising when one considers the game's hidebound past. As late as 1936, for instance, the major leagues fielded exactly one Jewish star, one bespectacled ballplayer, and barely weathered the storm surrounding "Frenchy" Bordagaray's cultivation of a mustache during that

The Detroit Stars, circa 1926. Norman "Turkey" Stearnes stands, third from right. (Dick Clark Collection)

year's spring training with Brooklyn. It was unspoken but abundantly clear that there was no room for a black man in a league that could not even accommodate facial hair. At the heart of such narrow-mindedness, of course, was the myth of white supremacy—the assumption that, Jim Crow aside, black athletes would not be able to compete with their white counterparts. That assumption was a constant sore point with all Negro Leaguers—and one that crumbled in the face of evidence.

Ray Sheppard came to the Stars on July 4, 1923, after his previous club, the Indianapolis ABC's, folded because of financial problems. In his first at bat for Detroit, he smashed a pinch hit, game-winning home run—a harbinger of an outstanding career that was never allowed to go further than the Negro Leagues.

"If we'd only been given the opportunity, a lot of us would have made the majors," said Sheppard, a retired Galveston, Texas, schoolteacher. "This isn't bragging, but over ten years I hit .300 or better each year. And the proof that our players were equal to, if not better than, the major leaguers was apparent whenever white all-star teams would play black all-star teams in exhibition games when both of their seasons were over."

Negro League clubs typically played between sixty and eighty "official" league games against each other but filled in their schedule with as many exhibition matches as possible. The most exciting of these were the contests between white and black all-star teams. Charley Gehringer, the Tigers' Hall of Fame second baseman from 1924–1942, played in many. "I traveled one year with a group of major league starts," he recalled, "and we traveled through the Dakotas, Kansas and Minnesota, barnstorming against Satchell Paige and his Chicago American Giants. I got to bat against Satchell almost every day, which wasn't much fun. He was a great pitcher.

"They had some great players. I remember that Chicago team had a big first baseman by the name of Mule Suttles. Gol', he could hit a ball nine miles. I remember we had a pretty good pitcher named Earl Whitehill pitching for us, and he couldn't get some of those guys out. Mule wore poor ol' Whitehill out." Although records are incomplete, it's estimated that black teams won sixty percent of their games against white teams.

The Great Depression dealt a crippling blow to the Negro National League. Some of the stronger clubs staggered through the Thirties before emerging stronger than ever in the Forties. Other clubs, like the Detroit Stars, went down for the count. With unemployment among Detroit blacks estimated at eighty percent during the dog days of the Depression, the black community was hard-pressed to support their families, much less a ball team.

In his old age, Charles "Red" House possesses the misshapen hands and gentle demeanor peculiar to so many boxers. Growing up in the Rivard-Hastings section of Detroit, House exhibited prowess in both boxing and baseball. He was the 1932 Golden Gloves Middleweight Champion, as well as an outstanding infielder on the Titus Stars, the immediate successor to the Detroit Stars.

"I loved both sports," said House, flipping through a scrapbook in the dining room of his River Rouge home. "But baseball was a little better because they didn't hit you back." House barnstormed with several Detroit-based semipro teams, including an outfit called the Zulu Giants.

Mack Park after a fire on July 7, 1929, that injured some two hundred spectators. After a decade of playing their home games at the field, the Stars moved to other sites in Detroit and Hamtramck. (Author's Collection)

"That was in 1933–34," he recalled. "We got all the best players that weren't working, and booked games every day from here to the West Coast. Phoenix, Butte, Seattle, Oakland, you name it. We wore straw skirts and painted our faces. Yeah, that's right. How do you think we drew crowds? Especially whites; they were crazy about it."

Embarrassing? "I felt okay," replied House, with the conviction of a practical man. "I made four or five dollars a game." House played the 1937 season with the rejuvenated Stars, making three hundred dollars a month. "Which was real good money, I'm tellin' you."

One of Red House's close friends, Joe Barrow, grew up on Catherine Street, näively dreaming of someday playing for his beloved Tigers. It wasn't until after Barrow changed his name to Joe Louis and became boxing's heavyweight champion that he was able to realize a watered-down version of his dream. Organizing twenty-two unemployed friends into the Brown Bomber Softball Team, and playing first base himself, Louis sunk thirty thousand dollars into a cross-country tour that eventually collapsed on the West Coast.

Other black teams flourished briefly in Detroit during the 1930s. Perhaps the most notable was the Detroit Cubs, which played its games at Dequindre Park on Modern and Dequindre, where a Vlasic pickle factory was later built. While Mickey Cochrane was leading the Tigers to pennants in 1934–1935, his black counterpart, catcher-manager Barney Jenkins, was exciting the north side of town with his own hitting and field leadership.

The 1940s witnessed both the high point and the swan song of the Negro Leagues. After Gus Greenlee, Pittsburgh's most prominent black gangster, reformed the Negro National League with a massive infusion of capital in 1933, a rival black league, the Negro American League, began operating in 1937. Together, the two leagues staged special events such as the Negro World Series and the East-West Classic. With the black population increasing dramatically in Northern cities, due largely to defense plant work during World War II, crowds of tens of thousands were commonplace. Turnstile counts weren't lost on major league owners, who were also under pressure from labor unions and civil rights groups to integrate the game.

In 1946, Branch Rickey, a University of Michigan graduate and president of the Brooklyn Dodgers, took the big first step toward ending the major leagues' color bar. He signed Jackie Robinson, a standout for the Kansas City Monarchs in the Negro National League, to a contract with the Dodgers' top farm club in Montreal.

Robinson's signing understandably caused a ripple of excitement in Detroit's black community. John R. Williams, a black sports promoter, arranged buses for five hundred blacks to witness Robinson's first game in Toronto. On another occasion, when a scheduled train trip to Montreal sponsored by the Frederick Douglass Non-Partisan Civic League of Detroit was suddenly canceled, half of the three hundred disappointed fans still made it on their own to Montreal's ballpark. Robinson responded by stroking the game-winning hit.

Robinson made it to the big time the following season, leading the Dodgers into the 1947 World Series and winning Rookie of the Year laurels. Robinson's courage in the face of racial slurs, threats on his life, and unfriendly teammates has been well-documented elsewhere. Suffice it to say that his example paved the way for scores of blacks during the 1950s, with the major leagues signing the finest players away from Negro League clubs at bargain basement prices.

By 1958, every major league team except Boston and Detroit was integrated. The Tigers' all-alabaster lineup was especially irritating to Wendall Smith, a native Detroiter who had gone on to become the most talented and influential advocate for baseball's integration as a sportswriter for the *Pittsburgh Courier,* the country's leading black weekly. In 1933, Smith had pitched his American Legion team to a 1–0 play-off victory in front of a Tigers scout, who then signed Smith's white catcher and the losing pitcher to contracts. "I wish I could sign you, too, kid," said the scout. "But, I can't." Smith cited this snub as the reason he decided to become a sportswriter whose life's mission was to see integration through. As a result, he never let up on Tigers' owner Walter O. Briggs.

In April 1958, an ad hoc civil rights group, the Briggs Stadium Boycott Commission, threatened a boycott of Tigers games if the club didn't integrate—and fast. On June 6, 1958, the Detroit Tigers finally entered the Twentieth Century, calling up infielder Ozzie Virgil from their Charleston farm club. Virgil, a man of color, was from the Dominican Republic. It wasn't until the following year, when the Tigers acquired aging Larry Doby—who had been the American's League's first black player when he signed with Cleveland in 1948—that the club could truly be considered integrated.

By 1960 the dismantling of the Negro Leagues was complete. The Negro National League shut down in 1948, while the Negro American League was able to last until 1960, although in the last several years it fielded only four clubs, including a revived version of the Detroit Stars. "We could've still survived, if only the majors had the desire to help the black leagues," contended Ted Rasberry, a Grand Rapids promoter who purchased the Stars in 1953. "We operated on a lot less money than their minor leagues. Instead, it was like sucking blood. They'd pay you a little money for players—nothing much, just enough to operate on. And we folded. They just took all the drawing power away from the Negro Leagues."

Turkey Stearnes's last season was 1945, two years before Jackie Robinson broke into the major leagues with the Dodgers. Stearnes found work in Ford's foundry, got married, and lived in a small, neat house on the east side of Detroit. According to his wife, Nettie, he never expressed any bitterness over the major leagues' failure to integrate earlier. "I never heard him say anything about it," she said. "He was a quiet man, but I guess he felt good that avenues were being opened up for our race."

To the very end, Stearnes attended almost all of the Tigers' home games, even when they carried on past midnight and he had to get up early the next morning to go to work. He died in 1979. One can only speculate how often the action on the grass drew an old man in the bleachers back in time, back to innings and afternoons spent on distant diamonds, when perhaps the finest ballplayer in all of Detroit was a young black man by the name of Norman "Turkey" Stearnes.

Eddie Bak, a sixteen-year-old Detroiter transplanted to the woods of Michigan's Upper Peninsula, in 1936. (Author's Collection)

TWENTY-FIVE
A Babe in the Woods

An aging member of "Roosevelt's Tree Army" of the 1930s returns with his son to the site of the best years of his life.

U.S. Route 2 runs as smooth as an office hallway between St. Ignace and Escanaba in Michigan's Upper Peninsula. We were somewhere west of Seul Choix Point, a forested finger that scratches the neck of Lake Michigan, when my father suddenly recalled the night he'd had too much blackberry wine. "It was two miles from this saloon in Cedar River to Camp Wells," he said. "I had to find my way home alone. It was pitch-black out. I remember the wind blowing, making those wires sing."

I tried to picture the wizened man sitting behind the steering wheel as a fresh-faced babe in the woods, alternately whistling and sprinting past curtains of tall pines. In the fertile imagination of a youngster slightly addled by wine, those trees probably sprouted legs and chased him halfway back to camp.

"I was just hoping no bear would jump out of the woods and get me," he admitted.

Such candor was unusual for my father, whose past, as far as his five children were concerned, had been tucked away like snapshots in a shoe box and never examined again. Growing up in Detroit in the 1950s and '60s, we knew the basics about the middle-aged man in the living room we called Dad, but that was all. His real name was Eddie, he was married to a mom named Lillian, he worked in an auto plant during the day, and liked peanuts on his ice cream at night.

Everything else was a blur. We were vaguely aware that he had served in the merchant marine during World War II and, before that, had spent time in some kind of camp with a lot of C's in its name. My younger brother and I got it into our heads that he had been in a concentration camp—a revelation that, to our father's chagrin, we shared with neighbors up and down the block. It wasn't until later that we learned that, while the Great Depression had been rough, no one had actually been put behind barbed wire for being poor.

Few young people today have heard of the Civilian Conservation Corps, or the CCC, one of the earliest and most successful work relief programs to come out of President Franklin D. Roosevelt's ambitious New Deal. Between 1933 and 1942, some 2.5 million unemployed single men between the ages of eighteen and twenty-five were part of the greatest conservation effort in history. Under the supervision of army officers, CCC members built roads, firebreaks, trails, dams, and lookout towers throughout hundreds of state and national forests and parks. They restocked lakes and streams, improved campgrounds and beaches, and battled fires. Most of all, they reforested countless acres of cutover land. In Michigan alone, the CCC planted a staggering 2.4 billion trees.

Included in what the press dubbed "Roosevelt's Tree Army" was a skinny sixteen-year-old from Detroit named Eddie Bak, who had been able to sneak in with his older brother, Rudy, because "no one checked birth certificates in those days," he said. Despite the culture shock of trading well-lit city sidewalks for dark dirt paths, my father once told me that the time he had spent in the CCC between 1936 and 1938 were the best years of his life.

He never elaborated. Perhaps he didn't think anyone would be that interested. After the concentration camp fiasco, I really wasn't—until I hit middle age and started developing a curiosity about a father who was rapidly running out of years. Certainly something had come before the age spots, thinning hair, and weathered face—dreams, disappointments, experiences, some kind of pre-history that had helped shape his character and determined the course of his life.

CCC members plant trees in one of Michigan's forests. (Author's Collection)

For this reason, one autumn day I impulsively invited my parents to join me in a two-day drive from Detroit to the western reaches of the Upper Peninsula. My father was excited about the prospect of visiting an area he had not seen in more than a half-century. My mother was excited that my father was excited. As it turned out, I probably got more out of the odyssey than anyone.

"We got paid a dollar a day," my father said as we headed for Cedar River, near the site of Camp Wells, the camp to which he had been assigned in the summer of 1936. "The government took twenty-five dollars out each month and sent it to our parents. That left us with five dollars to last a month."

Not much pocket change, to be sure, but then pockets weren't very deep in the Depression. My father's father, Stanley Bak, tried to support seven children with his on-again, off-again assembly line job at Hudson Motors. The Depression hit him particularly hard. The family had always raised chickens and rabbits in the carbarn, but even feed cost money. The fifty dollars my grandfather received each month from two boys in the CCC must have seemed heaven-sent.

Despite the unaccustomed spirit of openness during our trip up north, my father remained vague about his activities from the time he quit school in the fifth grade until he joined the CCC—a span of several years. The best that I could figure out was that while he was probably no angel during this period, he was no drugstore gangster, either. He was simply one of those many young men who, through no fault of their own, had had too much time on their hands in the 1930s.

The CCC wasted no time in filling those hands with shovels, hoes, and rakes. In the parking lot of a Big Boy restaurant in Manistique, where we stopped for coffee, my father reproduced the backbreaking choreography of "operating a Number 2 shovel." The thought that my father was personally responsible for tens of thousands of pines and birches that will almost certainly outlive my children's children produced an odd sensation. Not a bad legacy, when one thinks about it. I felt a surge in my chest, and it wasn't the caffeine.

It was clear from my father's enthusiasm that the CCC had restored human as well as natural resources. His recollections centered on the camaraderie of shared responsibilities and mutual fun. The young men of his company may have gotten up early each morning and labored long hours building dams and digging ditches, but there also was plenty of free time spent swimming, playing baseball and six-man football, pitching horseshoes, and exploring the natural wonders of their pine-scented surroundings. Shortly after my father arrived at Camp Wells, his company was ferried to Isle Royale. There they spent several weeks working twelve-hour shifts helping fight a devastating forest fire on the remote island. Until the end of his days he could always recall with delight the spindly-legged moose that emerged dripping from the cold, clear waters of Lake Superior at dusk—a magnificent and fascinating sight to a young man recently removed from the noise, concrete, and congestion of the big city.

In time my father was made a truckdriver. His first lesson behind the wheel was driving a load of drunk, singing campmates back from a saloon in Cedar River. CCC members were not allowed to have their own vehicles, but one camper managed to hide his Model A Ford in the woods. On weekends they pushed it out of earshot of camp officers,

Bak's first lesson behind the wheel of a truck was driving a load of drunk, singing campmates back from a saloon in Cedar River. (Author's Collection)

started it up, and then followed the single-lane blacktop into Escanaba. Roller-skating was the big attraction in town. One memorable Friday night, my father outlasted a field of skaters in a five-mile race that included his good friend Malott. "He was from Missouri," my father recalled. "He was always saying, 'I'm from Missouri, so you gotta show me.' So I showed him. I won a silver cup. It got all tarnished and then one day I lost it. It's the only thing I ever won in my life."

There also was a girlfriend, a red-haired secretary named Elaine Ferguson. "She was eighteen, a year older than me," he confided, out of earshot of my mother. "I broke it off with her. But don't worry, I didn't do anything that would make me ashamed if I saw her today." A reunion seemed unlikely, though there was a gray-haired woman peddling an adult tricycle down the sidewalk as we passed through Escanaba on the second day of our trip. "Who knows?" he said. "That may have been Elaine Ferguson pumping that bicycle."

A short while later we arrived in Cedar River, about forty miles southwest of Escanaba. We learned from a state policeman that whatever might still exist of old Camp Wells was now part of J. W. Wells State Park. The day we visited was a Wednesday afternoon in the fall, so the 970-acre park was practically empty. A helpful park ranger filled us in on what the CCC had accomplished here: the construction of parking lots, a vehicle bridge, miles of trails, and several beachfront cabins. The CCC also had developed scores of acres of picnic grounds and installed miles of telephone line.

All of this was still in use. While the CCC's handiwork was everywhere, casual park visitors would be hard-pressed to know it. There was a refurbished officer's cabin with a dusty wall display featuring a faded blue-and-yellow CCC pennant, but that was it. "There's been a reunion here in August for the last couple years," another ranger offered. "Of course, every year fewer and fewer show up."

That got my father to musing aloud: Jeez, whatever happened to Malott? He was from Missouri, you know, so you had to show him. How about Dragovich, the lanky first baseman who snored so loudly we once carried him and his bed onto the beach? "A lot of those boys went right into the service after Pearl Harbor," he said. "I'm sure some of them didn't come back from the war."

We made our way to the beach, where Camp Wells sat in the 1930s. Lake Michigan was hypnotically calm. There was no breeze and the temperature was in the sixties. The sky was so blue, it hurt our eyes. Despite the postcard setting, I was slightly disappointed. There was no flagpole, no barracks, no markers—nothing to signify that hundreds of young lives had once been shaped at this very spot. Watching my father move excitedly around the deserted beach, however, it occurred to me that although little of Camp Wells had been left behind, its members clearly had brought something back.

Surely the CCC accounted for my father's storied self-confidence. The skinny kid who had battled a forest fire, stubborn truck transmissions, and other youths in inter-camp boxing matches grew into the man who never backed down from a challenge. Whether it was wiring a room, overhauling an engine, or building a bathroom from scratch, he just picked up a how-to book and went at it. His home-improvement projects were notable for their ambition. "I'll have to knock out the kitchen wall, of course," he'd tell my mother. Of course. After all, the CCC's motto had been "We can do it!"

The seed of a marvelous entrepreneurial spirit also was planted in those drafty barracks. The boy who had supplemented his income by ironing his campmates' shirts for fifteen cents (twenty-five cents for trousers) had grown into the man who spent his lunch breaks in the factory selling cold soda and homemade sandwiches from a cooler. For as long as I can remember, my father made ends meet by painting a neighbor's living room or tuning a relative's car in his spare time. It was that kind of drive that spelled the difference between squeezing by on a factory hand's salary and giving a family of seven a few extras.

"I don't know where I would've wound up if not for the CCC," my father said. "It got us kids off the street corner, put us in the right direction . . ."

Daylight was fading as we left the park. Within an hour we had passed through Escanaba and were back on Route 2. I set the cruise control at sixty-five and glanced at my father. He was looking out the window, lost in thought. We drove in silence. The trees sprinted by, as fast as a city kid in the dark.

"Wild Bob" Burman. (Library of Congress)

TWENTY-SIX

The Final Lap of a Speed Imp

Away from the speedway, gentleman racer Bob Burman didn't live life in the fast lane, avoiding cussing, drinking, and scandal. But "Wild Bob" was a completely different fellow when he got behind the wheel of a racecar.

Down the Roaring Road they thunder on,
Like comets blazing along;
Their motors belching sheets of flame,
As they roar their mighty song.

—*JOHN C. DUVALL*
"Knights of the Roaring Road"

When death finally got around to claiming "Wild Bob" Burman, it was a shock to the public but was not entirely unexpected by those who knew him best. The young man from rural Lapeer County had been pushing the envelope for years, a "crazed speed imp" who would wipe the grime and oil off his face with an economical grin at the end of yet another record run. Ever since man first learned the joys of mechanical locomotion, there has been a primordial urge to go faster than the other guy—and Burman never liked being the other guy.

Although he is all but forgotten today, a century ago Wild Bob was racing royalty, with tire magnate Harvey Firestone fitting him with a jewel-encrusted crown prior to the inaugural running of the Indianapolis

500 in 1911. "As a driver he was a genius in point of skill and fearlessness," one Buick official said of Burman. "Whether he was in the lead or back in the ruck of the 'also-rans,' he never faltered, but drove his race always to the very best of his ability and with an unwavering spirit of pluck." Wild Bob's go-for-broke style burned out a lot of cars but never himself. "Hard luck and his grinding tactics eliminated him from many long races," observed a Detroit reporter, "but his driving skill and daring made him a big favorite."

Despite the spectacular implications of his nickname and the freewheeling nature of his exploits, away from the adoring crowds the popular racer was more mild than wild, admitted Dick Burman. "The name's a bit misleading," said the West Bloomfield Township resident, whose great-grandfather was the racer's brother. "He was quite dapper. He never swore. He never drank. He just loved racing."

Robert Burman was born on April 23, 1884, on a small farm outside Imlay City. He hated the dawn-to-dusk tedium of farm life and left when he was seventeen. Growing industrial centers like Detroit (fifty miles to the south) and Flint (thirty-five miles to the west) were magnets for mechanically inclined young men like Burman who didn't mind getting grease under their nails and bugs in their teeth.

Burman started off painting, then testing, engines at the small Buick plant, which was then located in Jackson. He moved to the Jackson Automobile Company as their chief road tester. One day in 1906, he talked his employer into letting him enter a widely publicized fifty-mile race at the Grosse Pointe racetrack. Among the familiar names on hand were Henry Ford and racer Barney Oldfield, who had helped make each other famous with a monstrous speed wagon known as the "999." The unheralded newcomer in a stock Jackson beat them all. "Burman took awful chances on the turns," Oldfield said. "But he won the contest and beat Ford and me." Burman followed up that victory with another, this time winning a grueling twenty-four-hour race in St. Louis. It was during this period that the young racer acquired the sobriquet "Wild Bob."

Paying attention was William C. "Billy" Durant, who had purchased the small, failing Buick company and was in the process of merging it with other car manufacturers to form General Motors. Durant extended an offer "too lucrative to turn down," recalled Burman, to join the racing team he was putting together at Buick.

For automakers, the philosophy of "win on Sunday, sell on Monday" was particularly important in the early days of the industry. Victories and headlines were essential in helping consumers and investors sort out a field crowded with hundreds of brands. Racing could also be seen as a form of public service. According to longtime track official Fred Wagner, author of the classic memoir *The Saga of the Roaring Road,* few people realize that "practically every improvement that has come to the modern motor car first made its appearance on the racing course. Without exception, everything the race has found advantageous has been adopted and everything found worthless has been discarded."

Shortly after signing Burman, Durant took him on a tour of the new Buick factory in Flint. "Bob," he said, "now that you have a good racing team, you drive your Buick car as hard and fast as you can. I don't care if you win races or not. When some part breaks, or wears out, you bring it to the factory immediately, and we'll build it better. And when better automobiles are built, Buick will build them." Henry Ewald, co-founder of the Campbell-Ewald advertising agency, later turned Durant's words to Burman into one of the industry's most memorable and effective slogans.

The Buick squad remains the greatest factory team ever assembled. In addition to Burman, the heart of the roster included the storied Chevrolet brothers, Louis and Arthur, and Lewis Strang, a handsome, strapping Georgian who was destined to die a couple of months after winning the pole position in the first Indianapolis 500. Between 1908 and 1911, the team won more than ninety percent of the events in which they competed—everything from hill climbs and reliability runs to endurance races. Grabbing his share of racing cups and bowls was Burman, whom Durant described as "happiest when the hazard was the greatest."

Burman never referred to himself as a race driver but as a "test driver." Because of frequent breakdowns, racecars during this era included a ride-along mechanic called a mechanician. While drivers often let the mechanic handle most of the diagnosing and repairs, Burman enjoyed this integral part of racing as much as he did the actual driving. In 1910 he had a hand in designing the famous Buick "Bug," a 2,600-pound racing machine with a 622-cubic-inch engine. Only two were ever built, one for Burman and the other for Louis Chevrolet. Burman used his "Space-Eater" to gobble up several short-distance sprint records.

Unlike many drivers of his era, Burman was not given to "dissipation," the popular term for drinking and carousing. A quiet, intense, and confident man, he made sure he stayed in top physical condition to handle the rigors of his profession. His 160 pounds were spread firmly over a five-foot-eleven frame. He had tremendous strength in his arms and shoulders, which he had built up over years of handling an oversize steering wheel and keeping a one-ton machine under control for hours on end. His vices, if they could be called that, were a love of oysters and fine clothes. For years he raced in a suit and tie, a cloth cap jammed backward on his head, until his manager convinced him that business attire was not necessary to win a race or the public. After that, "dressing down" on race day still meant wearing a silk shirt, a bow tie, and dark trousers under his coveralls. A diamond stickpin served as his ever-present good luck charm.

Knights of the Roaring Road they are,
With fearlessness their creed;
True sportsmen they, who drive to play
The game of skill and speed.

The Indianapolis Motor Speedway opened to great pomp in 1909. Burman and his Buick teammates were among the featured attractions of the first program at the 2.5-mile oval track. The culminating event of the day was a 250-mile race for the Prest-O-Lite Trophy, with Burman outlasting the field to win the speedway's first major race.

Fred Wagner, who flagged the events, later described the brick course as "Heaven's gift to morticians." Two young men from Massachusetts, driver William Bourque and mechanician Harry Holcomb, died in the Prest-O-Lite race. They were hurtling around the track aboard their Knox racer when the machine suddenly skidded out of control. "It was all over in an instant," reported an Indianapolis daily. "The maddened demon of speed rushed headlong into a ditch beside the track. The car was hurled and thrown end over end to the ground and against the fence, while the two unfortunate men were tossed helplessly to either side.

"Holcomb's head struck a fencepost and he was killed instantly. His brains were scattered on the post and the ground." Bourque, barely alive, was rushed to the hospital with a crushed skull, mangled legs, and several broken ribs that had punctured his right lung. "The blood was pouring into the lung at such a rate that the driver drowned, as the physicians termed it, in his own blood."

After the race, a Knox official declared an end to the company's participation in racing. "It is simply suicide," he said, "that's all it is." The characterization wasn't far off the mark. The cars and their drivers lacked even rudimentary safety devices, such as seat belts, helmets, and roll cages. The dirt tracks threw up thick clouds of dust that cut visibility down to practically nothing. Hot oil sprayed into the drivers' faces, and flying rocks shattered their goggles. (Racecars did not yet have windshields.) By one account, between 1904 and 1911 more than two hundred drivers and mechanicians around the country lost their lives through mechanical or human error. The toll didn't include the unlucky bystanders also killed in the frequent mishaps, nor the number of drivers too seriously injured to continue racing.

Burman had his share of close calls. Throughout his career tires blew, throttles stuck, and exploding cylinder heads whizzed past his face. He wrapped one car around a tree in Atlanta and went airborne in major races in San Francisco and Indianapolis. One Christmas Day his car caught fire on the beach in San Diego, and he drove it into the Pacific Ocean to douse the flames. A similar episode saw him plow his burning machine into the Atlantic. Throughout all the narrow escapes, Burman remained fatalistic about his livelihood. "What is to be, will be," was a favorite expression.

In the summer of 1910, a firestorm erupted when owners of the Indianapolis Speedway considered having Jack Johnson—the first black heavyweight boxing champion in the world and a motoring enthusiast—participate in an exhibition race at the track. The sport's licensing body was the American Automobile Association, which refused to issue permits to African Americans. The idea of sanctioning Johnson, a larger-than-life character who delighted in antagonizing his many detractors by squiring around white women and whizzing through towns in his high-powered automobiles, was particularly galling to member drivers.

Interviewed in Detroit, both Burman and his Buick stablemate, Louis Chevrolet, stated "in forceful terms" that they would permanently boycott the course if the controversial "Papa Jack" was allowed on it. "I am not willing to allow my name to be used in the same race program as that of Jack Johnson," Chevrolet said, "and if the Indianapolis motor speedway management can not confine itself to automobile racing without bringing [in] a Negro barn-storming pugilist, I believe it is time for the white drivers to quit the game on that track." According to the reporter, "Burman seconded the sentiments of Chevrolet." The newspaper account continued: "The two objecting pilots maintain that the only virtue in Johnson's automobile driving is the fact that he puts money in circulation by paying fines for speeding. They assert it would be fool-hardiness itself to race against Johnson, who has no knowledge of the mechanical end of an automobile. They feel it would place him on a par with them—a position which they do not choose to occupy."

Barney Oldfield, as much of a high-living renegade as Johnson, risked opprobrium and the loss of his racing license by agreeing to a series of unsanctioned five-mile races with Johnson that fall. Before five thousand people at a track in Brooklyn, New York, Oldfield easily outdistanced Johnson in the first heat. In the second he slowed down just long enough to allow newsreel cameramen to get both cars in the frame. There was no need for a third heat. Oldfield won five thousand dollars, and Papa Jack was uncharacteristically humble. "No more of that automobile racing for Jack Johnson," he said. "I may be able to drive a car fast on a straight road, but I never will take any chances on the turns like Oldfield does."

To nobody's great surprise, Johnson barreled into the afterworld at the wheel of a high-performance automobile. On June 9, 1946, en route to New York to attend the Joe Louis–Billy Conn title fight, he crashed his Lincoln Zephyr near Raleigh, North Carolina, after speeding away from a whites-only restaurant that had just refused to serve him.

Bob Burman (*second from right*) and his record-setting "Blitzen" Benz. (Library of Congress)

They live to thrill, they thrill to live
Their lives of swift romance;
They stake their all, to heed the call,
Of the fickle gods of chance.

Wild Bob's reputation was cemented on the packed sands of Ormond Beach, Florida, in the spring of 1911. By that time Burman had hired Ernie Moross to manage his personal career, and the promoter wasted no time in scheduling various exhibitions and record runs to enrich both of them. After Oldfield was given his first of many "lifetime suspensions" by the AAA for racing Johnson, Burman and Moross bought Oldfield's beloved Benz racer for $13,500. Oldfield had set records all around the country in the German-made machine, which was dubbed "Blitzen" (German for "lightning").

Over the course of two days, April 23–24, 1911, Burman drove his new acquisition harder and faster than its former owner ever had. After shattering Oldfield's records for the fastest kilometer and mile, he trained his sights on establishing a new mark for the fastest two-mile run. The Benz leaped forward and in quick order was eating up 208 feet of sand per second. The force of the rushing wind threatened to pop the lens out of Burman's goggles. Keeping the rushing Benz on course was like riding a bucking bull. One tremendous bump shot Burman straight into the air, causing his foot to slip off the pedal. He immediately recovered, "and old 'Blitzen' and I were chasing up the beach again after that two-mile mark," he recalled. "My death-grip on that steering wheel was the only thing that had kept me from flying out [of] the seat."

In less than a minute it was all over. Officials looked at their stopwatches and shook their heads. Burman had covered two miles in 51.28 seconds, shooting through space at better than 141 mph, or roughly one-tenth the speed of a bullet. "God knows how I ever reached the end of that death-ride without smashing the car and myself," he exclaimed afterward. "Every moment in that ride seemed to me the last on earth, and I'm glad it's over." He wasn't so glad, however, that he didn't continue to better his own times in various straightaway categories. This particular land-speed record stood for eight years. Various other marks he set lasted for a decade.

A few weeks after the record runs at Ormond Beach, Harvey Firestone ceremoniously placed a crown embedded with pearls and gems on Burman's head. The crown was modeled after the one King George V had worn at his recent coronation and was valued at a reported ten thousand dollars. With trumpets sounding and the viewers in packed stands at Indianapolis Speedway cheering, Firestone declared Burman "Speed King of the World."

Burman raced in the first five Indy 500s, 1911 through 1915, always finishing out of the money; however, his heavily hyped presence helped establish "The Brickyard" as the mecca of American motorsports and instituted the Memorial Day race as a popular cultural mainstay. In one promotion he took an adventurous soul named Betty Blythe for a bone-jarring, mile-a-minute ride. Her carbonated account of being the first woman around the famous course appeared in papers across the country. "Talk about going like the wind!" she wrote. "Well, I have never traveled on the crest of a gale, but you have got to show me that

Ralph DePalma and Burman tear around the Indianapolis track. In 1915 DePalma won the Indianapolis 500 while Burman finished sixth. (Library of Congress)

it can get you around the Speedway any quicker than 'Wild Bob's' racer carried me."

The world's speed king, described by one historian as an "aw-shucks, toe-in-the-sand American archetype," had no royal affectations. After his first marriage fell apart—the woman was a bit too wild for Wild Bob's taste—he married a young lady named Helen who encouraged his passion for high speeds even as she feared its consequences. They had two daughters, Eugenia and Florence, and in 1914 the family moved into a house at 70 Chandler Avenue in Detroit, near Chandler Park. When he could find some time away from the track or the garage, he enjoyed a quiet day of fishing or a genial gathering with childhood pals back in Imlay City.

Once a friend came upon Burman parked outside a store on Woodward Avenue, waiting patiently for his wife to finish shopping. He remarked that probably only a handful of passersby recognized the quiet, well-dressed man as the daredevil who tore into turns with such wild

Bob Burman on a Detroit street in 1913. (Janet Lowry Collection)

abandon. "That is my work," Burman responded, "and now I am just an ordinary family man."

His compensation was far from ordinary. In 1915, a year when the average annual salary of American workers was $687 and a new house could be bought for two or three thousand dollars, Burman pulled down $18,000 in winnings. Other money came in from sponsorships, equipment testimonials, and such. It was a good life, but it was going to end soon.

And if the "Referee" calls them "Home,"
When Fortune flags them down;
They are not done, they still live on,
To wear the hero's crown.

Early in 1916, Burman left for California. He was approaching his thirty-second birthday and was still finishing in the money. He won a boulevard race in San Diego and grabbed second place in two events at the Ascot Speedway in Los Angeles. Afterward he turned his attention to the upcoming race at Corona, a small, tidy community known far and wide for its lemons. A dozen top drivers were set to fly around the leafy Grand Boulevard in pursuit of a hefty $12,000 purse put up by local citizens.

Burman had helped develop the annual three-hundred-mile race, which was in its third running. Later, some claimed the course never should have been sanctioned by city fathers or the American Automobile Association, as large shade trees prevented the banking of curves and spectators were allowed to stand dangerously close on the curbs. At least two people had uncanny premonitions. Prior to the start of the race, Helen Burman tearfully pleaded with her husband to withdraw; the night before the race she'd had a vivid dream about him crashing. W. D. Edenburn, who covered motorsports for the *Detroit News-Tribune,* convinced his editor to pull a photo of Burman that had been scheduled to run on the day of the event. "I've got a hunch that Bob will be killed this afternoon," Edenburn said.

April 8, 1916, was a muggy, breezeless Sunday in Corona. Burman climbed into his pale blue Peugeot, a temperamental machine he had bought from Jules Goux, a Frenchman who three years earlier had steered it to victory in the Indianapolis 500. Riding along in the mechanic's bucket was Eric Schroeder, a former jockey from a wealthy family in Chicago. He considered racing a thrill, and riding with Burman a privilege. After leading for the first five laps, Burman fell back into a seesaw battle for the front position, bedeviled by a slipping clutch and eleven tire changes. Schroeder, who was feeling sick, at one point asked to be relieved, then thought better of it.

On the ninety-sixth lap, Burman was tearing around the track at nearly 100 mph, attempting to claw back into contention, when the right rear tire exploded. The car careened out of control, skidding upon a culvert before hitting a guideline and flipping over. In scythelike fashion the hurtling Peugeot sheared off two posts and the top of a parked car before mowing into the crowd. A policeman was killed, and nearly a score of spectators were injured, some critically.

The victims were rushed to Riverside Hospital. Schroeder was dead, and Burman was breathing his last. His skull had been fractured, his chest crushed, and both legs broken. As he was being hurriedly prepared for surgery, his frantic wife asked if she could hold onto his good-luck diamond stickpin. It was then that nurses discovered that a square of the patient's silk shirt had been expertly cut out by an unknown woman who had helped bring the injured to the hospital. The thief was discovered a while later hiding inside a bathroom, the missing stickpin in her girdle. By then Burman was dead.

A train brought Burman's body and his sobbing widow back to Imlay City. Twenty-five hundred people, twice the population of his hometown, paid their respects as he lay in state at the Masonic Hall. The next day, hundreds of mourners and banks of floral tributes were squeezed into the small Baptist church he had attended since childhood. "Henry Ford, Louis Chevrolet, Harvey Firestone, Barney Oldfield, and Eddie Rickenbacker were all at the funeral," Dick Burman said. "Rickenbacker had a funeral wreath made to resemble a checkered flag."

Burman was one of six Indy 500 drivers to die in 1916. Oldfield was spooked enough by the carnage to build his famous "Golden Submarine," an odd-looking, one-of-a-kind machine with a caged cockpit that was the first fully enclosed racecar. A more practical lifesaving innovation was the use of vertical roll bars in open-cockpit cars.

Burman was buried in a cemetery a short distance from his birthplace. He was joined six years later by his much younger brother, Earl, who was killed in his very first race. The speed-related tragedies didn't end there. According to Dick Burman, one of the racer's daughters, Eugenia, died a few years later in a scandalous crash. "She was speeding down Dixie Highway with a young man who was not her husband," he said—a highballing exit that mirrored that of Wild Bob, speed king in a silk shirt.

CHEVROLET: THE MAN BEHIND THE NAMEPLATE

A story has it that Louis Chevrolet was driving a tad too fast through Royal Oak one day when he was pulled over by a constable. The judge that heard his case slapped him with a twenty-dollar fine. "Ten dollars for speeding," he said, "and ten dollars for assuming the name of a noted race driver."

Louis Chevrolet and his ride-along mechanic prepare to take to the track. (Library of Congress)

Obscurity was the cruel fate of the namesake of one of the most enduring brands in automotive history. Born in Switzerland on Christmas morning in 1878 and raised in France, Chevrolet lived briefly in Montreal before settling in the States in about 1900. The burly, mustachioed, cigar-chomping Chevrolet was blessed with a stout heart and a knack for mechanics. This combination made him a true giant of the roaring road, as he won roughly one-third of the 250 races in which he competed during his career. In 1911 his fame and engineering prowess caused Billy Durant, the recently ousted president of General Motors, to team up with him in starting a new company. The two men knew each other well, Durant having hired Louis (and his equally fearless brother, Arthur) for the famous Buick racing team of the early 1900s.

Durant never personally cared for Chevrolet, constantly chastising him about his tobacco habit; however, he loved the lyrical sound of his name and appropriated it for their new venture. Durant also borrowed from a wallpaper pattern he'd discovered inside a Paris hotel room to create the now-iconic "bow tie" emblem, which first appeared on the 1914 models.

Chevrolet's prototype, built inside a Detroit garage, retailed for triple the cost of a Ford Model T. Although technologically advanced, sales were low. Durant insisted that his partner create economical cars that would appeal to the masses, but Chevrolet wanted to build high-performance luxury vehicles on a par with those produced by the best European carmakers. After numerous run-ins, one day in 1915 he told Durant he'd had enough: "I sold you my car, and I sold you my name, but I'm not going to sell myself to you. I'm going to smoke my cigarettes as much as I want. And I'm getting out."

Chevrolet was merged into GM in 1917 and became its best-selling division, a distinction it holds to this day. Meanwhile, Louis Chevrolet's activities included building cars that won the Indianapolis 500 in 1920 and 1921. The first was driven by his younger brother, Gaston, who was killed a few months later in a Thanksgiving Day race in Los Angeles. Arthur, a partner in most of Louis's ventures, committed suicide in 1946.

For all of his success as a racer and designer, Chevrolet was a terrible businessman. He dumped his stock before GM took off, costing him a fortune, and mismanaged the various enterprises he became involved with. While broke and in his fifties, he returned to the company he had co-founded, working briefly at the axle plant during the Depression before moving on to a minor sales position with an oil company. Reflecting the auto pioneer's lack of pull, his only child, Alfred, spent his life toiling anonymously on a GM assembly line.

Louis Chevrolet, one of the most important and glamorous figures of the early automobile age, lived his last years as a diabetic amputee confined to his Detroit home. He died there one spring morning in 1941, in a house filled with tarnished trophies. Today he and his brothers rest side by side in an Indianapolis cemetery while the family name speeds on via millions of vehicles around the world.

TWENTY-SEVEN
Wings of Pride

In the summer of 1927, intrepid aviators Ed Schlee and Billy Brock did Detroit proud with their ill-fated attempt to fly around the world.

In aviation circles, 1927 is remembered as the "summer of eagles," though the *Pride of Detroit* could be more aptly described as a giant yellow canary, with the brightly colored monoplane darting across the headlines for several weeks as its pilots attempted to set a record for flying around the world. Some thought Ed Schlee and Billy Brock nuts—or worse, sane but suicidal. But Schlee and Brock were as dauntless a pair of adventurers ever to do Detroit proud. They were determined to see their dream through or, as so many other aviators had done, die trying. Friends and family members were equally determined to keep them alive.

The story of the Schlee–Brock world flight really begins with the exploits of an infinitely more famous pilot, Charles Lindbergh, a native Detroiter who on May 20–21, 1927, flew the *Spirit of St. Louis* nonstop from New York to Paris. Young, tall, handsome, and modest, Lindbergh was tailor-made for the role of the modern world's first great international hero. His feat—the first direct flight between the two great cities and the first solo crossing of the Atlantic—touched off an unprecedented wave of public celebration and mindless idolatry that inspired a slew of copycat flights. It seems almost incredible that something as dangerous and expensive as transoceanic flying could become a fad, but it did. Some were flights straight into oblivion.

Would-be world fliers Billy Brock (*left*) and Ed Schlee. (Author's Collection)

Edward F. Schlee was a balding thirty-nine-year-old risktaker who owned about a hundred gas stations around Detroit. He had made his fortune by "picking the right corners." He also was an amateur pilot who used the golf course as an airfield when he visited Mackinac Island—a sign of how far aviation still had to go to be mainstream.

To help sell the public on the idea of traveling by air, Henry Ford—who in the 1920s had opened the world's most modern airport on Oakwood in Dearborn—created the Ford Reliability Tour. The annual event showcased aviation's commercial possibilities as contenders flew thousands of miles between cities. Schlee operated a small air taxi service of Stinson biplanes, which were manufactured locally. His chief pilot was William S. Brock, a chubby, jovial Ohio native who had some 4,500 hours of flying experience.

"My dad was on Mackinac Island when he heard the news about Lindbergh," remembered Edward "Ted" Schlee, Jr., a retired industrial

The *Pride of Detroit* was a single-engine Stinson monoplane that had already proved its worth in the Ford Reliability Tour. (Author's Collection)

salesman now living in northern Michigan. "He basically said, 'Well, if he's going to fly the ocean, I'm going to fly around the world.'" Brock, who was thirty-one, was always open to new flying challenges. He had flown a pet collie to Mrs. Calvin Coolidge at the summer White House in the Black Hills and rushed a medical team to Bath, Michigan, after a schoolhouse explosion had killed and injured scores of children.

Schlee and Brock devised a plan to break the existing record for circumnavigating the globe: 28 days, 14 hours, and 30 minutes. While Brock worked on navigational charts, Schlee arranged for fuel and supplies to be stored at twenty stops along the way. Their mode of transportation was to be a single-engine Stinson monoplane that had already been put through its paces in the Ford air tour. Originally called the *Miss Wayco,* it was re-christened the *Pride of Detroit.* The fuselage was "doped" fabric stretched over a frame. Inside, every possible inch of space was given over to storing several hundred gallons of fuel and oil. The instrumentation was primeval. There was no radio. "You look at that plane today," Ted Schlee said, "and you wouldn't go to Flint in it, much less around the world."

The fliers left Detroit on August 23, 1927, bound for Harbor Grace, Newfoundland, the jumping-off point for crossing the Atlantic. "Our flight is not a stunt," Schlee insisted. "Our main purpose is to demonstrate, dramatically perhaps, but definitely, how practical and serviceable travel by air is today."

Early on the morning of August 26, the *Pride of Detroit* rolled down the gravel runway at Harbor Grace. It climbed steadily until it was at 1,500 feet, flying into the rising sun. Gulping coffee and munching bananas and sandwiches, the men guided the little plane through rain, fog, and mist for much of the next twenty hours. After almost a full day in the air, they dropped through the overcast sky and found themselves over a coastline. But where were they? England? France? Ireland?

After trying in vain to locate an identifiable landmark, they circled a lighthouse. Brock wrote a note on a piece of cardboard asking someone on the ground to spell out the location's name in the sand, attached the note to a rag, and threw it out the window. It fluttered away, unnoticed. He tried again, bundling a new message in some cloth and weighing it down with an orange. This time several men came out and chalked some letters on the street, but the fliers couldn't read them. Finally, somebody thought to run the Union Jack up the flagpole. Brock and Schlee got their bearings and adjusted course for Croydon Airfield in London.

Landing safely in England was a feat in itself for the would-be world fliers. Today transoceanic flights are as common and safe as a stroll to the corner store, but at that time the *Pride of Detroit* was one of only a handful of planes to safely cross the Atlantic. However, this was just the first leg of their dangerously ambitious itinerary. Brock was confident: "With every break of luck, and allowing four or five hours' sleep a night with no time out for accidents, engine trouble, or other unforeseen contingency, we might make it under eighteen days."

The following day they were off to Munich. *Die amerikanischen Flieger* were photographed clinking mugs of beer with the mayor, an image that caused a mixture of outrage and jealousy back in the States, where Prohibition was the law of the land.

The next morning, they set out for Belgrade, Yugoslavia, intending to refuel bodies and plane before quickly heading to Constantinople;

The *Pride of Detroit* is escorted by two French planes as it passes over France. (Author's Collection)

however, bad weather and red tape kept them grounded for the better part of two days. "Flying over the Atlantic is a cinch compared with crossing Turkey," Brock grumbled before the *Pride of Detroit* was finally allowed to depart Constantinople for Baghdad, 1,075 miles away. Schlee blamed the costly delays in obtaining government permits on the "good luck bead" given him in Turkey, which somehow was working against the rabbit's foot he had carried since leaving Detroit.

On they flew, touching down in Bender Abbas, Persia (present-day Iran), one day and in Karachi, India, the next. By the time the self-described "aerial hoboes" reached Rangoon on September 7, a revolt was brewing. Since late August, an unremitting string of tragedies had the public finally questioning the sanity and purpose of transoceanic flying. The biggest catastrophe was the Dole Race, in which ten people lost their lives during a mad dash from California to Hawaii. The victims included Mildred Doran, a twenty-two-year-old Flint schoolteacher riding along as a gimmick. Despite the toll, nearly a dozen more long-distance flights between various points on the globe were launched through the end of September. Some of the planes were forced down by bad weather or mechanical problems; others were never seen again. Not a single one completed its journey.

Schlee and Brock both had a wife and two young children worrying about them at home. However, of immediate concern as they darted from Hanoi to Hong Kong to Shanghai was making up lost time. Headwinds cut into their speed. From China the *Pride of Detroit* winged its way toward Japan. A thunderstorm forced them down on Kiushiu Island, 600 miles shy of their destination, which was Tokyo. A typhoon and tidal wave hit Kiushiu, killing 791 people and keeping the plane in its hangar until September 14, when the fliers finally made it to Tokyo.

By then they were hopelessly behind schedule. They had flown 12,275 miles in 19 days, averaging 646 miles per day. They needed to nearly double that pace over the next nine days if they were to break the record—an impossible task. Nonetheless, they stubbornly insisted on continuing—and they started talking about the $50,000 prize being offered for the first flight between Hong Kong and Dallas.

To continue home by air, Schlee and Brock still had to make it over the Pacific, a series of water jumps that was the most intimidating part of their journey. Locating Midway Island, a speck of sand some 2,500 miles from Tokyo, promised to be a Herculean task, especially without the aid of a radio beacon. The flight was made more hazardous by the early arrival of typhoon season, whose winds could easily blow the little plane off course. After Midway there was a 1,440-mile hop to Honolulu, to be followed by a 2,400-mile flight to San Francisco—the same stretch of the Pacific that had just swallowed up several Dole racers. It was a daunting itinerary.

Amid a flurry of frantic messages from Detroit asking the government to intercede, Washington officials said that they had no the authority over the movements of private citizens. However, the Department of the Navy could—and did—withhold any offers of help, including shipping fuel to Midway and having its vessels provide navigational assistance. Over the last several weeks the navy had spent millions of dollars searching for lost fliers, but now the Detroit airmen were on their own.

Telegrams continued to pour into the U.S. embassy in Tokyo. Friends, family members, and politicians beseeched the fliers to stop what the press and top aviation experts were now calling a suicide flight. "In the name of the people of Detroit . . . I beg you to abandon your intended flight over the Pacific," cabled Mayor John W. Smith. "Daddy," pleaded ten-year-old Rosemarie Schlee, "please take the next boat home to us. We want you."

Finally, on September 15, the men caved in. They announced that they would take a liner back to the states. "We quit," said Brock, "because the whole world is fighting us." Two weeks later, the *Korea Maru* pulled into San Francisco harbor, the *Pride of Detroit* "hanging tailless by ropes on the upper afterdeck, looking like a yellow jacket that had alighted in the rigging." The dejected pilots criticized the navy, but, more than eighty years later, Ted Schlee sees things differently. "It's a good thing the Navy decided not to cooperate," he said. "They probably wouldn't have made it." Schlee points out that the pilots gained more admiration for their near-triumph than if they had actually completed the trip. One aviation publication praised their difficult decision to quit as "a sane interlude in a succession of disastrous ventures."

The fliers reassembled their plane and flew home, landing at Ford Airport on the afternoon of October 4. "As they landed, crowds surged in upon them," reported *Time* magazine, which had followed the men's exploits. "Into Mr. Schlee's arms rushed his wife. As he was pushed through the crowds on his way to City Hall, congratulatory hands clapped him on the back, hundreds of people shouted at him from all directions, automobile sirens shrieked in his ears." After being received by Mayor Smith and other dignitaries, the pilots attended a banquet given by their friends. Schlee was called upon to speak, but he could get out only a half-dozen words before collapsing. The strain of the adventure had finally caught up with him. The mayor helped carry him out of the room and the banquet was adjourned.

Was the truncated flight a legitimate attempt to push aviation's envelope or was it just two more pilots succumbing to the siren call of fame? Detroit dailies gave the local heroes the benefit of the doubt. The *Free Press* reminded readers: "Schlee and Brock flew more than halfway

Ten-year-old Rosemarie Schlee jumps into her father's arms upon his return to Detroit. (Author's Collection)

around the world with only brief stops, traversing oceans and continents, mountain ranges and deserts, combating fierce storms in strange lands and waters. Their skill and courage never failed them and their machine proved staunch. They demonstrated the practicability of sustained, long distance flying. All these things combine to make their trip 'the greatest flight.'"

Over the next couple of years, Schlee and Brock undertook a variety of endurance and distance flights around the country, though nothing nearly as ambitious as their globe-girdling "greatest flight." Bad luck continued to dog them. One summer day in 1929, Schlee was hand-starting a plane when the propeller kicked back. The blades sliced his shoulder, fractured his arm, cracked his skull, and left him permanently deaf in one ear. He survived, but the small aircraft company he and Brock operated didn't. The Great Depression hit both men hard. In 1931, the *Pride of Detroit*—which Schlee had once praised as "more faithful than a woman"—was auctioned by the county sheriff to satisfy a debt. It sold for seven hundred dollars. The following year, Brock died of cancer at age thirty-six. Schlee drifted into obscurity. His last job was working as an aircraft inspector at Packard during World War II. He died in 1969, the year *Apollo XI* traveled to the moon and back—the ultimate long-distance flight.

Today the flying machine that once carried two dreamers halfway around the world hangs inside the Henry Ford Museum in Dearborn, though its original canvas skin—bearing the faded signatures of new friends made in Belgrade, Baghdad, Karachi, and other exotic ports of call along the way—was unaccountably replaced by a curator. Tucked away in the archives is a full-page newspaper tribute published the day of the airmen's homecoming: "Detroit is proud of the *Pride of Detroit* and its Intrepid Pilots—Ed Schlee and Billy Brock."

INDEX